INFOCOMP 2018

The Eighth International Conference on Advanced Communications and Computation

July 22 - 26, 2018

Barcelona, Spain

INFOCOMP 2018 Editors

Claus-Peter Rückemann, Westfälische Wilhelms-Universität Münster / Leibniz Universität Hannover / North-German Supercomputing Alliance, Germany
Ian Flood, Rinker School, College of Design, Construction and Planning | University of Florida, USA
Sebastiano Fabio Schifano, University of Ferrara and INFN-Ferrara, Italy
Enrico Calore, University of Ferrara and INFN-Ferrara, Italy

Printed from e-media with permission by:

Curran Associates, Inc.
57 Morehouse Lane
Red Hook, NY 12571

Some format issues inherent in the e-media version may also appear in this print version.

Printed by Curran Associates, Inc. (2018)

International Academy, Research, and Industry Association (IARIA)
412 Derby Way
Wilmington, DE 19810

Phone: (408) 893-6407
Fax: (408) 527-6351

petre@iaria.org

Additional copies of this publication are available from:

Curran Associates, Inc.
57 Morehouse Lane
Red Hook, NY 12571 USA
Phone: 845-758-0400
Fax: 845-758-2633
Email: curran@proceedings.com
Web: www.proceedings.com

Table of Contents

INFOCOMP 2018

Foreword

The Eighth International Conference on Advanced Communications and Computation (INFOCOMP 2018), held between July 22 - 26, 2018- Barcelona, Spain, continued a series of events dedicated to advanced communications and computing aspects, covering academic and industrial achievements and visions.

The diversity of semantics of data, context gathering and processing led to complex mechanisms for applications requiring special communication and computation support in terms of volume of data, processing speed, context variety, etc. The new computation paradigms and communications technologies are now driven by the needs for fast processing and requirements from data-intensive applications and domain-oriented applications (medicine, geo-informatics, climatology, remote learning, education, large scale digital libraries, social networks, etc.). Mobility, ubiquity, multicast, multi-access networks, data centers, cloud computing are now forming the spectrum of de factor approaches in response to the diversity of user demands and applications. In parallel, measurements control and management (self-management) of such environments evolved to deal with new complex situations.

We take here the opportunity to warmly thank all the members of the INFOCOMP 2018 Technical Program Committee, as well as the numerous reviewers. The creation of such a broad and high quality conference program would not have been possible without their involvement. We also kindly thank all the authors who dedicated much of their time and efforts to contribute to INFOCOMP 2018. We truly believe that, thanks to all these efforts, the final conference program consisted of top quality contributions.

Also, this event could not have been a reality without the support of many individuals, organizations, and sponsors. We are grateful to the members of the INFOCOMP 2018 organizing committee for their help in handling the logistics and for their work to make this professional meeting a success.

We hope that INFOCOMP 2018 was a successful international forum for the exchange of ideas and results between academia and industry and for the promotion of progress in the areas of communications and computations.

We are convinced that the participants found the event useful and communications very open. We hope that Barcelona provided a pleasant environment during the conference and everyone saved some time to enjoy the charm of the city.

INFOCOMP 2018 Chairs:

INFOCOMP Steering Committee

Claus-Peter Rückemann, Leibniz Universität Hannover / Westfälische Wilhelms-Universität Münster / North-German Supercomputing Alliance (HLRN), Germany [Chair]
Kei Davis, Los Alamos National Laboratory, USA
Malgorzata Pankowska, University of Economics, Katowice, Poland
Subhash Saini, NASA, USA
Hans-Joachim Bungartz, Technische Universität München (TUM) - Garching, Germany
Almadena Chtchelkanova, National Science Foundation - Arlington, USA

INFOCOMP 2018

COMMITTEE

INFOCOMP Steering Committee

Claus-Peter Rückemann, Leibniz Universität Hannover / Westfälische Wilhelms-Universität Münster / North-German Supercomputing Alliance (HLRN), Germany [Chair]
Kei Davis, Los Alamos National Laboratory, USA
Malgorzata Pankowska, University of Economics, Katowice, Poland
Subhash Saini, NASA, USA
Hans-Joachim Bungartz, Technische Universität München (TUM) - Garching, Germany
Almadena Chtchelkanova, National Science Foundation - Arlington, USA

INFOCOMP Industry/Research Advisory Committee

Bernhard Bandow, Max Planck Institute for Solar System Research (MPS), Göttingen, Germany
Alfred Geiger, T-Systems Solutions for Research GmbH, Germany
Edgar A. Leon, Lawrence Livermore National Laboratory, USA
Lutz Schubert, Institute of Information Resource Management, University of Ulm, Germany
Walter Lioen, SURFsara, Netherlands
Huong Ha, School of Business, Singapore University of Social Sciences (SUSS), Singapore
Manfred Krafczyk, Institute for Computational Modeling in Civil Engineering (iRMB) - Braunschweig, Germany
Hans-Günther Müller, Cray, Germany

INFOCOMP Publicity Chair

Ustijana Rechkoska-Shikoska, University for Information Science and Technology "St. Paul the Apostle" - Ohrid, Republic of Macedonia

INFOCOMP 2018 Technical Program Committee

Mohamed Riduan Abid, Al Akhawayn University, Morocco
Ayaz Ahmad, COMSATS Institute of Information Technology, Pakistan
Mehmet Aksit, University of Twente, Netherlands
Daniel Andresen, Kansas State University, USA
Andres Ignacio Avila Barrera, Universidad de La Frontera, Chile
Marc Baaden, Institut de Biologie Physico-Chimique, Paris, France
Raymond Bair, Argonne National Laboratory / University of Chicago, USA
Bernhard Bandow, Max Planck Institute for Solar System Research (MPS), Göttingen, Germany
Valeria Bartsch, Fraunhofer ITWM in Kaiserslautern, Germany
Md Zakirul Alam Bhuiyan, Fordham University, USA
Tekin Bicer, Argonne National Laboratory, USA
Suhaimi Bin Ishak, Universiti Utara Malaysia, Kedah, Malaysia
Fernanda Maria Brito Correia, University of Aveiro / Polytechnic Institute of Coimbra, Portugal
Hans-Joachim Bungartz, Technische Universität München (TUM) - Garching, Germany

Xiao-Chuan Cai, University of Colorado Boulder, USA
Nicola Calabretta, Institute for Photonic Integration (IPI), The Netherlands
Ralph H. Castain, Intel Inc., USA
Hsi-Ya Chang, National Center for High-Performance Computing, Taiwan
Jian Chang, Bournemouth University, UK
Shuai Che, Advanced Micro Devices, USA
Albert M. K. Cheng, University of Houston, USA
Almadena Chtchelkanova, National Science Foundation, USA
Christian Contarino, University of Trento, Italy
Noelia Correia, University of Algarve | CEOT (Center for Electronics, Optoelectronics and Telecommunications), Portugal
Vitalian Danciu, Ludwig-Maximilians-Universität München, Germany
Kei Davis, Los Alamos National Laboratory, USA
Amine Dhraief, ESEN/HANA Research Lab - University of Manouba, Tunisia
Vanessa End, GWDG, Germany
Iman Faraji, Nvidia Corp., Canada
Ian Flood, Rinker School, College of Design, Construction and Planning - University of Florida, USA
Felix Freitag, Politechnical University of Catalonia, Spain
Steffen Frey, Visualization Research Center - University of Stuttgart, Germany
Munehiro Fukuda, University of Washington, Bothell, USA
Alfred Geiger, T-Systems Solutions for Research GmbH, Germany
Birgit Gersbeck-Schierholz, Leibniz Universität Hannover, Germany
Franca Giannini, IMATI-CNR, Italy
Vincenzo Gulisano, Chalmers University of Technology, Sweden
Yanfei Guo, Argonne National Laboratory, USA
Shakhmametova Gyuzel, Ufa State Aviation Technical University, Russia
Huong Ha, School of Business, Singapore University of Social Sciences (SUSS), Singapore
Mahantesh Halappanavar, Pacific Northwest National Laboratory, USA
Raoudha Den Djemaa Hamza, Higher Institute of Computer Sciences and Technology Communication of Hammam Sousse / MIRACL - Sfax University, Tunisia
Houcine Hassan, Universitat Politècnica de València, Spain
Thomas Heller, Friedrich-Alexander-Universität Erlangen-Nürnberg, Germany
Enrique Hernández Orallo, Universidad Politécnica de Valencia, Spain
Gonzalo Hernandez, Universidad de Santiago de Chile, Chile
Daniel Holmes, EPCC | The University of Edinburgh, Scotland, UK
Friedrich Hülsmann, Gottfried Wilhelm Leibniz Bibliothek, Hannover, Germany
Miaoqing Huang, University of Arkansas, USA
Sergio Ilarri, University of Zaragoza, Spain
Neena Imam, Oak Ridge National Laboratory, USA
Haziq Jeelani, Galgotias University, India
Jinlei Jiang, Tsinghua University, Beijing, China
Eugene B. John, The University of Texas at San Antonio, USA
Seifedine Kadry, Beirut Arab University, Lebanon
Izabela Karsznia, University of Warsaw, Poland
Nicolas Kemper Valverde, Universidad Nacional Autónoma de México, Mexico
Amin Khan, UiT The Arctic University of Norway, Tromsø, Norway
Jinoh Kim, Texas A&M University-Commerce, USA
Alexander Kipp, Robert Bosch GmbH, Germany

Stefanos Kollias, University of Lincoln, UK
Zlatinka Kovacheva, Department of Mathematics and Applied Sciences, Middle East College - Muscat, Oman
Manfred Krafczyk, Institute for Computational Modeling in Civil Engineering (iRMB) – TU Braunschweig, Germany
Bettina Krammer, MoRitS, Bielefeld University & Bielefeld University of Applied Sciences, Germany
Rolf Krause, Università della Svizzera italiana, Switzerland
Herbert Kuchen, Westfälische Wilhelms-Universität Münster, Institut für Wirtschaftsinformatik, Germany
Kalyan Kumaran, Argonne Leadership Computing Facility, USA
Sonal Kumari, Robert BOSCH, Bangalore, India
Robert S. Laramee, Swansea University, UK
Edgar A. Leon, Lawrence Livermore National Laboratory, USA
Yiu-Wing Leung, Hong Kong Baptist University, Kowloon Tong, Hong Kong
Elżbieta Lewańska, Poznan University of Economics and Business, Poland
Xin Li, Johns Hopkins University, USA
Yanting Li, City University of HongKong, China
Jaehan Lim, Kwangwoon University, South Korea
Walter Lioen, SURFsara, Netherlands
Iryna Lishchuk, Institut für Rechtsinformatik | Leibniz Universität Hannover, Germany
Maciej Liskiewicz, Universität zu Lübeck, Germany
Chin-Jung Liu, Michigan State University, USA
Piotr Luszczek, University of Tennessee, USA
Filippo Mantovani, Barcelona Supercomputing Center, Spain
António Manuel Duarte Nogueira, University of Aveiro - Instituto de Telecomunicações, Portugal
Alessandro Margara, Politecnico di Milano, Italy
Antonio Martí-Campoy, Universitat Politècnica de València, Spain
Nikolaos Matsatsinis, Technical University of Crete, Greece
Artis Mednis, Akero Systems, Latvia
Roderick Melnik, MS2Discovery Interdisciplinary Research Institute | Wilfrid Laurier University (WLU), Canada
Gabriele Mencagli, University of Pisa, Italy
Mariofanna Milanova, UA Little Rock, USA
Sangman Moh, Chosun University, Korea
Sébastien Monnet, University Savoie Mont Blanc - LISTIC, France
Hans-Guenther Mueller, Cray, Germany
Mithun Mukherjee, Guangdong University of Petrochemical Technology, China
Marian Mureșan, Babes-Bolyai University, Cluj-Napoca, Romania
Katsuhiro Naito, Aichi Institute of Technology, Japan
Syed Naqvi, Birmingham City University, UK
Lena Noack, Free University of Berlin, Germany
Ulrich Norbisrath, University of Applied Sciences Upper Austria (FH UA) Linz, Austria / George Mason University, USA
Krzysztof Okarma, West Pomeranian University of Technology, Szczecin, Poland
Aida Omerovic, SINTEF ICT, Norway
Malgorzata Pankowska, University of Economics in Katowice, Poland
Giuseppe Patane', CNR-IMATI, Italy
Ripon Patgiri, National Institute of Technology Silchar, India

Andrew J. Younge, Sandia National Laboratories, USA
Quan Yuan, The University of Texas of the Permian Basin,USA
Na Zhang, VMware Inc., USA
Sotirios Ziavras, New Jersey Institute of Technology, USA
Jason Zurawski, Lawrence Berkeley National Laboratory / Energy Sciences Network (ESnet), USA

Copyright Information

Global Exponential Stability of the Periodic Solution of a Discrete-Time Complex-Valued Hopfield Neural Network with Delays and Impulses

Valéry Covachev
Institute of Mathematics and Informatics
Bulgarian Academy of Sciences
Sofia, Bulgaria
Email: vcovachev@hotmail.com

Zlatinka Covacheva
Middle East College
Muscat, Sultanate of Oman
Email: zkovacheva@hotmail.com

Abstract—**The global stability of the periodic solution of a discrete-time complex-valued Hopfield neural network is studied. By introducing an appropriate Lyapunov functional it is proved that any two solutions of the system exponentially approach each other with time.**

Keywords-complex neural networks; periodic solution; stability.

I. Introduction

Over the past three decades, neural networks have been widely studied since they have been successfully applied to various processing problems such as optimization, image processing, associative memory and many other fields (see [10][12] and references given therein). Different types of applications depend on the dynamical behaviors of the neural networks. The existence and stability of equilibrium points and periodic solutions are of particular interest.

In order to solve problems in the fields of optimization, neural control and signal processing, neural networks have to be designed such that there is only one equilibrium point and this equilibrium point is globally asymptotically stable so as to avoid the risk of having spurious equilibria and local minima. In the case of global stability, there is no need to be specific about the initial conditions for the neural circuits since all trajectories starting from anywhere settle down at the same unique equilibrium. If the equilibrium is exponentially asymptotically stable, the convergence is fast for real-time computations. The unique equilibrium depends on the external stimulus. When the parameters of the neural network and the external stimulus are not constants but periodic functions of time, which is the case in many real-life problems, the role of the equilibrium point is played by a periodic solution.

Numerical algorithms of Hopfield-type differential equations lead to discrete-time dynamic systems and such discrete-time systems should not give rise to any spurious behavior if either system is to be used for coding equilibrium as associative memories corresponding to temporally uniform external stimuli obtained. The discrete-time models serve as global numerical methods on unbounded intervals for the continuous-time systems [18].

A. Hirose wrote in the introduction to [13]: "Complex-valued neural networks (CVNNs) are effective and powerful in particular to deal with wave phenomena such as electromagnetic and sonic waves, as well as to process wave-related information ... Researchers extend the world of computation to pattern processing fields based on a novel use of the structure of complex-amplitude (phase and amplitude) information." Further on, he listed the following major application fields of CVNNs: antenna design, estimation of direction of arrival and beamforming of electromagnetic waves, radar imaging, acoustic signal processing and ultrasonic imaging, communications signal processing, image processing, traffic-lights and electric-power systems, quantum devices such as superconductive devices, optical/lightwave information processing including carrier-frequency multiplexing. CVNNs also find applications in fields such as speech synthesis, spatiotemporal analysis of physiological neural devices and systems and artificial neural information processing [23]. CVNNs can be considered as an extension of real-valued neural networks; however, they can be used to solve problems which cannot be solved using their real-valued counterparts [20]. The existence, global asymptotic and exponential stability of equilibrium points of CVNNs have been actively studied in the recent years [6][14][22]. On the other hand, there are very few results on the existence, global asymptotic and exponential stability of periodic solutions of CVNNs [11][21]. These papers deal with delayed CVNNs, respectively of neutral type and with impulses. In [23], sufficient conditions are obtained for the existence and global asymptotic stability of periodic solutions for delayed complex-valued simplified Cohen-Grossberg neural networks.

In our previous paper [7], we constructed a discrete-time counterpart of a complex-valued Hopfield network with time-varying delays and impulses by using the semi-discretization method. We found sufficient conditions for the existence of periodic solutions of the discrete-time system thus obtained by using the continuation theorem of coincidence degree theory. The goal of the present paper is to find sufficient conditions for the uniqueness and global exponential stability of the periodic solution of the aforementioned discrete-time system. The motivation for our study was the possibility to apply to CVNNs methods previously applied to real-valued neural network. The exposition is self-contained: its understanding does not require reading of [7].

The rest of the paper is organized as follows: Section II recalls the original continuous-time neural network of [7], its discrete-time counterpart and representation as a real-valued discrete-time neural network of double dimension, and the sufficient conditions for the existence of periodic solutions. In Section III, under some additional conditions including time-independence of the delays, we prove the uniqueness and global exponential stability of the periodic solution by introducing an appropriate Lyapunov functional. More precisely, it is shown that any two solutions of the discrete-time system exponentially approach each other. The proof is more difficult than in the case of real-valued neural networks because of the more complicated form of the Lyapunov functional. Finally, Section IV is Discussion, and Section V is Conclusion and Further Work.

II. Preliminaries

In [7], we consider the following impulsive neural network with time-varying delays:

$$\dot{z}_i(t) = -a_i(t)z_i(t) + \sum_{j=1}^{m} b_{ij}(t)f_j(z_j(t)) + \sum_{j=1}^{m} c_{ij}(t)g_j(z_j(t-\tau_{ij}(t))) + I_i(t), \quad t>0, \quad t \neq t_k, \tag{1}$$

$$\Delta z_i(t_k) = -\alpha_{ik}z_i(t_k) + \sum_{j=1}^{m} \beta_{ijk}\Phi_j(z_j(t_k)) + \sum_{j=1}^{m} \gamma_{ijk}\Gamma_j(z_j(t_k - \tau_{ij}(t_k))) + \zeta_{ik}, \quad k \in \{0\}\cup\mathbb{N}, \tag{2}$$

$$z_i(s) = \varphi_i(s), \quad s \in [-\tau, 0], \quad i = \overline{1,m}, \tag{3}$$

where $z_i(t)$ is the complex-valued state of the i-th neuron at time t; $a_i(t)$ is the rate with which the i-th unit resets its potential to the equilibrium state when isolated from the network and external inputs; $f_j(\cdot)$, $g_j(\cdot)$ denote complex activation functions, respectively without and with delay; the functions $b_{ij}(t)$, $c_{ij}(t)$ represent the weights (or strengths) of the synaptic connections between the j-th neuron and the i-th neuron, respectively without and with transmission delay $\tau_{ij}(t)$; $I_i(t)$ denotes the complex-valued external bias on (input signal introduced from outside the network to) the i-th unit at time t; t_k ($k \in \{0\}\cup\mathbb{N}$) are the moments (instants) of impulse effect satisfying $0 = t_0 < t_1 < t_2 < \cdots < t_k < \cdots$ and $\lim_{k\to\infty} t_k = \infty$; $\Delta z_i(t_k) := z_i(t_k+0) - z_i(t_k-0) \equiv z_i(t_k+0) - z_i(t_k)$ represents the instantaneous change of the state of the i-th neuron at time t_k; $\Phi_j(\cdot)$, $\Gamma_j(\cdot) : \mathbb{C} \to \mathbb{C}$ are some functions; α_{ik}, β_{ijk}, γ_{ijk}, ζ_{ik} are some complex constants; and $\tau = \max_{i,j=\overline{1,m}} \sup_{t>0} \tau_{ij}(t)$.

We included a real-life example which is a real-valued neural network of the form (1)–(3) (see, for instance, [1] and [16]):

$$C_i\dot{u}_i(t) = -\frac{u_i(t)}{R_i} + \sum_{j=1}^{m} a_{ij}f_j(u_j(t)) + \sum_{j=1}^{m} b_{ij}(t)g_j(u_j(t-\tau_{ij}(t))) + I_i, \quad t>0,\ t\neq t_k,$$

$$\Delta u_i(t_k) = J_{jk}(u_i(t_k)), \qquad k \in \mathbb{N},$$

$$u_i(s) = \varphi_i(s), \quad s \in [-\tau, 0], \quad i = \overline{1,m},$$

where $u_i(t)$ denotes the state (voltage) of the i-th neuron at time t, the positive constants C_i and R_i are the neuron amplifier input capacitance and resistance, respectively.

For system (1)–(3) we made the following assumptions:

[H1] There exists a positive number ω and a positive integer p such that

$a_i(t+\omega) = a_i(t)$, $I_i(t+\omega) = I_i(t)$ for $t \geq 0$ and $i = \overline{1,m}$,

$b_{ij}(t+\omega) = b_{ij}(t)$, $c_{ij}(t+\omega) = c_{ij}(t)$, $\tau_{ij}(t+\omega) = \tau_{ij}(t)$ for $t \geq 0$ and $i,j = \overline{1,m}$,

$t_{k+p} = t_k + \omega$ for $k \in \{0\}\cup\mathbb{N}$,

$\alpha_{i,k+p} = \alpha_{ik}$, $\zeta_{i,k+p} = \zeta_{ik}$ for $k \in \{0\}\cup\mathbb{N}$ and $i = \overline{1,m}$,

$\beta_{ij,k+p} = \beta_{ijk}$, $\gamma_{ij,k+p} = \gamma_{ijk}$ for $k \in \{0\}\cup\mathbb{N}$ and $i,j = \overline{1,m}$.

[H2] The complex-valued functions $a_i(t)$, $b_{ij}(t)$, $c_{ij}(t)$ are continuous on $[0,\infty]$; $\mathrm{Re}\,a_i(t) > 0$ for $t \geq 0$ and $0 < \mathrm{Re}\,\alpha_{ik} < 1$ for $k \in \{0\}\cup\mathbb{N}$, $i = \overline{1,m}$.

[H3] There exist positive constants F_j, G_j, $\mathcal{F}_j$, $\mathcal{G}_j$ ($j = \overline{1,m}$) such that

$$\max\{|\mathrm{Re}\,f_j(u) - \mathrm{Re}\,f_j(v)|, |\mathrm{Im}\,f_j(u) - \mathrm{Im}\,f_j(v)|\} \leq F_j(|\mathrm{Re}\,u - \mathrm{Re}\,v| + |\mathrm{Im}\,u - \mathrm{Im}\,v|),$$
$$\max\{|\mathrm{Re}\,g_j(u) - \mathrm{Re}\,g_j(v)|, |\mathrm{Im}\,g_j(u) - \mathrm{Im}\,g_j(v)|\} \leq G_j(|\mathrm{Re}\,u - \mathrm{Re}\,v| + |\mathrm{Im}\,u - \mathrm{Im}\,v|),$$
$$\max\{|\mathrm{Re}\,\Phi_j(u) - \mathrm{Re}\,\Phi_j(v)|, |\mathrm{Im}\,\Phi_j(u) - \mathrm{Im}\,\Phi_j(v)|\} \leq \mathcal{F}_j(|\mathrm{Re}\,u - \mathrm{Re}\,v| + |\mathrm{Im}\,u - \mathrm{Im}\,v|),$$
$$\max\{|\mathrm{Re}\,\Gamma_j(u) - \mathrm{Re}\,\Gamma_j(v)|, |\mathrm{Im}\,\Gamma_j(u) - \mathrm{Im}\,\Gamma_j(v)|\} \leq \mathcal{G}_j(|\mathrm{Re}\,u - \mathrm{Re}\,v| + |\mathrm{Im}\,u - \mathrm{Im}\,v|)$$

for any $u, v \in \mathbb{C}$.

[H4] The functions $\tau_{ij}(t)$ ($i,j = \overline{1,m}$) are nonnegative and continuous for $t \geq 0$.

[H5] The functions $\varphi_i(s)$ ($i = \overline{1,m}$) are piecewise continuously differentiable on the interval $[-\tau, 0]$, with points of possible discontinuity of the form $t_k - \omega$.

To find an ω-periodic solution of system (1), (2) means to determine the initial functions $\varphi_i(s)$ so that the solution of the initial-value problem (1)–(3) is ω-periodic.

In their paper [15] T. Insperger and G. Stépán presented an efficient numerical method for the stability analysis of linear delayed systems. The semi-discretization method is based on discretization with respect to the past effect only. It was shown that the semi-discretization method is much more effective than the full discretization for the stability analysis. The semi-discretization does not preserve the solutions of the original system. However, it does preserve their exponential stability if the semi-discretization is fine enough in some sense.

A modification of the semi-discretization method was used for the stability analysis of neural networks by S. Mohamad and K. Gopalsamy in [19] and numerous subsequent papers of the same authors. In particular, it can be applied to not necessarily linear neural networks if the nonlinearities satisfy certain conditions.

Similarly to our previous papers [2][3][4], next we derived a discrete counterpart of system (1)–(3) using a modification of the semi-discretization method and obtained sufficient conditions for the existence of periodic solutions of the latter.

For the sake of definiteness we assumed that $\tau \le \omega$. For a positive integer N we chose the discretization step $h = \omega/N$. For the moment we assume N so large that $h < \min_{k=\overline{1,p}}(t_{k+1} - t_k)$. Then each interval $[nh, (n+1)h]$ contains at most one instant of impulse effect t_k.

For convenience we denoted $n = [t/h]$, the greatest integer in t/h, $n_k = [t_k/h]$, and $N_0 = [\tau/h]$.

Omitting the details, we present the derived discrete-time counterpart of system (1)–(3):

$$\Delta z_i(n) = -A_i(n) z_i(n) + I_i(n)$$
$$+\begin{cases} \sum_{j=1}^{m} b_{ij}(n) f_j(z_j(n)) + \sum_{j=1}^{m} c_{ij}(n) g_j(z_j(n-\tau_{ij}(n))), \\ \qquad n \ne n_k, \\ \sum_{j=1}^{m} \beta_{ijk} \Phi_j(z_j(n_k)) + \sum_{j=1}^{m} \gamma_{ijk} \Gamma_j(z_j(n_k - \tau_{ij}(n_k))), \\ \qquad n = n_k, \end{cases} \tag{4}$$
$$n \in \{0\} \cup \mathbb{N},$$
$$z_i(s) = \varphi_i(s) \quad \text{for} \quad s = 0, -1, \ldots, -N_0, \quad i = \overline{1,m}, \tag{5}$$

where $z_i(n)$ is the complex-valued state of the i-th neuron at time nh ($n \in \mathbb{Z}$, $n \ge -N_0$; $A_i(n)$ is a complex-valued function with a positive real part; n_k ($k \in \{0\} \cup \mathbb{N}$) are integers satisfying $0 = n_0 < n_1 < n_2 < \cdots < n_k < \cdots$ and $\lim_{k\to\infty} n_k = \infty$; $\Delta z_i(n) := z_i(n+1) - z_i(n)$; $\Phi_j(\cdot)$, $\Gamma_j(\cdot) : \mathbb{C} \to \mathbb{C}$ are some functions; α_{ik}, β_{ijk}, γ_{ijk}, ζ_{ik} are some complex constants; $\varphi(s) = (\varphi_1(s), \varphi_2(s), \ldots, \varphi_m(s))^T$, $s = 0, -1, \ldots, -N_0$, are given initial vectors, and $N_0 = \max_{i,j=\overline{1,m}} \sup_{n\ge 0} \tau_{ij}(n)$.

From the assumptions H1, H2, H4, it follows that

[H6] There exist positive integers N and p such that

$$A_i(n+N) = A_i(n),\ I_i(n+N) = I_i(n) \ \text{for}\ i = \overline{1,m}, \quad n \in \{0\} \cup \mathbb{N},$$

$$\tau_{ij}(n+N) = \tau_{ij}(n) \ \text{for}\ i,j = \overline{1,m},\ n \in \{0\} \cup \mathbb{N},$$

$$b_{ij}(n+N) = b_{ij}(n),\ c_{ij}(n+N) = c_{ij}(n) \ \text{for}\ i,j = \overline{1,m}, \quad n \in \mathbb{N} \setminus \{n_k\}_{k\in\mathbb{N}},$$

$$n_{k+p} = n_k + N \quad \text{for} \quad k \in \{0\} \cup \mathbb{N},$$

$$\beta_{ij,k+p} = \beta_{ijk},\ \gamma_{ij,k+p} = \gamma_{ijk} \ \text{for}\ k \in \{0\} \cup \mathbb{N} \quad \text{and} \quad i,j = \overline{1,m}.$$

[H7] $0 < \operatorname{Re} A_i(n) < 1$ for $i = \overline{1,m}$, $n \in I_N := \{0, 1, \ldots, N-1\}$.

To find an N-periodic solution of system (4) means to determine the initial vectors $\varphi_i(s)$ so that the solution of the initial-value problem (4), (5) is N-periodic. For the sake of definiteness, we assume that $N_0 \le N$.

In order to formulate the main result of [7], we introduced the following notation:

For an N-periodic sequence $v(n)$, we denote $\tilde{v} = \sum_{n=0}^{N-1} v(n)$ (if $v(n)$ is given by a long formula, we write $v\tilde{}$ or $(v)\tilde{}$ instead);

$$\overline{b}_{ij} = \max\{\sup_{n\ne n_k} |\operatorname{Re} b_{ij}(n)|,\ \sup_{n\ne n_k} |\operatorname{Im} b_{ij}(n)|\},$$
$$\overline{c}_{ij} = \max\{\sup_{n\ne n_k} |\operatorname{Re} c_{ij}(n)|,\ \sup_{n\ne n_k} |\operatorname{Im} c_{ij}(n)|\},$$
$$\overline{\beta}_{ij} = \max\{\max_{k=\overline{1,p}} |\operatorname{Re} \beta_{ijk}|,\ \max_{k=\overline{1,p}} |\operatorname{Im} \beta_{ijk}|\},$$
$$\overline{\gamma}_{ij} = \max\{\max_{k=\overline{1,p}} |\operatorname{Re} \gamma_{ijk}|,\ \max_{k=\overline{1,p}} |\operatorname{Im} \gamma_{ijk}|\}, \quad i,j = \overline{1,m};$$

$$\rho_i = (N-p)\sum_{j=1}^{m} \left[\overline{b}_{ij}(|\operatorname{Re} f_j(0)| + |\operatorname{Im} f_j(0)|) + \overline{c}_{ij}(|\operatorname{Re} g_j(0)| + |\operatorname{Im} g_j(0)|)\right]$$
$$+p\sum_{j=1}^{m} \left[\overline{\beta}_{ij}(|\operatorname{Re} \Phi_j(0)| + |\operatorname{Im} \Phi_j(0)|) + \overline{\gamma}_{ij}(|\operatorname{Re} \Gamma_j(0)| + |\operatorname{Im} \Gamma_j(0)|)\right], \quad i = \overline{1,m};$$

$$\mathcal{B}_{ij} = 2[(N-p)(\overline{b}_{ij} F_j + \overline{c}_{ij} G_j) + p(\overline{\beta}_{ij} \mathcal{F}_j + \overline{\gamma}_{ij} \mathcal{G}_j)], \quad i,j = \overline{1,m}.$$

Next, we introduced the condition

[H8] $\min_{i=\overline{1,m}} \left(\widetilde{\operatorname{Re} A_i} - |\operatorname{Im} A_i|\tilde{} - \sum_{j=1}^{m} \mathcal{B}_{ji} \right) > 0.$

We introduce the $m \times m$ matrices

$$\tilde{A}_R = \operatorname{diag}\left(\widetilde{\operatorname{Re} A_i} \frac{1 - \widetilde{\operatorname{Re} A_i}}{1 + \widetilde{\operatorname{Re} A_i}},\ i = \overline{1,m} \right),$$
$$\tilde{A}_I = \operatorname{diag}\left(|\operatorname{Im} A_i|\tilde{},\ i = \overline{1,m}\right), \quad \mathcal{B} = (\mathcal{B}_{ij})_{i,j=1}^{m},$$

and the condition

[H9] The $2m \times 2m$ matrix $\mathcal{A} = \begin{pmatrix} \tilde{A}_R - \mathcal{B} & -\tilde{A}_I - \mathcal{B} \\ -\tilde{A}_I - \mathcal{B} & \tilde{A}_R - \mathcal{B} \end{pmatrix}$ is an M-matrix.

This condition implies that the matrix $\mathcal{A}$ is nonsingular and its inverse has only nonnegative entries [5][8].

The main result of [7] is the following theorem.

Theorem 1: Suppose that conditions H3, H6–H9 hold. Then the system (4) has at least one N-periodic solution.

The theorem was proved using Mawhin's continuation theorem [9, p. 40]. To this end, we denoted $x_i = \operatorname{Re} z_i$, $y_i = \operatorname{Im} z_i$ ($i = \overline{1,m}$), $x = (x_1, x_2, \ldots, x_m)^T$, $y = (y_1, y_2, \ldots, y_m)^T$, and considered $z = (x, y)^T$ as a vector in $\mathbb{R}^{2m}$. Next, we rewrote the complex system (4) as the real system

$$
\Delta x_i(n) = -\mathrm{Re}\,A_i(n)x_i(n) + \mathrm{Im}\,A_i(n)y_i(n) + \mathrm{Re}\,I_i(n)
+ \begin{cases} \sum_{j=1}^{m} [\mathrm{Re}\,b_{ij}(n)\mathrm{Re}\,f_j(z_j(n)) - \mathrm{Im}\,b_{ij}(n)\mathrm{Im}\,f_j(z_j(n)) \\ \quad + \mathrm{Re}\,c_{ij}(n)\mathrm{Re}\,g_j(z_j(n-\tau_{ij}(n))) \\ \quad - \mathrm{Im}\,c_{ij}(n)\mathrm{Im}\,g_j(z_j(n-\tau_{ij}(n)))], \quad n \neq n_k; \\ \sum_{j=1}^{m} [\mathrm{Re}\,\beta_{ijk}\mathrm{Re}\,\Phi_j(z_j(n_k)) - \mathrm{Im}\,\beta_{ijk}\mathrm{Im}\,\Phi_j(z_j(n_k)) \\ \quad + \mathrm{Re}\,\gamma_{ijk}\mathrm{Re}\,\Gamma_j(z_j(n_k-\tau_{ij}(n_k))) \\ \quad - \mathrm{Im}\,\gamma_{ijk}\mathrm{Im}\,\Gamma_j(z_j(n_k-\tau_{ij}(n_k)))], \quad n = n_k, \end{cases} \tag{6}
$$

$$
\Delta y_i(n) = -\mathrm{Re}\,A_i(n)y_i(n) - \mathrm{Im}\,A_i(n)x_i(n) + \mathrm{Im}\,I_i(n)
+ \begin{cases} \sum_{j=1}^{m} [\mathrm{Re}\,b_{ij}(n)\mathrm{Im}\,f_j(z_j(n)) + \mathrm{Im}\,b_{ij}(n)\mathrm{Re}\,f_j(z_j(n)) \\ + \mathrm{Re}\,c_{ij}(n)\mathrm{Im}\,g_j(z_j(n-\tau_{i-m,j}(n))) \\ + \mathrm{Im}\,c_{ij}(n)\mathrm{Re}\,g_j(z_j(n-\tau_{i-m,j}(n)))], \ n \neq n_k; \\ \sum_{j=1}^{m} [\mathrm{Re}\,\beta_{ijk}\mathrm{Im}\,\Phi_j(z_j(n_k)) + \mathrm{Im}\,\beta_{ijk}\mathrm{Re}\,\Phi_j(z_j(n_k)) \\ + \mathrm{Re}\,\gamma_{ijk}\mathrm{Im}\,\Gamma_j(z_j(n_k-\tau_{i-m,j}(n_k))) \\ + \mathrm{Im}\,\gamma_{ijk}\mathrm{Re}\,\Gamma_j(z_j(n_k-\tau_{i-m,j}(n_k)))], \ n = n_k, \end{cases} \tag{7}
$$

for $i = \overline{1,m}$.

In the next section, under some additional assumptions, we prove the global exponential stability of any N-periodic solution of system (4).

III. Main Result

Let us denote

$$
B_{ij} = 2\max(\overline{b}_{ij}F_j, \overline{\beta}_{ij}\mathcal{F}_j),
$$
$$
C_{ij} = 2\max(\overline{c}_{ij}G_j, \overline{\gamma}_{ij}\mathcal{G}_j). \tag{8}
$$

Next, we introduce the conditions

[H10] The delays τ_{ij} $(0 \le \tau_{ij} \le N_0)$ are independent of n.

[H11] The inequalities

$$
\mathrm{Re}\,A_i(n) - |\mathrm{Im}\,A_i(n)| - \sum_{j=1}^{m}(B_{ji} + C_{ji}) > 0
$$

are satisfied for all $n \in I_N$ and $i = \overline{1,m}$.

It is easy to see that condition H11 implies H8.

Our main result is the following theorem.

Theorem 2: Let conditions H3, H6, H7, H10, H11 hold. Let $z^*(n) = (x^*(n), y^*(n))^T$ be an N-periodic solution of system (4). Then there exist constants $M > 1$ and $\overline{\lambda} > 1$ such that for any $\lambda \in (1, \overline{\lambda}]$ and for any other solution $z(n) = (x(n), y(n))^T$ of system (4) defined at least for $n \ge -N_0$ the following estimate holds

$$
\sum_{i=1}^{m}(|x_i(n) - x_i^*(n)| + |y_i(n) - y_i^*(n)|) \tag{9}
$$
$$
\le M\lambda^{-n}\sum_{i=1}^{m} \max_{-N_0 \le s \le 0}(|x_i(s) - x_i^*(s)| + |y_i(s) - y_i^*(s)|)
$$

for all $n \in \{0\} \cup \mathbb{N}$.

In the proof of the theorem, we use the following lemma.

Lemma 1: Let condition H11 hold. Then there exists a constant $\overline{\lambda} > 1$ such that for any $\lambda \in (1, \overline{\lambda}]$

$$
\lambda\left(1 - \mathrm{Re}\,A_i(n) + |\mathrm{Im}\,A_i(n)| + \sum_{j=1}^{m} B_{ji}\right)
+ \sum_{j=1}^{m} C_{ji}\lambda^{1+\tau_{ji}} - 1 \le 0
$$

for all $n \in I_N$ and $i = \overline{1,m}$.

Proof: Consider the functions

$$
\chi_i(n,\lambda) := \lambda\left(1 - \mathrm{Re}\,A_i(n) + |\mathrm{Im}\,A_i(n)| + \sum_{j=1}^{m} B_{ji}\right)
+ \sum_{j=1}^{m} C_{ji}\lambda^{1+\tau_{ji}} - 1, \quad n \in I_N,\ i = \overline{1,m}.
$$

For each $n \in I_N$ and $i = \overline{1,m}$, $\chi_i(n,\lambda)$ is a continuous function of $\lambda \in [1,\infty)$ such that

$$
\chi_i(n,1) = -\left(\mathrm{Re}\,A_i(n) - |\mathrm{Im}\,A_i(n)| - \sum_{j=1}^{m}(B_{ji} + C_{ji})\right) < 0
$$

by virtue of condition H11, and $\lim_{\lambda\to\infty}\chi_i(n,\lambda) = +\infty$. Then there exists $\overline{\lambda}_{in} > 1$ such that $\chi_i(n, \overline{\lambda}_{in}) = 0$ and $\chi_i(n,\lambda) \le 0$ for $\lambda \in (0, \overline{\lambda}_{i,n}]$. It suffices to choose $\overline{\lambda} = \max\{\overline{\lambda}_{in} | \ i = \overline{1,m},\ n \in I_N\}$. ■

Proof of Theorem 2: Let $z^*(n)$ and $z(n)$ be as in the statement of Theorem 2. Our goal will be to construct a Lyapunov functional $V(n)$ of the difference $z(n) - z^*(n)$, which is decreasing with respect to $n \in \{0\} \cup \mathbb{N}$. First, we denote

$$
X(n) := x(n) - x^*(n), \qquad Y(n) := y(n) - y^*(n).
$$

Then, from (6) for $n \in \{0\} \cup \mathbb{N}$, $n \neq n_k$, we have

$$
X_i(n+1) = (1 - \mathrm{Re}\,A_i(n))X_i(n) + \mathrm{Im}\,A_i(n)Y_i(n)
+ \sum_{j=1}^{m}\{\mathrm{Re}\,b_{ij}(n)[\mathrm{Re}\,f_j(z_j(n)) - \mathrm{Re}\,f_j(z_j^*(n))]
- \mathrm{Im}\,b_{ij}(n)[\mathrm{Im}\,f_j(z_j(n)) - \mathrm{Im}\,f_j(z_j^*(n))]\}
$$
$$
+ \sum_{j=1}^{m}\{\mathrm{Re}\,c_{ij}(n)[\mathrm{Re}\,g_j(z_j(n-\tau_{ij})) - \mathrm{Re}\,g_j(z_j^*(n-\tau_{ij}))]
- \mathrm{Im}\,c_{ij}(n)[\mathrm{Im}\,g_j(z_j(n-\tau_{ij})) - \mathrm{Im}\,g_j(z_j^*(n-\tau_{ij}))]\}
$$

and, by virtue of H3, we derive

$$
|X_i(n+1)| \le (1 - \mathrm{Re}\,A_i(n))|X_i(n)| + |\mathrm{Im}\,A_i(n)|\,|Y_i(n)|
+ \sum_{j=1}^{m} 2\overline{b}_{ij}F_j(|X_j(n)| + |Y_j(n)|)
+ \sum_{j=1}^{m} 2\overline{c}_{ij}G_j(|X_j(n-\tau_{ij})| + |Y_j(n-\tau_{ij})|). \tag{10}
$$

In a similar way, we obtain

$$
\begin{aligned}
&|X_i(n_k+1)| \\
&\le (1-\operatorname{Re} A_i(n_k))|X_i(n_k)| + |\operatorname{Im} A_i(n_k)|\,|Y_i(n_k)| \\
&+\sum_{j=1}^{m} 2\overline{\beta}_{ij}\mathcal{F}_j(|X_j(n_k)|+|Y_j(n_k)|) \\
&+\sum_{j=1}^{m} 2\overline{\gamma}_{ij}\mathcal{G}_j(|X_j(n_k-\tau_{ij})|+|Y_j(n_k-\tau_{ij})|). \qquad (11)
\end{aligned}
$$

Using the notation (8), inequalities (10) and (11) can be written by one formula as

$$
\begin{aligned}
&|X_i(n+1)| \\
&\le (1-\operatorname{Re} A_i(n))|X_i(n)| + |\operatorname{Im} A_i(n)|\,|Y_i(n)| \\
&+\sum_{j=1}^{m} B_{ij}(|X_j(n)|+|Y_j(n)|) \\
&+\sum_{j=1}^{m} C_{ij}(|X_j(n-\tau_{ij})|+|Y_j(n-\tau_{ij})|) \qquad (12)
\end{aligned}
$$

for all $n \in \{0\}\cup\mathbb{N}$.

Similarly, from (7) we derive

$$
\begin{aligned}
&|Y_i(n+1)| \\
&\le (1-\operatorname{Re} A_i(n))|Y_i(n)| + |\operatorname{Im} A_i(n)|\,|X_i(n)| \\
&+\sum_{j=1}^{m} B_{ij}(|X_j(n)|+|Y_j(n)|) \\
&+\sum_{j=1}^{m} C_{ij}(|X_j(n-\tau_{ij})|+|Y_j(n-\tau_{ij})|) \qquad (13)
\end{aligned}
$$

for all $n \in \{0\}\cup\mathbb{N}$.

Next, we define the quantities

$$
W_i(x)=\lambda^n|X_i(n)|, \qquad \Psi_i(n)=\lambda^n|Y_i(n)|
$$

for $\lambda\in(1,\overline{\lambda}]$, $n\ge -N_0$ and $i=\overline{1,m}$. Then, in view of (12) and (13), we obtain

$$
\begin{aligned}
&W_i(n+1) \\
&\le \lambda(1-\operatorname{Re} A_i(n))W_i(n) + \lambda|\operatorname{Im} A_i(n)|\Psi_i(n) \\
&+\lambda\sum_{j=1}^{m} B_{ij}(W_j(n)+\Psi_j(n)) \\
&+\sum_{j=1}^{m} C_{ij}\lambda^{1+\tau_{ij}}[W_j(n-\tau_{ij})+\Psi_j(n-\tau_{ij})], \qquad (14)
\end{aligned}
$$

$$
\begin{aligned}
&\Psi_i(n+1) \\
&\le \lambda(1-\operatorname{Re} A_i(n))\Psi_i(n) + \lambda|\operatorname{Im} A_i(n)|W_i(n) \\
&+\lambda\sum_{j=1}^{m} B_{ij}(W_j(n)+\Psi_j(n)) \\
&+\sum_{j=1}^{m} C_{ij}\lambda^{1+\tau_{ij}}[W_j(n-\tau_{ij})+\Psi_j(n-\tau_{ij})]. \qquad (15)
\end{aligned}
$$

Inequalities (14), (15) suggest us to define the Lyapunov functional

$$
V(n)=\sum_{i=1}^{m}\Bigg[W_j(n)+\Psi_j(n) + \sum_{j=1}^{m} C_{ij}\lambda^{1+\tau_{ij}}\sum_{s=n-\tau_{ij}}^{n-1}(W_j(s)+\Psi_j(s))\Bigg]
$$

for all $n\in\{0\}\cup\mathbb{N}$. Then, we have

$$
\begin{aligned}
V(n+1) &= \sum_{i=1}^{m}\Bigg[W_j(n+1)+\Psi_j(n+1) \\
&+\sum_{j=1}^{m} C_{ij}\lambda^{1+\tau_{ij}}\sum_{s=n+1-\tau_{ij}}^{n}(W_j(s)+\Psi_j(s))\Bigg] \\
&\le \sum_{i=1}^{m}\Bigg\{\lambda\Bigg[(1-\operatorname{Re} A_i(n)+|\operatorname{Im} A_i(n)|)(W_i(n)+\Psi_i(n)) \\
&\quad+\sum_{j=1}^{m} B_{ij}(W_j(n)+\Psi_j(n))\Bigg] \\
&+\sum_{j=1}^{m} C_{ij}\lambda^{1+\tau_{ij}}\sum_{s=n-\tau_{ij}}^{n}(W_j(s)+\Psi_j(s))\Bigg\}
\end{aligned}
$$

and

$$
\begin{aligned}
\Delta V(n) &\le \sum_{i=1}^{m}\Bigg\{\lambda\Bigg[1-\operatorname{Re} A_i(n)+|\operatorname{Im} A_i(n)|+\sum_{j=1}^{m} B_{ji}\Bigg] \\
&\quad+\sum_{j=1}^{m} C_{ji}\lambda^{1+\tau_{ji}}-1\Bigg\}(W_i(n)+\Psi_i(n)) \\
&= \sum_{i=1}^{m}\chi_i(n,\lambda)(W_i(n)+\Psi_i(n))\le 0
\end{aligned}
$$

in view of Lemma 1. This means that $V(n+1)\le V(n)$ for all $n\in\{0\}\cup\mathbb{N}$. In particular,

$$
V(n)\le V(0) \quad \text{for all } \; n\in\{0\}\cup\mathbb{N} \; \text{ and } \; \lambda\in(1,\overline{\lambda}].
$$

Taking into account that

$$
V(n)\ge\lambda^n\sum_{i=1}^{m}(|x_i(n)-x_i^*(n)|+|y_i(n)-y_i^*(n)|)
$$

and

$$
\begin{aligned}
V(0) &= \sum_{i=1}^{m}\Bigg[|x_i(0)-x_i^*(0)|+|y_i(0)-y_i^*(0)| \\
&+\sum_{j=1}^{m} C_{ji}\lambda^{1+\tau_{ji}}\sum_{s=-\tau_{ji}}^{-1}(|x_i(s)-x_i^*(s)|+|y_i(s)-y_i^*(s)|)\Bigg] \\
&\le \max_{i=\overline{1,m}}\left(1+\overline{\lambda}^{1+N_0}\sum_{j=1}^{m} C_{ji}\right) \\
&\times\sum_{i=1}^{m}\max_{-N_0\le s\le 0}(|x_i(s)-x_i^*(s)|+|y_i(s)-y_i^*(s)|),
\end{aligned}
$$

we derive the estimate (9) with

$$M = \max_{i=\overline{1,m}} \left(1 + \overline{\lambda}^{1+N_0} \sum_{j=1}^{m} C_{ji} \right).$$

The proof of this estimate did not use the assumption that the solution $z^*(n)$ is N-periodic. In fact, it shows that system (4) can have at most one N-periodic solution and such a solution is globally exponentially stable. ■

IV. Discussion

Our previous experience with papers devoted to neural networks has shown us that most of these papers can be assigned to one of two quite distinct classes — theoretical and applied (practical).

The papers of the first class usually list some real-life applications in their introductions. These applications are normally taken from surveys on neural networks or the introductions of other papers of the same class. Then, the authors study a mathematical model, which is usually a far-going generalization of an application of neural networks to a real-life problem. The properties of the mathematical model are examined using methods, often much more complicated than in the present paper. Finally, a few examples of low-dimensional neural networks satisfying the conditions obtained may be given, and some computations may be carried out. However, applications of the results obtained to real-life problems are very seldom given.

The papers of the second class are usually devoted to a quite concrete real-life problem, say, the identification of people by their fingerprints. Experimental data are usually given, but very little mathematics is used and models to be studied by papers of the first class are seldom given.

The present paper, as well as our previous papers devoted to neural networks, belong to the first class. So it is not easy to give applications to real-life problems.

To the best of our knowledge, the above mentioned two classes of papers grow (maybe exponentially) quite independently of each other. We hope that a cooperation between "theoreticians" and "practicians" could prove fruitful for both trends.

V. Conclusion and Future Work

In the present paper, we obtained sufficient conditions for any two solutions of a discrete-time complex-valued Hopfield neural network with delays and impulses to infinitely approach each other with time. The proof was accomplished by constructing an appropriate Lyapunov functional. The result obtained implies the uniqueness and global exponential stability of a periodic solution, provided that it exists.

In future, in the theoretical aspect, we can extend our research to quaternionic neural networks, which are a generalization of CVNNs. On the other hand, in case of an available "practician" as a co-author, we can concentrate on finding real-life examples and applications of the CVNNs considered in the present paper and the results obtained.

References

[1] H. Akça, R. Alassar, and V. Covachev, "Stability of neural networks with time varying delays in the presence of impulses," *Adv. Dyn. Syst. Appl.*, vol. 1, no. 1, pp. 1–15, 2006.

[2] H. Akça, R. Alassar, V. Covachev, and Z. Covacheva, "Discrete counterparts of continuous-time additive Hopfield-type neural networks with impulses," *Dyn. Syst. Appl.*, vol. 13, no. 1, pp. 77–92, 2004.

[3] H. Akça, E. Al-Zahrani, V. Covachev, and Z. Covacheva, "Existence of periodic solutions for the discrete-time counterpart of a neutral-type cellular neural network with time-varying delays and impulses," *Int. J. Appl. Math. Stat.*, vol. 57, no. 1, pp. 154–166, 2018.

[4] H. Akça, V. Covachev, Z. Covacheva, and S. Mohamad, "Global exponential periodicity for the discrete analogue of an impulsive Hopfield neural network with finite distributed delays," *Funct. Differ. Equ.*, vol. 16, no. 1, pp. 53–72, 2009.

[5] A. Berman and R. J. Plemmons, *Nonnegative Matrices in Mathematical Sciences*, New York: Academic Press, 1979.

[6] M. Bohner, S. H. Rao, and S. Sanyal, "Global stability of complex-valued neural networks on time scales," *Differ. Equ. Dyn. Syst.*, vol. 19, no. 1–2, pp. 3–11, 2011.

[7] V. Covachev and Z. Covacheva, "Existence of periodic solutions for the discrete-time counterpart of a complex-valued Hopfield neural network with time-varying delays and impulses," accepted to IJCNN 2018, Rio de Janeiro.

[8] M. Fiedler, *Special Matrices and Their Applications in Numerical Mathematics*, Dordrecht: Martinus Nijhoff, 1986.

[9] R. E. Gaines and J. L. Mawhin, *Coincidence Degree and Nonlinear Differential Equations*, Berlin-Heidelberg: Springer-Verlag, 1977.

[10] A. I. Galushkin, *Neural Networks Theory*, Berlin-Heidelberg: Springer-Verlag, 2007.

[11] S. Guo and B. Du, "Global exponential stability of periodic solution for neutral-type complex-valued recurrent neural networks," *Discrete Dyn. Nat. Soc.*, vol. 2016, Article ID 1267954, 10 pp., 2016.

[12] J. Heaton, *Introduction to the Math of Neural Networks*, Heaton Research, ISBN: 9781604390339, 2011.

[13] A. Hirose (Ed.), *Complex-Valued Neural Networks: Advances and Applications*, Wiley-IEEE Press, 2013.

[14] J. Hu and J. Wang, "Global stability of complex-valued recurrent neural networks with time-delays," *IEEE Trans. Neural Netw. Learn. Syst.*, vol. 23, no. 6, pp. 853–865, 2012.

[15] T. Insperger and G. Stépán, "Semi-discretization method for delayed systems," *Int. J. Numer. Math. Engng.*, vol. 55, pp. 503–518, 2002.

[16] Y. Li and M. Hua, "The stability analysis for a kind of impulsive Hopfield cellular neural networks," *3rd International Conference on Mechatronics, Robotics and Automation (ICMRA 2015)*, Atlantic Press, 4 p., 2015.

[17] Y. Li, L. Zhao, and X. Chen, "Existence of periodic solutions for neural type cellular neural networks with delays," Appl. Math. Model., vol. 36, no. 3, pp. 1173–1183, 2012.

[18] G. Meinardus and G. Nurnberger (Eds.), *Delay Equations, Approximation and Application*, Boston: Birkhäuser, 1985.

[19] S. Mohamad and K. Gopalsamy, "Dynamics of a class of discrete-time neural networks and their continuous-time counterparts," *Math. Comput. Simulation*, vol. 53, pp. 1–39, 2000.

[20] T. Nitta, "Solving the XOR problem and the detections of symmetry using a single complex-valued neuron," *Neural Netw.*, vol. 16, no. 8, pp. 1101–1105, 2003.

[21] D. Xie and Y. P. Jiang, "Global exponential stability of periodic solutions for delayed complex-valued neural networks with impulses," *Neurocomputing*, vol. 207, pp. 528–538, 2016.

[22] Y. Zhang and C. Lin, "Global stability criterion for delayed complex-valued recurrent neural networks," *IEEE Trans. Neural Netw. Learn. Syst.*, vol. 25, no. 9, pp. 1704–1708, 2014.

[23] Z. Zhang and T. Zheng, "Global asymptotic stability of periodic solutions for delayed complex-valued Cohen-Grossberg neural networks by combining coincidence degree theory with LMI method," *Neurocomputing*, vol. 289, pp. 220–230, 2018.

Computation and Knowledge Mapping for Data Entities

Claus-Peter Rückemann
Westfälische Wilhelms-Universität Münster (WWU),
Leibniz Universität Hannover,
North-German Supercomputing Alliance (HLRN), Germany
Email: ruckema@uni-muenster.de

Abstract—**This paper presents the research and results from developing resources and knowledge based methods for the creation of new context for objects and entities, based on the methodology of knowledge mapping. The results are an architecture allowing advanced knowledge mapping including flexible deployment of computational sequences and an implementation of resources and application components. The knowledge mapping enables to put knowledge objects in new context, which can be used in arbitrary scenarios, e.g., with knowledge mining and decision making. The paper shows the importance of facilities for different implementations and presents a resulting architecture and case studies of two different implementations for a task. The implementation cases are based on a computational case of spatial visualisation. For demonstration, a publicly available central data object was used for data entity analysis. The paper presents practical examples and discusses the high level views of implementations and case study. The main goal of this research is to create a functional architecture based on sustainable long-term multi-disciplinary knowledge resources, which can provide a wide range of flexibility for knowledge mapping and different computational solutions.**

Keywords–Knowledge Mining and Mapping; Computational Procedures; Context Creation; Universal Decimal Classification; Advanced Data-centric Computing.

I. INTRODUCTION

Resources of knowledge are steadily increasing and so is the complexity and heterogeneity of the associated knowledge. In most cases, it is not possible to find satisfying results even though the basis of data is rapidly growing. New approaches are needed in order to find answers to challenging knowledge mining requests.

Concepts used in the past mostly provided non consistent and insufficient approaches when dealing with the complexity of knowledge. In most cases, those concepts basically consider dealing with 'data' and claim to result in 'knowledge' or even 'wisdom' of some kind [1]. For example, the Data-Information-Knowledge-Wisdom (DIKW) approach widely used in Data Mining (DM) lacks an understanding of data being only one aspect of knowledge [2].

Implementations are mostly neglecting the knowledge associated with originary resources and referred knowledge and therefore deal with the applications and isolated technical features, which are neither able to be integrated for improving results nor do they provide reasonable freedom of solutions.

Concepts like DIKW are lacking a profound relation of data and information [3]. Terms like "knowledge hierarchy" and "information hierarchy" are more misleading than constructive, especially when we have to deal with complex and long-term resources. Approaches used with data warehousing [4] on that basis, e.g., Extract, Transform, Load (ETL) and Extract, Load, Transform (ELT) for integrating data newly also resulted in requiring hybrid approaches but have not been based on a profound understanding of knowledge.

The described deficits are a major motivation for this long-term research. The fundaments of terminology and of understanding knowledge are layed out by Aristotle [5][6], being an essential part of 'Ethics' [7]. Information sciences can very much benefit from Aristotle's fundaments and a knowledge-centric approach [8] but for building holistic and sustainable solutions they need to go beyond the available technology-based approaches and hypothesis [9] as analysed in Platons' Phaidon. Making a distinction and creating interfaces between methods and applications [10], the principles are based on the methodology of knowledge mapping [11], which fundaments are not outlayed here again. The implementation can make use of objects and conceptual knowledge [12] and shows being able to build a base for applications scenarios like associative processing [13] and advanced knowledge discovery [14].

Considering this state-of-the-art, the methodology deployed in this research and the accompanying implementation of methods consequently focusses on the complex knowledge basis, which allows to integrate the different aspects of knowledge and the complexity of knowledge context. In result, the methodology allows to create methods focussing on alternative contexts based on a wide range of criteria and solutions provided by knowledge context. Implementations are considered knowledge-centric, with data being one complementary facet of knowledge. Therefore, the methodology and, in consequence, the method implementations based on this methodology, are vastly scalable. Scalability support ranges from fixed associations to arbitrarily fuzzy understanding.

This paper is organised as follows. Section II introduces to the state-of-the-art, architecture, and frame of universal knowledge. Section III presents an exemplary case study with different implementations. Section IV discusses the results of the case study, evaluates them based on the sequences and architecture and delivers a computational footprint in context with referred knowledge. Section V summarises the results and lessons learned, conclusions, and future work.

II. ARCHITECTURE AND UNIVERSAL KNOWLEDGE

An understanding of the essence and complexity of universal, multi-disciplinary knowledge can be achieved by taking a closer look on classification. The state-of-the-art of classifying 'universal knowledge' is the Universal Decimal Classification (UDC) and its solid background and long history. The LX knowledge resources' structure and the classification references [15] based on UDC [16] are essential means for the processing workflows and evaluation of the knowledge objects and containers. Both provide strong multi-disciplinary and multi-lingual support. For the research, all small unsorted excerpts of the knowledge resources objects only refer to main UDC-based classes, which for this publication are taken from the Multilingual Universal Decimal Classification Summary (UDCC Publication No. 088) [17] released by the UDC Consortium under the Creative Commons Attribution Share Alike 3.0 license [18] (first release 2009, subsequent update 2012). Nevertheless, the research conducted here in deploying knowledge provides a new solution not precedented by comparable approaches, from the view of methodology and implemented methods.

A. Architecture

The implementation architecture is shown in Figure 1.

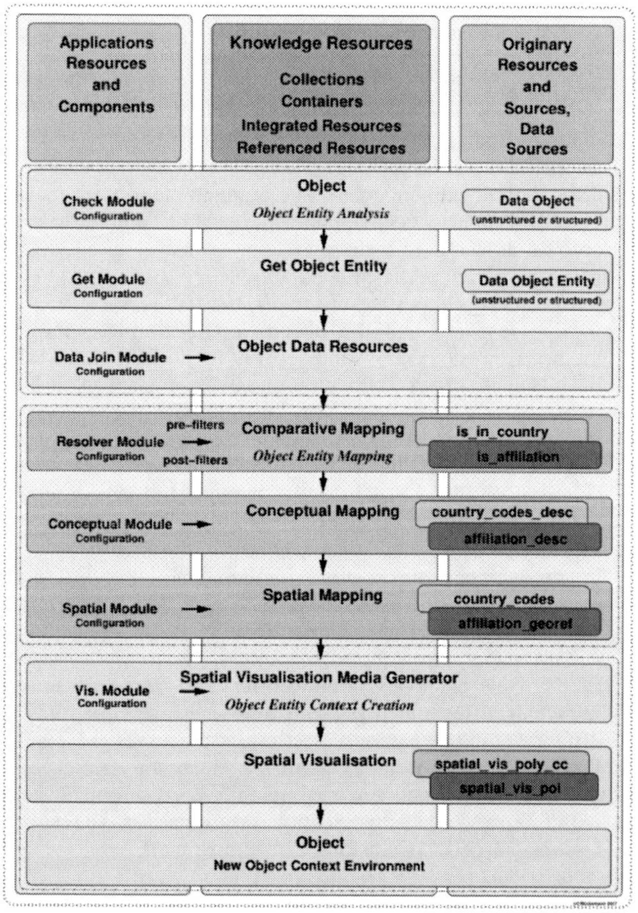

Figure 1. Architecture for mapping arbitrary objects / entities to new context environments, allowing different methods (yellow/red) for implementations.

The illustration of the architecture for knowledge mapping of arbitrary objects and entities to new object context environments also takes into account that the context of objects and their entities can contain many different facets and references from different origin. The target for the case studies is a knowledge mapping providing two different mapping views. The spatial visualisation is an illustrative step, providing insights on new context. Data and modules are provided by Knowledge Resources, originary resources, and application resources and components. The architecture is also aware of allowing different methods (e.g., highlighted in yellow/red) for implementations regarding the same resources and target.

The core of the knowledge mapping in this case consists of comparative mapping, conceptual mapping, and spatial mapping. All the examples in the case studies are based on the methodology of knowledge mapping [11]. The integration of originary sources provides a generic view for terms like 'knowledge integration' and 'knowledge representation' as such might be used in less generic approaches.

Here, in the mapping and the consecutive steps (here, a visualisation for illustration purposes), we do have the major differences of different methods for implementing alternative ways for the same resources and target.

The following case study demonstrates the different characteristics of implementations based on the same universal knowledge. From a multitude of applications scenarios, a term to location association providing ways of knowledge mapping of textual context to space and place were choosen for case studies.

B. Data and Universal Knowledge

The next passages show some major steps for creating spatially linked context from plain text, which were used in the workflows required for the cases. The single data object in this case study implementation (Figure 2) contains mostly unstructured text [19] markup, and formatting instructions.

```
<!DOCTYPE html PUBLIC "-//W3C//DTD␣XHTML␣1.0␣Transitional//EN" ... <title>
 GEOProcessing 2018 ...</title>
..., Leibniz Universit&auml;t Hannover / Westf&auml;lische
 Wilhelms-Universit&auml;t M&uuml;nster / North-German Supercomputing Alliance
      (HLRN), Germany ...
...., Technion - Israel Institute of Technology, Haifa,      Israel<br />
..., Consiglio Nazionale delle Ricerche - Genova,       Italy <br />
..., Centre for Research in Geomatics - Laval University,       Quebec, Canada <
 br />
..., Curtin University, Australia <br />
..., Lomonosov Moscow State University, Russia  <br />
..., FH Aachen, Germany</p> ...
        <p>..., Universiti Tun Hussein Onn Malaysia, Malaysia<br />
          ..., Cardiff University, Wales, UK<br />
          ..., Universidade  Federal do Rio Grande, Brazil<br />
          ..., GIS unit Kuwait Oil  Company, Kuwait<br />
          ..., Middle East Technical  University, Turkey<br />
          ..., University of  Sharjah, UAE<br />
          ..., Georgia State University, USA<br />
          ..., Centre for Research  in Geomatics - Laval University, Quebec,
           Canada<br />
          ..., Environmental Systems  Research Institute (ESRI), USA<br />
          ..., ORT University -  Montevideo, Uruguay<br /> ...
```

Figure 2. Mapping target: Single object, unstructured text (excerpt).

The sample object is the committees' page of the GEOProcessing 2018 conference in Rome [19]. Passages not relevant for demonstration were reduced to ellipses. The spatial visualisation can result from identifying and mapping entities in the text of an object to various knowledge context. The identification of entities is resulting from automated analysis.

Figure 3 shows the object content after automatically integrated with the Knowledge Resources via a join module. The Object Entity Mapping facilitates to associate relevant objects, e.g., via conceptual knowledge and comparative methods. The objects and their entities can contain any knowledge, e.g., factual and conceptual knowledge.

```
GEOProcessing 2018 [...]: ...
  ..., Leibniz Universität Hannover / Westfälische Wilhelms-Universität Münster
   / North-German Supercomputing Alliance (HLRN), Germany ...
  ..., Technion - Israel Institute of Technology, Haifa, Israel
  ..., Consiglio Nazionale delle Ricerche - Genova, Italy
  ..., Centre for Research in Geomatics - Laval University, Quebec, Canada
  ..., Curtin University, Australia
  ..., Lomonosov Moscow State University, Russia
  ..., FH Aachen, Germany ...
  ..., Universiti Tun Hussein Onn Malaysia, Malaysia
  ..., Cardiff University, Wales, UK
  ..., Universidade  Federal do Rio Grande, Brazil
  ..., GIS unit Kuwait Oil  Company, Kuwait
  ..., Middle East Technical  University, Turkey
  ..., University of  Sharjah, UAE
  ..., Georgia State University, USA
  ..., Centre for Research  in Geomatics - Laval University, Quebec, Canada
  ..., Environmental Systems  Research Institute (ESRI), USA
  ..., ORT University -  Montevideo, Uruguay ...
```

Figure 3. Object instance representation after integration (excerpt).

In this case, dealing with space and place data, the references, e.g., referred conceptual knowledge, carried in objects are most relevant. The complement knowledge used with the mapping contains multi-disciplinary and multi-lingual knowledge, it can contain names and synonyms in different languages, dynamically usable geocoordinates, geoclassification, and so on.

Example excerpts of possibly relevant main classification codes of the UDC references are shown in Table I.

TABLE I. UDC CODES OF SPATIAL FEATURES AND PLACE: MAIN CLASSIFICATION CODES USED FOR CONCEPTUAL MAPPING (EXCERPT).

UDC Code	*Description*
UDC:(1)	Place and space in general. Localization. Orientation
UDC:(2)	Physiographic designation
UDC:(3)	Places of the ancient and mediaeval world
UDC:(4/9)	Countries and places of the modern world

The references, e.g., classification, facets, concordances, and textual description, are usable in all the procedures and steps and allow to consider and implement arbitrary flexibility of fuzziness. During the research, two computational sequences were implemented for illustration. These sequences show different characteristics in content and context, as well as different characteristics in architecture and computational requirements.

III. IMPLEMENTATION: MULTIPLE WAYS TO SPACE

The following case study presents two different methods for implementing object/entity knowledge mapping to space and place targets and discusses major insights. Computational knowledge mapping procedures are presented for both methods, as well as the visualisation of the results. The computational application components are part of the available resources. The Generic Mapping Tools (GMT) [20] suite application components were used for handling the spatial data, applying related criteria, and for the visualisation. All provided spatial presentations are using the same Mercator projection (region: -180/180/-60/84) in order to provide a common base for the comparison.

A. Space and place: Affiliation based knowledge mapping

This method implements the knowledge mapping based on affiliations. Table II gives the computational sequence of the core computational procedures.

TABLE II. AFFILIATION BASED MAPPING: COMPUTATIONAL SEQUENCE OF CORE COMPUTATIONAL PROCEDURES AND REFERRED MODULES.

Procedure	*Module*
Comparative Mapping Configuration	`is_affiliation`
Conceptual Mapping Configuration	`affiliation_desc`
Spatial Mapping Configuration	`affiliation_georef`

The means, regarding space and place: Affiliation mapping, affiliation association via conceptual knowledge and textual description, and affiliation georeferencing.

Figure 4 shows an excerpt of affiliation references from the Knowledge Resources as associated with the comparison.

```
...
9.7196969 52.3829641 Leibniz Universitaet Hannover, Germany
...
7.6131826 51.9635705 Westfaelische Wilhelms-Universitaet Muenster
...
-61.5289325 16.2242724 Universite des Antilles - LAMIA, France, Guadeloupe
...
```

Figure 4. Knowledge Resources: Affiliation references used in comparative mapping (excerpt).

In practice, the number of such place references can be very large. In case of this study, the numbers are in the range of millions of places. The visualisation of the results (red bullets) from the affiliation based procedures was done on a spatial map (Figure 5).

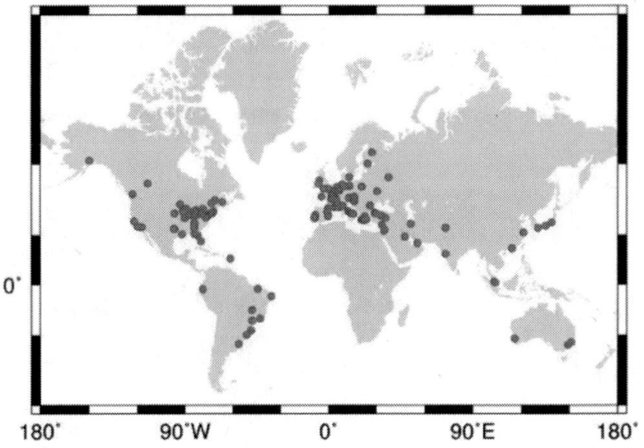

Figure 5. Visualisation of the result of affiliation based knowledge mapping: Geo-referenced place association.

The computing task can be parallelised for objects and entities. For demanding application scenarios, e.g., dynamical implementations, this implementation benefits to a small extend from parallelisation.

B. Space and place: Country code based knowledge mapping

This method implements the knowledge mapping based on country codes. Table III gives the computational sequence of the core computational procedures.

TABLE III. COUNTRY CODE BASED MAPPING: COMPUTATIONAL SEQUENCE OF CORE COMPUTATIONAL PROCEDURES AND REF. MODULES.

Procedure	*Module*
Comparative Mapping	`is_in_country`
Configuration	
Conceptual Mapping	`country_codes_desc`
Configuration	
Spatial Mapping	`country_codes`
Configuration	

That means, regarding space and place: Country mapping, association of country codes via codes description, and evaluation of country codes and visualisation.

Figure 6 shows an excerpt of country code references from the Knowledge Resources as associated with the comparison.

```
...
"Germany|Deutschland" 1xcoco-DE
"Ghana"  1xcoco-GH
"Gibraltar" 1xcoco-GI
"Greece" 1xcoco-GR
"Greenland|Grønland" 1xcoco-GL
"Grenada" 1xcoco-GD
"Guadeloupe" 1xcoco-GP
...
```

Figure 6. Knowledge Resources: Country Codes used for comparative mapping (excerpt).

In practice, the number of such country code references have several hundred pattern-code entities for a certain year or era. In case of this study, the numbers are in the range of about 300 pattern rules per language. Resolving can be done automatically via geo-referencing and visualisation application components.

The visualisation of the results (yellow country colourisation) from the country code based procedures was done on a spatial map (Figure 7). The country codes are based on the standard of the International Standards Organisation (ISO).

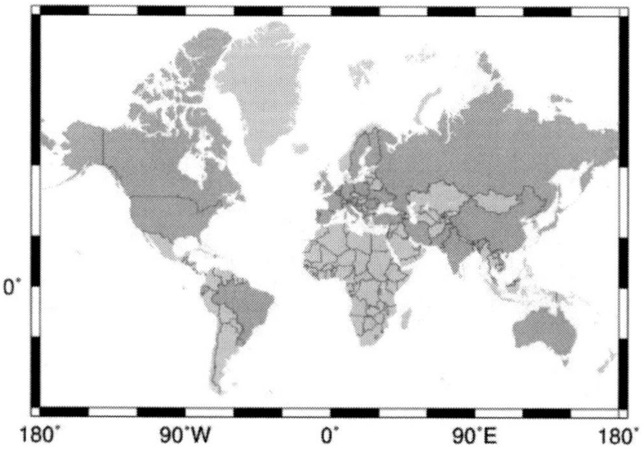

Figure 7. Visualisation of the result of country code based knowledge mapping: ISO referenced state association.

The computing task can be parallelised for objects and entities. For demanding application scenarios, e.g., dynamical implementations, this implementation widely benefits from parallelisation.

IV. DISCUSSION

Implementations can range from generic to specialised, as granted by the methodology, all the components and the illustrated architecture. A reason for illustrating the methodology with a well defined implementation is that from many experiences made from working with methodologies, specialised implementations tend to be better comprehensible by the majority of researchers in various disciplines.

The methodology of knowledge mapping, as illustrated via implementation of two methods discussed here, allows a versatile number of methods to be created for a purpose, based the same knowledge and data.

A. Comparison and discussion of results

The two sequences show different characteristics

- in content and context, as well as
- in architecture and computational requirements.

Country code based and affiliation based solutions result in visualisation of different distribution patterns. While an affiliation based solution can have a higher granularity it can be more precise in detail. In that context, a country code based solution is associated with more dependencies in the results – border lines, different country context, especially for handling and visualising long-term intervals. For example, considering the same data, on the one hand geo-references of a place do not really change much over time, on the other hand border lines of states change much faster on a global scale.

For a visual comparison, the results from both the affiliation based and country code based sequences were placed on the same spatial map (Figure 8).

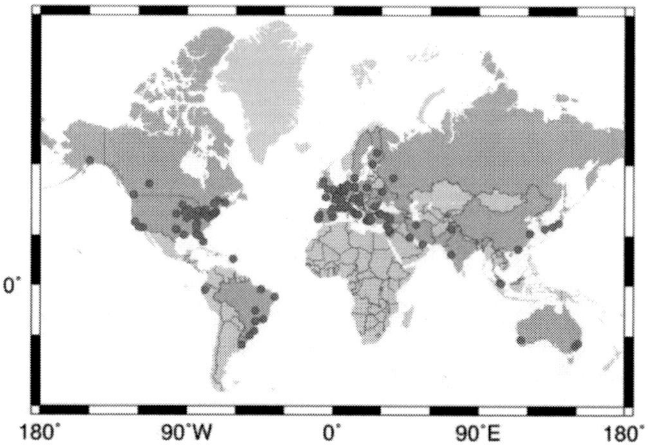

Figure 8. Comparison of both affiliation and country code based knowledge mapping: Geo-referenced place and ISO referenced state results.

There are more differences in detail, which can influence decisions on applicability and implementation. In general, there are arbitrary ways of implementing a knowledge mapping target based on the same Knowledge Resources. An implementation will in most cases be triggered by a combination of items, e.g., purpose, implementation efficiency, and computational performance. The characteristics and resolvability achieved via different knowledge mapping may be different. The number of countries is much more limited and the identification can be much more standardised than for geo-references places. The distribution of affiliation associated places can create a different impression than a visualisation based on country data. The sizes of mapped country areas can create a different impression than a visualisation based on country data. Associations based on both results can be significantly different, leading to further different knowledge context.

A further significant difference of the two case study implementations is the fact that the computational requirements are much more complex for affiliation mapping than for country code mapping. Depending on the objects and entities and the selected knowledge resources the factor of complexity can go up by millions. This is foremost relevant for the computation of comparative modules and analysis and visualisation of results.

B. *Knowledge and its computational footprint*

Based on the case studies, the characteristics of both solutions result in different computational requirements. Table IV compares the solutions regarding the numbers of computational checks required, done for the same object and entities.

TABLE IV. CORE PROCEDURES AND OBJECTS: COMPARISON OF COUNTRY CODE AND AFFILIATION BASED MAPPING.

Procedure	*Country Code*	*Affiliation*
Comparative Mapping		
pre-filter Checks	5,500	72,000
Knowledge Mapping Checks	40,000	570,000
post-filter Checks	7,000	75,000
Conceptual Mapping		
Checks UDC	300	5,000,000
Checks, other references	300	500,000
Spatial Mapping		
Results	> 50 Polygons	>50 Points
Context, object level	> 120 Polygons	0 Polygons
Context, basic	1 Basemap	1 Basemap

Different implementations involve different knowledge. As can be reasoned from the comparison, the case of affiliation based knowledge mapping might be a challenge for certain architectures, e.g., a distributed service implementation.

On the opposite, country code mapping can mean higher requirements for supportive data and higher load on spatial mapping application components, e.g., polygons provided by additional data, requests, application bound features, and visualisation. The supportive data can easily get into the range of millions of entities and Giga Bytes of data size per single request. If considering that country shapes will differ for a certain year or era, then multiple supportive data set might be needed. Therefore, load distribution is very much different for the implementations due to the nature of the different methodologies. The core sequences required for the knowledge mapping result in significant computational loads, especially at two steps: Comparisons and visualisation. These result in both comparative mapping load and supportive application load. Configuration of resources and modules can help to scale the computational load, nevertheless, any different configurations will have additional impact on the associated knowledge involved, which can be a significant reason for decision: For most component implementations and investments it does make a difference if a computational step takes two seconds or two days and if the required knowledge and data are involved or not. In addition to different knowledge being associated during the sequences, there is another difference: Most of the procedures are not bidirectional. If the affiliation based knowledge mapping is used in order to compute a consecutive country code based knowledge mapping and even if the result would be identical to the plain country code mapping this does not indicate that the country code mapping could also provide a consecutive affiliation mapping in the same manner.

V. CONCLUSION

The paper presented the research and results based on the developments of resources and advanced knowledge based methods. The methodology of knowledge mapping is deployed for the creation of new context for objects and entities as successfully demonstrated via two different methods.

The result of this research is a functional architecture, which proved to provide most flexible facilities for creating knowledge mapping and different and very scalable computational solutions. In consequence, the further development of resources and methods allows to consider different constraints when implementing solutions for a certain task. It was shown that the architecture allows to efficiently create implementations with significantly different characteristics.

The knowledge resources and the knowledge based solutions provide comprise universal knowledge and are not limited to a certain discipline or task. Nevertheless, examples limited to a defined task had to be taken for demonstration. The presented case studies illustrated how the knowledge mapping is applied for different solutions, namely country code based knowledge mapping and affiliation based knowledge mapping. The knowledge objects involved for these solutions however were not limited to a single discipline and task and are truly multi-disciplinary and multi-lingual as are all the components and referenced knowledge involved in the scenarios. Both solutions are very much visualisations of object entities. Regardless of that fact, both workflows are significantly different in steps, methods, algorithms, details of involved knowledge, and computational characteristics.

The facts, which become visible when the case study examples are discussed as an example of general abstraction, while still accessing the same resources: The large range of flexibility from knowledge, algorithmic, and computational perspectives. The complements of possibly required solutions share the complementary knowledge. Here, results comparable to the country code solution can be created with geo-referenced place data. In contrast, from the data involved with the country code solution it is not possible to create a geo-referenced view based on the associated data. Therefore, besides the individual context and results delivered by different implementations, it holds "The journey is the reward". The methodology of knowledge mapping as described can be used for any knowledge and context. The conducted case study is using terms in arbitrary text on the one hand, which can be associated with geo-referencing on the other hand. A different application scenario can be regional floras and faunas being mapped to an biological context, in which case even no geo-referencing or cartographic visualisation needs to be involved. Instead, the results can show the level of complexity for certain cases.

In conclusion, one can choose solutions under different constraints of application scenarios, e.g., knowledge involved, flexibility of sequences, and computational requirements. That way, it is possible to create scalable solutions considering the implementation of required procedures and methodologies, as well as the implementation of required infrastructures. Future research will be spent on extending the dimensional extent of knowledge resources and on the creation of advanced methodologies for deploying the complements of knowledge, further improving knowledge mapping, integration, and handling.

ACKNOWLEDGEMENTS

We are grateful to the "Knowledge in Motion" (KiM) long-term project, Unabhängiges Deutsches Institut für Multidisziplinäre Forschung (DIMF), for partially funding this implementation, case study, and publication under grants D2016F1P04683, D2017F1P04708, D2017F1P04812 and to its senior scientific members, especially to Dr. Friedrich Hülsmann, Gottfried Wilhelm Leibniz Bibliothek (GWLB) Hannover, to Dipl.-Biol. Birgit Gersbeck-Schierholz, Leibniz Universität Hannover, to Dipl.-Ing. Martin Hofmeister, Hannover, and to Olaf Lau, Hannover, Germany, for fruitful discussion, inspiration, practical multi-disciplinary case studies, and the analysis of advanced concepts. We are grateful to Dipl.-Ing. Hans-Günther Müller, Cray, Germany, for his work and support providing practical private cloud and storage solutions and excellent technical support. We are grateful to all national and international partners in the Geo Exploration and Information cooperations for their constructive and trans-disciplinary support. We thank the Science and High Performance Supercomputing Centre (SHPSC) for long-term support of collaborative research since 1997, including the GEXI developments and case studies and The International ARS Science and History Network for providing multi-disciplinary reference data.

REFERENCES

[1] R. L. Ackoff, "From data to wisdom," Journal of Applied Systems Analysis, vol. 16, 1989, pp. 3–9, ISSN: 0308-9541.

[2] M. Frické, "The knowledge pyramid: a critique of the DIKW hierarchy," Journal of Information Science, vol. 35, no. 2, 2009, pp. 131–142, SAGE, DOI: 10.1177/0165551508094050.

[3] J. Rowley, "The wisdom hierarchy: representations of the DIKW hierarchy," Journal of Information Science, vol. 33, no. 2, 2007, pp. 163–180, SAGE, DOI: 10.1177/0165551506070706.

[4] A. Bauer and H. Günzel, Eds., Data-Warehouse-Systeme - Architektur, Entwicklung, Anwendung. dpunkt, 2013, ISBN: 3-89864-785-4.

[5] Aristotle, Nicomachean Ethics, 2008, (Written 350 B.C.E.), Translated by W. D. Ross, Provided by The Internet Classics Archive, URL: http://classics.mit.edu/Aristotle/nicomachaen.html [accessed: 2018-05-12].

[6] Aristotle, Nicomachean Ethics, Volume 1, 2009, Project Gutenberg, eBook, EBook-No.: 28626, Release Date: April 27, 2009, Digitised Version of the Original Publication, Produced by Sophia Canoni, Book provided by Iason Konstantinidis, Translator: Kyriakos Zambas, URL: http://www.gutenberg.org/ebooks/12699 [accessed: 2018-05-12].

[7] Aristotle, The Ethics of Aristotle, 2005, Project Gutenberg, eBook, EBook-No.: 8438, Release Date: July, 2005, Digitised Version of the Original Publication, Produced by Ted Garvin, David Widger, and the DP Team, Edition 10, URL: http://www.gutenberg.org/ebooks/8438 [accessed: 2018-01-01].

[8] L. W. Anderson and D. R. Krathwohl, Eds., A Taxonomy for Learning, Teaching, and Assessing: A Revision of Bloom's Taxonomy of Educational Objectives. Allyn & Bacon, Boston, MA (Pearson Education Group), USA, 2001, ISBN-13: 978-0801319037.

[9] Plato, Phaedo, 2008, (Written 360 B.C.E.), Translated by Benjamin Jowett, Provided by The Internet Classics Archive, URL: http://classics.mit.edu/Plato/phaedo.html [accessed: 2018-05-12].

[10] C.-P. Rückemann and F. Hülsmann, "Significant Differences: Methodologies and Applications," KiMrise, Knowledge in Motion Meeting, November 27, 2017, Knowledge in Motion, Hannover, Germany, 2017.

[11] C.-P. Rückemann, "Methodology of Knowledge Mapping for Arbitrary Objects and Entities: Knowledge Mining and Spatial Representations – Objects in Multi-dimensional Context," in Proceedings of The Tenth International Conference on Advanced Geographic Information Systems, Applications, and Services (GEOProcessing 2018), March 25 – 29, 2018, Rome, Italy. XPS Press, Wilmington, Delaware, USA, 2018, pp. 40–45, ISSN: 2308-393X, ISBN-13: 978-1-61208-617-0, URL: http://www.thinkmind.org/index.php?view=article&articleid=geoprocessing_2018_3_20_30078 [accessed: 2018-05-12].

[12] C.-P. Rückemann, "Creation of Objects and Concordances for Knowledge Processing and Advanced Computing," in Proceedings of The Fifth International Conference on Advanced Communications and Computation (INFOCOMP 2015), June 21–26, 2015, Brussels, Belgium. XPS Press, 2015, ISSN: 2308-3484, ISBN-13: 978-1-61208-416-9, URL: http://www.thinkmind.org/index.php?view=article&articleid=infocomp_2015_4_30_60038 [accessed: 2018-05-12].

[13] C.-P. Rückemann, "Advanced Association Processing and Computation Facilities for Geoscientific and Archaeological Knowledge Resources Components," in Proceedings of The Eighth International Conference on Advanced Geographic Information Systems, Applications, and Services (GEOProcessing 2016), April 24 – 28, 2016, Venice, Italy. XPS Press, 2016, pages 69–75, ISSN: 2308-393X, ISBN-13: 978-1-61208-469-5.

[14] C.-P. Rückemann, "Advanced Knowledge Discovery and Computing based on Knowledge Resources, Concordances, and Classification," International Journal On Advances in Intelligent Systems, vol. 9, no. 1&2, 2016, pp. 27–40, ISSN: 1942-2679.

[15] C.-P. Rückemann, "Enabling Dynamical Use of Integrated Systems and Scientific Supercomputing Resources for Archaeological Information Systems," in Proc. INFOCOMP 2012, Oct. 21–26, 2012, Venice, Italy, 2012, pp. 36–41, ISBN: 978-1-61208-226-4.

[16] "UDC Online," 2018, URL: http://www.udc-hub.com [ac.: 2018-05-12].

[17] "Multilingual Universal Decimal Classification Summary," 2012, UDC Consortium, 2012, Web resource, v. 1.1. The Hague: UDC Consortium (UDCC Publication No. 088), URL: http://www.udcc.org/udcsummary/php/index.php [accessed: 2018-05-12].

[18] "Creative Commons Attribution Share Alike 3.0 license," 2012, URL: http://creativecommons.org/licenses/by-sa/3.0/ [accessed: 2018-05-02].

[19] "GEOProcessing 2018: Committees," 2018, the Tenth International Conference on Advanced Geographic Information Systems, Applications, and Services (GEOProcessing 2018) March 25–29, 2018 – Rome, Italy, URL: https://www.iaria.org/conferences2018/ComGEOProcessing18.html [accessed: 2018-03-04].

[20] "GMT - Generic Mapping Tools," 2018, URL: http://imina.soest.hawaii.edu/gmt [accessed: 2018-05-12].

Fitness Switching Strategy for Developing Genetic Algorithm that Utilizes Infeasible Solutions

Kim Jun Woo
Department of Industrial and Management Systems Engineering
Dong-A University
Busan, South Korea
e-mail: kjunwoo@dau.ac.kr

Abstract—**This paper introduces a general search strategy for genetic algorithm, which is called fitness switching. This strategy is developed to utilize the infeasible solutions during search procedure, and it provides two important benefits. First, it helps to find good solutions more effectively, since useful infeasible solutions can be exploited. Second, conventional feasibility handling strategies such as repair and penalization are not needed in fitness switching genetic algorithm, where fitness switching strategy is applied. Moreover, this strategy can be applied to a wide range of combinatorial optimization problems, while repair and penalization procedures are typically problem-specific.**

Keywords-genetic algorithm; fitness switching strategy; combinatorial optimization; meta heuristic; infeasible solution

I. Introduction

Genetic Algorithm (GA), proposed by Holland, is a well-known meta heuristic search method for solving combinatorial optimization problems [1]. Typically, meta heuristic search methods provide general search methodologies for exploring the search space of given problem effectively, and the search methodology of GA is usually defined by three genetic operators, selection, crossover, and mutation [2]. While the search methodology of GA is generally applicable to various problems, the genetic operators must be tailored to a specific problem, which is sometimes very difficult [3][4].

Feasibility is an important factor that can increase the complexities of genetic operators in that the infeasible solutions are not considered by conventional GAs. There are two approaches for handling the solution feasibility. One is to use carefully designed genetic operators which does not produce infeasible solutions at all, and the other is to apply additional procedures such as repair and penalization [5]. However, both approaches have two important limitations. First, they do not allow the infeasible solutions to be included within population, while such solutions can sometimes contain some features useful for finding better solutions. Second, both approaches are problem-specific, and complex genetic operators or additional procedures can be required.

Fitness switching can be used to address such problems, although it has been initially developed to solve specific combinatorial optimization problem with rare feasible solutions [5][6]. In this context, this paper introduces generalized form of fitness switching strategy and its application examples.

The remainder of this paper is organized as follows: In Section 2, the generalized structure of fitness switching strategy is introduced. The application examples of the strategy are illustrated in Section 3, and finally, the concluding remarks follow in Section 4.

II. Fitness Switching Genetic Algorithm

Fitness switching strategy is characterized by three additional procedures, fitness switching, fitness leveling and simple local search, which are generally applicable to various combinatorial optimization problems [5][6][7].

A. Fitness Switching

Let us assume that desirability of a solution s can be measured by a function $X(s)$. For example, total value of a solution for knapsack problem and total length of a solution for traveling salesman problem can be used as $X(s)$. If a maximization problem is given, we have to increase the value of $X(s)$. However, too large $X(s)$ is typically obtained by infeasible solutions. Consequently, we have to decrease the value of $X(s)$ if s is infeasible, and fitness switching procedure suggests that

$$fitness^{+}(s) \propto X(s) \propto \frac{1}{fitness^{-}(s)}, \tag{1}$$

where fitness value of s, $fitness(s)$, is computed as follows:

$$fitness(s) = \begin{cases} fitness^{+}(s) & \text{, if } s \text{ is feasible} \\ fitness^{-}(s) & \text{, if } s \text{ is infeasible} \end{cases} \tag{2}$$

Note that (1) indicates that feasible solutions are enhanced when their fitness values increase, while infeasible ones are enhanced by decreasing their fitness values. Of course, fitness switching procedure can be written in additive form, for example, $fitness^{+}(s) = X(s)$ and

$fitness^{-}(s) = T - X(s)$. However, we have to determine the value of additional parameter T in this case.

The fitness switching procedure proposed in this paper is applied to evaluation phase of standard GA (SGA) [8]. For details on the original version of FSWGA based on SGA, see Fig. 3 in [5].

B. Fitness Leveling

It is straightforward that the fitness of a feasible solution should be larger than the fitness of an infeasible one. This is satisfied if $fitness^{+}(s) \geq 0$. However, too large difference between $fitness^{+}(s)$ and $fitness^{-}(s)$ is not desirable in that it can cause too high selection pressure.

Fitness leveling procedure is used to maintain appropriate selection pressure by adjusting $fitness(s)$ as follows:

$$fitness'(s) = \begin{cases} fitness^{+}{}'(s) & \text{, if } s \text{ is feasible} \\ fitness^{-}{}'(s) & \text{, if } s \text{ is infeasible} \end{cases}, \quad (3)$$

where

$$fitness^{+}{}'(s) = 1 + L \times \frac{fitness(s) - \min_{x \in F} fitness(x)}{\max_{x \in F} fitness(x) - \min_{x \in F} fitness(x)} \quad (4)$$

and

$$fitness^{-}{}'(s) = (1-\alpha) \times \frac{fitness(s)}{\max_{x \in I} fitness(x)} \quad (5)$$

F and I denote the sets of feasible and infeasible solutions within population, respectively. Moreover, factor L (≥ 1) defines the relative desirability of feasible solutions, while factor α ($0 \leq \alpha < 1$) is used to guarantee that $fitness^{-}{}'(s) < fitness^{+}{}'(s)$. Consequently, $1 \leq fitness^{+}{}'(s) \leq L$ and $0 \leq fitness^{-}{}'(s) \leq 1$, if and only if $fitness^{+}(s) \geq 0$.

Note that fitness leveling procedure is not needed if current population consists of only feasible solutions or only infeasible ones, and this procedure can be incorporated into evaluation or selection phase of SGA.

C. Simple Local Search

Fitness Switching GA (FSWGA) allows infeasible solutions to be included within population. However, they are not suitable for solving given problems, inherently. In this context, the infeasible solutions can be slightly modified by applying simple local search procedure in hopes that they would be converted into better solutions, not necessarily feasible.

Unlike fitness switching and fitness leveling, this procedure is optional and problem-specific. This procedure is incorporated into evaluation phase of SGA.

III. APPLICATION EXAMPLES

FSWGA has been applied to Maze-type shortest path problem and 0-1 knapsack problem, and the details of fitness switching strategy for those problems are summarized in Table 1.

Table 1 indicates that $fitness^{-}(s)$ can be defined flexibly, as long as it is inversely proportional to $fitness^{+}(s)$. Moreover, no repair and penalization procedure are needed, and FSWGA has successfully solved given problem in both cases. For example, Fig. 2 shows the experiment result of FSWGA for maze-type shortest path problem with a maze-type network as shown in Fig. 1, where node 1 and node 27 are source node and destination node, respectively, and lengths of all edges are assumed to be 1 [5]. Then, it is straightforward that the optimal path from node 1 to node 27 is <1, 9, 11, 15, 26, 27> with length 5, while there are some competitive local optima such as <1, 9, 11, 15, 16, 26, 27> and <1, 2, 9, 11, 15, 26, 27> with length 6. Moreover, the network contains a number of dead-ends such as node 6, 8, and 10, etc. and we have many infeasible paths that fail to arrive at the destination node, such as <1, 2, 4, 6> and <1, 3, 5, 8>.

Nevertheless, FSWGA found the optimal solution successfully as shown in Fig. 2, where the search procedure of FSWGA for combinatorial optimization problems with rare feasible solutions consists of three periods. In initial period, there is no feasible solution in population, since it is not easy to find any feasible ones from scratch. During initial period, FSWGA aims to find longer paths in hopes that some feasible paths that arrives at the destination node would be found.

TABLE I. APPLICATION OF FITNESS SWITCHING STRATEGY.

Target problem	Maze-type Shortest Path Problem [5][6]	0-1 Knapsack Problem [7]
Problem type	Rare feasible solutions	Many feasible solutions
Objective	To find the shortest feasible path from source node to destination node	To find a set of items with maximum total value, satisfying pre-specified total weight limit
Feasible solution	A path from source node to destination node	A set of items with total weight does not exceed pre-specified upper limit
Infeasible solution	A path from source node to a non-destination node	A set of items that total weight exceeds pre-specified upper limit
$X(s)$	Length of path s	Total value of a set of some items s
$fitness^{+}(s)$	$\frac{\text{sum of all edges' lengths}}{\text{length of path}}$	Total value
$fitness^{-}(s)$	$\frac{\text{length of path}}{\text{sum of all edges' lengths}}$	(1) 1/total value (2) 1/total weight (3) 1/total (value × weight)
Simple local search	Randomly modify the last move	Exclude a randomly chosen item

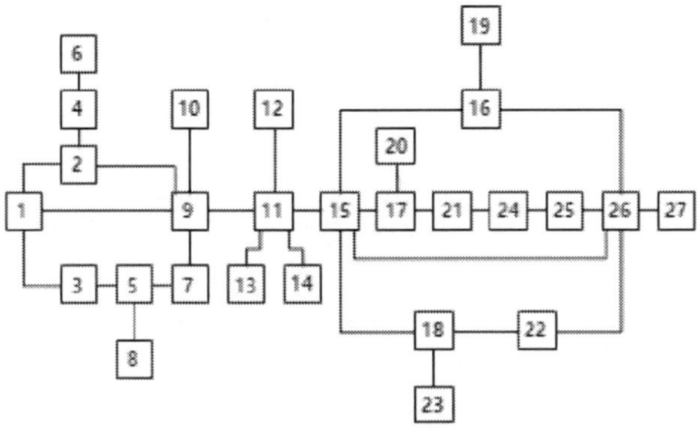

Figure 1. Example of a maze-type network [5].

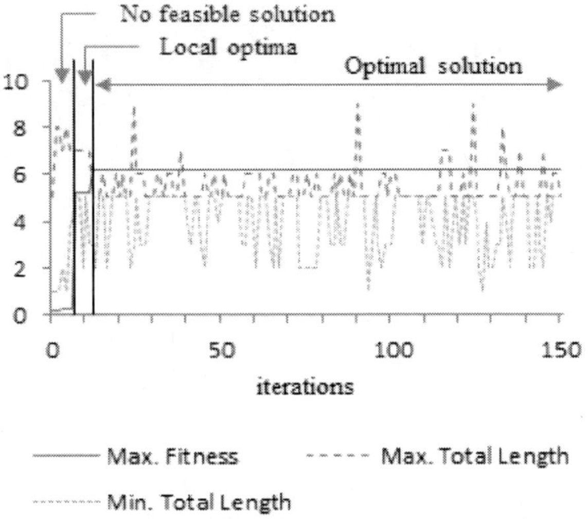

Figure 2. Experiment result of FSWGA for maze-type shortest path problem [5].

The second period begins when any feasible path is found, and FSWGA focuses on finding shorter feasible paths in this period. Finally, the optimal solution, the shortest feasible path is identified and maintained during the last period. Note that conventional GAs for classical shortest path problems have failed to find the optimal solution for the maze-type network shown in Fig. 1. On the contrary, Fig. 3 shows the experiment result of FSWGA for classical 0-1 knapsack problem with 50 items [7], which has many feasible solutions. In other words, it is easy to generate a number of feasible solutions that contain few items, and the graph in Fig. 3 represents the change in maximum total value, total value of the best feasible solution within current population. In this case, we can see that the initial population also has a number of feasible solutions and the maximum total value continuously increases until the optimal solution is found.

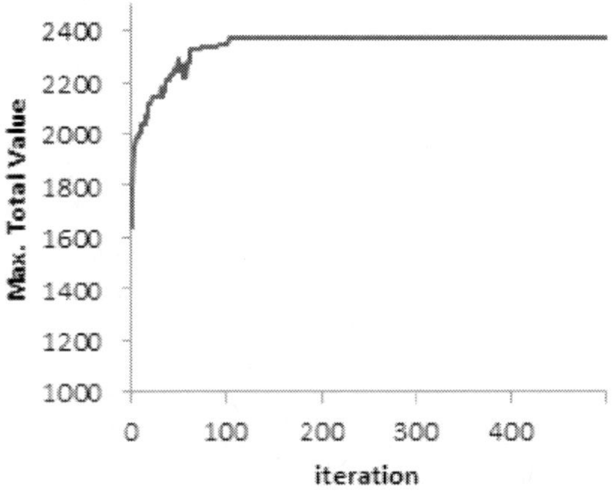

Figure 3. Experiment result of FSWGA for 0-1 knapsack problem [7].

The maze-type shortest path problem and 0-1 knapsack problem are quite different from each other for two reasons: (i) maze-type shortest path problem is inherently a sort of sequencing problem, but 0-1 knapsack problem is not. (ii) maze-type shortest path problem has rare feasible solutions, while 0-1 knapsack problem typically has many feasible solutions. Nevertheless, both problems have been successfully addressed by applying the fitness switching strategy, and we can conclude that the strategy can be widely applied to various combinatorial optimization problems.

IV. Conclusions

FSWGA utilizes infeasible solutions during search procedure, and it can be easily implemented. The fitness switching strategy is easy to implement and widely applicable in that it is applied to fitness values and solutions are not modified, and parameters are relatively intuitive. In this context, it will help to explore the search spaces of various combinatorial optimization problems efficiently.

Although the fitness switching strategy has been applied only to two types of combinatorial optimization problems, maze-type shortest path problem with rare feasible solutions and 0-1 knapsack problem with many feasible solutions, yet, the author plans to apply the strategy to various problems with complex constraints, in order to demonstrate its applicability.

Acknowledgment

This work was supported by the National Research Foundation of Korea(NRF) grant funded by the Korea government(Ministry of Science, ICT & Future Planning) (NRF-2017R1C1B1008650).

References

[1] J. H. Holland, Adaptations in Natural and Artificial Systems, University of Michigan Press, Michigan, 1975.

[2] J. W. Kim, "Candidate Order based Genetic Algorithm (COGA) for Constrained Sequencing Problems," Int. J. Ind. Eng-Appl. P. USA, vol. 23, pp. 1-12, 2016.

[3] K. Chakhlevitch and P. Cowling, "Hyperheuristics: Recent Developments," In Adaptive and Multilevel Metaheuristics, Springer Berlin Heidelberg, pp. 3-29, 2008.

[4] E. Burke et al., "Hyper-heurisrics: A Survey of the State of the Art," J. Oper. Res. Soc. Am. USA, vol. 64, pp. 1695-1724, 2013.

[5] J. W. Kim and S. K. Kim, "Fitness Switching Genetic Algorithm for Solving Combinatorial Optimization Problems with Rare Feasible Solutions," J. Supercomput. Netherlands, vol. 72, pp. 3549-3571, 2016.

[6] J. W. Kim and S. K. Kim, "Genetic Algorithms for Solving Shortest Path Problem in Maze-Type Network with Precedence Consrtraints," Wireless Pers. Commun. Netherlands, in press.

[7] J. W. Kim, "Application of Fitness Switching Genetic Algorithm for Solving 0-1 Knapsack Problem," unpublished.

[8] Z. Michalewicz, Genetic Algorithm + Data Structure = Evolution Programs, 3rd ed., Springer-Verlag, New York, 1996.

A Model of a Source-Retrial Open Exponential Queuing Network with Finite Shared Buffers in Multi-Queue Nodes

Miron Vinarskiy
Institute of Control Sciences of Russian Academy of Science
Moscow, Russia
Corresponding address: 3709 Mariana Way, Santa Barbara, California, 93105 USA
e-mail: mironvin@yahoo.com

Abstract— **We study a model of an open exponential queuing network where each node comprises several M/M/1 queues that share a common waiting space (a buffer) of limited capacity. A customer arriving to a node with a fully occupied buffer is blocked and re-injected by the source after a delay into the network. The process is repeated until the customer completes his service in the network and exits it. Input flow to each node is a superposition of the external Poisson flow, the flows coming from other nodes, and the retrials. The assumption made is that input flow to a node is a Poisson process. Under this assumption, two results are presented: an analytical evaluation of the network throughput and a method of an approximate analysis of the network model. The approach for both is based on iteratively solving a system of non-linear equations for unknown nodal flow rates. Existence and uniqueness of the solutions, obtained by the iterative algorithms, are rigorously proven in both cases. Required network and node performance characteristics are presented. The method provides low bound estimates for a moderately loaded (non-congested) network.**

Keywords- queuing network; multi-queue node; finite buffer; retrial; delay.

I. INTRODUCTION

Limited waiting spaces (finite buffers) in real-life nodes (service centers) lead to a so-called "blocking" when a customer cannot get into a fully occupied buffer. In many applications, such as computer communications, telephone systems, and distributed data processing a blocked customer tries to re-enter a network after some random time. The framework of retrial queues and networks seems to be an adequate approach for these applications. Most of the work on retrial models has been done on single queues (see, e.g., [1], [2], [3]). Retrial queuing network models have mostly concentrated on tandem queues. An exact analysis of these network models does not seem to be feasible for the general case, and therefore almost all known retrial tandem models use approximate approaches (see, e.g., [4], [5]).

The works by Irland et al. [4] and Avrachenkov et al. [5] give some details for tandem queuing systems with retrials of blocked customers. Irland et al. [4] considered a single isolated source-destination path in a packet-switching network as a tandem of single-queue nodes with a limited waiting space in each node. They compared two retrial techniques for a blocked customer (packet): local retrials (switch-retransmission) and source retrials (host-retransmission). The former retransmits a customer backup copy from the preceding switch, while the latter resends it from the network subscriber. Assuming Poisson flows in each node, they used a decomposition of a tandem queue network into simple M/M/1/N node models to approximate the unknown node input rates.

Avrachenkov et al. [5] considered a tandem network of two M/M/1/1 queues with blocking and with an M/M/1/∞ source-retrial (orbit) queue. The model formalized the interaction of data flow generated by a short TCP connection with a network of finite buffers. Authors explicitly solved the model and derived a stability condition. For more complex networks, it was suggested to use a fixed point approximation [6] with an assumption of a Poisson flow in each queue. It was shown in [7] that a fixed point approximation for a retrial queue with a Poisson assumption works well only when the nominal load is small. This fact was confirmed in [8] for a tandem network with an arbitrary number of M/G/K/K queues.

Lam [9] studied a model of a packet-switching network with local retrials and multi-queue nodes. A blocked customer (packet) is unlimitedly retransmitted from an adjacent node until the nodal buffer becomes open. Under the Poisson flow assumption, a system of non-linear equations was built for the unknown nodal blocking probabilities, and solved iteratively. No proof of iterations convergence was presented.

The network model under study in this paper is an extension of the single-class queuing network model with losses and multi-queue nodes [10] to the case of source-retrials. The model description and solution methodology have a lot in common with the model in [10], but we focus specifically on the source-retrial. Adding retrials to the network model with losses makes flow balance equations more complex. In turn, it requires different approaches to prove the solution. The goal of the paper is to show that the model can be solved analytically by an approximate numerical method.

Blocked customers are dispatched back to the network after a random delay in the M/M/ ∞ retrial queue with infinite exponential servers. Thus, the model uses the classic retrial policy: each blocked customer generates a stream of repeated requests independently of the rest of the customers in the retrial group.

The model can be used for performance evaluation of distributed data processing systems with nodes implemented as shared-memory architecture multiprocessor service centers, telecommunication systems and computer communication networks with source-retransmission of undelivered packets. In a distributed data processing system a customer (data request) can travel between nodes in order to get access to a distributed database. Upon completing its service by a node processor, a customer can leave the system from the node, or continue service at either the next node, or at the same node by a different processor.

Our network model is based on multi-queue nodes with a finite common buffer in each node. Buffer sharing policy is Complete Sharing (CS), where no restrictions on buffer occupancy are imposed for any queue. Output queuing structures in shared-memory switches/routers are good examples of such nodes [11]. In this application, a packet memory pool is shared among output ports.

Retrial queues are very complex objects. Even for a single retrial M/M/C queue, a closed form solution is only available for the number of servers $C \leq 2$. An approximate analysis for C>>2 is performed by replacing a retrial queue with a loss queue, under a Poisson input. The latter represents the mixture of a primary Poisson flow and retrials. This approximation works really well for not overloaded queue [1].

To make our network model analytically tractable, we also use a Poisson process to represent a node input. The input flow is a superposition of an external Poisson stream, a traffic coming from other nodes, and a retrial flow. Under this assumption, two results are presented: - 1) an analytical evaluation of the network throughput, which determines a permissible network load; - 2) a method of an approximate analysis of the network model. In both cases, the result is achieved by decomposing the network into separate simple nodal models and combining the nodal results in a system of non-linear equations for the unknown nodal flow rates. It is shown that the systems can be solved iteratively, and a proof is provided that the iterations converge to a unique solution. The solution for the nodal flow rates in the network model is used to receive several all-network and node performance measures.

The approach provides reasonable low bound estimates for a moderately loaded (non-congested) network. We use the term "moderately loaded" to approximately define a network mode, where an internal traffic, including retrials, loads any server in a node under 80% of capacity, and node blocking probabilities lower than 0.05.

The remainder of this paper is organized as follows. In Section II, we provide a formal description of the network model, including notation and the node product-form state distribution. In Section III, we present equations and a computational procedure for the network throughput. In Section IV, we concentrate on the network flow balance equations. Direct substitution iterations are used to solve the equations. In Section V, we define the required network performance measures. In Section VI, we present some numerical results computed by our analytic method in comparison with simulation results.

II. NETWORK MODEL

The network model under consideration here is a modification of the single-class queuing network model with losses [10]. Some model notation and description from [10] is included in this paper to provide a clear foundation for the model's expansion.

Let us consider an open queuing network with W nodes. The retrial (orbit) queue Figure 1 formalizes the random delay associated with a retrial of a blocked customer. The queue has infinitely many exponential servers (M/M/ ∞) with service rate μ_0.

The node-i (i = 1, 2,.., W) comprises $Q_i > 1$ of M/M/1 queues sharing finite common buffer of size N_i units Figure 1. The buffer contains all Q_i queues, including customers in service. The queuing system q (q = 1,2,.., Q_i) is characterized by an exponentially distributed service time with mean μ_q^{-1}, and queuing discipline FCFS (first come first served).

A customer arriving at node-i when its buffer is fully occupied is blocked, and transferred to the orbit queue that dispatches the customer back to the network after some random time. Retrials are distributed between nodes with probabilities γ_{0i}, i=1,2,.., W, $\sum_{i=1}^{W}\gamma_{0i} = 1$.

If there are free spots in the buffer of node-i, then an arriving customer joins the q -th queue system with probability α_{iq}, q =1,2.., Q_i, $\sum_{q=1}^{Q_i}\alpha_{iq} = 1$. Customers initially arrive to the network from an external source, which generates a Poisson flow with rate λ_0. This flow is distributed between nodes according to probabilities p_{0i}, i = 1, 2,.., W, $\sum_{i=1}^{W} p_{0i} = 1$. A customer, that has completed his service in node-i, is either transferred to node-j with routing probability p_{ij} , i,j = 1, 2,.., W , $\sum_{j=1}^{W} p_{ij} < 1$, or completes his service in the network and leaves with probability $p_{iE} = (1 - \sum_{j=1}^{W} p_{ij}) > 0$.

Figure 1 shows traffic in a node in the network. Node-i receives an "original" Poisson flow from an external source with the rate $\lambda_0 p_{0i}$. A secondary flow (dashed lines) is produced by other nodes in the network and possibly by node-i itself, as well as by the source-retrials. Superposition of the original and secondary flows forms the node-i input flow with rate λ_i . A part of this flow with the rate $\lambda_{i0}^{(R)}$ is blocked, initiating the source-retrial. The rest goes through node-i and then splits into a secondary flow with probability $1 - p_{iE} = \sum_{j=1}^{W} p_{ij}$ and traffic with flow rate λ_{iE} exiting the network after node-i.

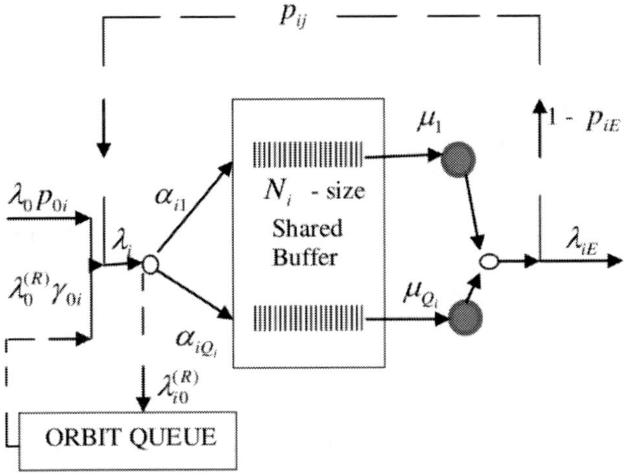

Figure1. Flows in the node-i of the network.

To determine traffic rates λ_i (i = 1, 2, .., W), we assume that the superposition of the original external Poisson flow and all secondary flows to the node-i is a Poisson process. This approach provides acceptable low bounds for moderately loaded networks (see Section VI). We have observed that the method works really well for networks where each node is connected to at least two nodes and traffic after a node splits according to a Markovian routing, merging with other flows as input arrivals.

It should be noted that the buffer overflow is a bursty stream. It can be efficiently approximated by Interrupted Poisson Process (IPP) [12] with a squared coefficient of variation $c^2 = (\mathrm{var}/mean^2) > 1$. However, even an individual queue with limited waiting space and IPP input does not have a closed form solution. Analysis is performed numerically. For a multi-queue node, even this approach fails in general because the number of the Markov equations grows exponentially with the number of queues.

A. Notation

The multi-queue node-i state is given by Q_i - dimensional vector $\mathrm{n}_i = (n_{i1}, n_{i2}, ..., n_{iQ_i})$, where n_{iq} $(0 \le n_{iq} \le N_i$, $q = 1, 2, .., Q_i)$ denotes the number of customers in the q -th queue system, including the customer in service. It is convenient to introduce the following notation:

$n_{i,k}^{m} = (n_{i1}, ..., n_{i,k-1}, \mathbf{m}, n_{i,k+1}, ..., n_{iQ_i})$,

$n_i = \sum_{q=1}^{Q_i} n_{iq}$ = total number of customers in node-i,

$\bar{n}_i(N_i)$ = mean number of customers in node-i.

Let

D_i = the set of permissible states that determined by CS buffer sharing policy in the node-i

$$D_i = \{\mathbf{n}_i : \sum_{q=1}^{Q_i} n_{iq} \le N_i,\ 0 \le n_{iq} \le N_i\}.$$

For queue- q we have

$\rho_{iq} = \lambda_i\, \alpha_{iq} / \mu_q$ = offered traffic intensity for queue- q in node-i.

The following is for the network,

$\mathbf{\Lambda} = (\lambda_1, \lambda_2, ..., \lambda_W)^{`}$ = column-vector of input flow rates in all $W$ nodes, (` denotes transposition).

$\| \mathbf{\Lambda} \| = \sum_{i=1}^{W} |\lambda_i|$ = norm of the vector $\mathbf{\Lambda}$.

B. The node product-form state distribution

The node-i model in Figure 1 can be considered as an open exponential queuing sub network under Poisson arrivals with input rate

$$\lambda_i(N_i) = \begin{cases} 0 & \text{– if buffer is fully occupied} \\ \lambda_i & \text{- otherwise.} \end{cases}$$

The equilibrium state probability distribution for this type of queuing network is given by product form [13], [14]

$$P(\mathbf{n}_i) = G(N_i)^{-1} \prod_{q=1}^{Q_i} \rho_{iq}^{n_{iq}}, \tag{1}$$

where

$$G(N_i) = \sum_{\mathbf{n}_i \in D_i} \prod_{q=1}^{Q_i} \rho_{iq}^{n_{iq}} \tag{2}$$

is the normalization constant. From (1, 2) the stationary probability that the node-i is available for a customer is

$$\pi_i(\lambda_i) = G(N_i - 1) / G(N_i) \tag{3}$$

The output flow rate from the node-i is

$$\lambda_i^{out} = \lambda_i \pi_i(\lambda_i) \tag{4}$$

In the following statement, imported from [10, Proposition 3.2], the index i is dropped to simplify the notation.

Proposition 1. The node output $\lambda\pi(\lambda)$ is an increasing function of $\lambda > 0$, and $\lim_{\lambda\to\infty} \lambda\pi(\lambda) = \hat{G}(N-1) / \hat{G}(N)$, where $\hat{G}(N)$ is the normalization constant of the closed queuing network that is a node model under a constantly full buffer.

III. NETWORK THROUGHPUT

Let us consider the network output rate

$$O(\mathbf{\Lambda}) = \sum_{i=1}^{W} \lambda_i \pi_i(\lambda_i)\ (1 - \sum_{j=1}^{W} p_{ij}). \tag{5}$$

In the network's stationary mode, $O(\mathbf{\Lambda})$ is equal to the source flow rate λ_0. To determine the network's permissible load λ_0, let us find the network throughput $O_{\max}$, which has to satisfy the following inequality

$$O_{\max} \le \lim_{\mathbf{\Lambda}\to\infty} O(\mathbf{\Lambda}) = \sum_{i=1}^{W} a_i (1 - \sum_{j=1}^{W} p_{ij}), \tag{6}$$

where $a_i = \lim_{\lambda_i\to\infty} \lambda_i \pi_i(\lambda_i) = \hat{G}(N_i - 1) / \hat{G}(N_i)$ (see Proposition 1).

To calculate $O_{\max}$ we assume the infinite network load $\lambda_0 = \infty$. Under this assumption, a group of nodes will have constantly full buffers. Among them will be the nodes that receive initial arrivals from an external source according to positive probabilities $p_{0i} > 0$. Also, the group will have nodes that receive retrials that are generated by all nodes, including those with always full buffers.

Let us assume that there will be v ($0 \le v < W$) nodes with not always full buffers and (W - v) nodes with constantly full buffers. Let $I_1 = \{1,2,..,v\}$ and $I_2 = \{v+1, v+2,...,W\}$. Then $O_{\max}$ can be expressed from (5 and 6) as

$$O_{\max} = [\sum_{i\in I_2} a_i + \sum_{i\in I_1} \lambda_i \pi_i(\lambda_i)](1 - \sum_{j=1}^{W} p_{ij}). \tag{7}$$

Unknown flow rates λ_i, $i \in I_1$, are solutions of the following system of non-linear flow balance equations

$$\lambda_i = \sum_{j\in I_2} a_j p_{ji} + \sum_{j\in I_1} \lambda_j \pi_j(\lambda_j) p_{ji} \qquad i \in I_1. \tag{8}$$

The structure of (8) is very similar to the flow balance equations in the single-class network model with losses [10, expression (2.6) for $R = 1$]. Thus, a positive unique solution of (8) $\boldsymbol{\lambda}^* = (\lambda_1^*, \lambda_2^*,..,\lambda_v^*)$ can be found by direct substitution iterations as in [10, expression (3.4)]. We omit here the proof of the iterations convergence. An interested reader is referred to [10, Theorem 3.1].

With vector $\boldsymbol{\lambda}^*$ the network throughput $O_{\max}$ is fully determined by (7), that in turn defines the network permissible load $\lambda_0 < O_{\max}$.

IV. NETWORK FLOW BALANCE EQUATIONS

The following system of non-linear equations establishes flow balance for nodes in the network

$$\lambda_j = \lambda_0 p_{0j} + \sum_{i=1}^{W} \lambda_i \pi_i(\lambda_i) p_{ij} + \gamma_{0j} \sum_{i=1}^{W} \lambda_i (1 - \pi_i(\lambda_i)),$$

$$j = 1, 2, .., W. \tag{9}$$

The flow rate into the orbit queue is determined by λ_j (j =1, 2, .., W) as

$$\lambda_0^{(R)} = \sum_{j=1}^{W} \lambda_{j0}^{(R)} = \sum_{j=1}^{W} \lambda_j (1 - \pi_j(\lambda_j)). \tag{10}$$

It is convenient rewrite (9) in vector form

$$\mathbf{\Lambda} = \mathbf{\Psi}(\mathbf{\Lambda}), \tag{11}$$

where $\mathbf{\Psi}(\mathbf{\Lambda}) = (\ \Psi_1(\mathbf{\Lambda}),..., \Psi_W(\mathbf{\Lambda})\ )'$,

$$\Psi_j(\mathbf{\Lambda}) = \lambda_0 p_{0j} + \sum_{i=1}^{W} \lambda_i \pi_i(\lambda_i) p_{ij} +$$

$$\gamma_{0j} \sum_{i=1}^{W} \lambda_i (1 - \pi_i(\lambda_i)), \qquad j = 1, 2,...W. \tag{12}$$

Operator $\mathbf{\Psi}(\mathbf{\Lambda})$ is defined in $\Omega = \{\ \mathbf{\Lambda} : \lambda_i \ge 0$, $i = 1,2,.., W\ \}$ and maps $\Omega \to \Omega$.

Proposition 2. Operator $\mathbf{\Psi}(\mathbf{\Lambda})$ is an increasing operator.

Proof. Proposition immediately follows from [10, expression (D.1) in Appendix D] for node-k

$$\frac{\partial(\lambda_k \pi_k(\lambda_k))}{\partial \lambda_k} = \pi_k(\lambda_k)\ [\bar{n}_k(N_k-1) - \bar{n}_k(N_k) + 1] > 0$$

and

$$\frac{\partial \Psi_i(\mathbf{\Lambda})}{\partial \lambda_k} = p_{ki}\pi_k(\lambda_k)[\bar{n}_k(N_k-1) - \bar{n}_k(N_k)+1] +$$

$$\gamma_{0i}\ \{\ 1 - \pi_k(\lambda_k)[\bar{n}_k(N_k-1) - \bar{n}_k(N_k)+1]\ \} =$$

$$p_{ki}\omega_k + \gamma_{0i}(1 - \omega_k) > 0, \qquad (13)$$

where $i,k = 1,2,..,W$, and

$$0 < \omega_k = \pi_k(\lambda_k)[\bar{n}_k(N_k-1) - \bar{n}_k(N_k)+1] < 1. \quad (14)$$

The system (11) can be solved iteratively by using the following relation

$$\mathbf{\Lambda}^{(m+1)} = \mathbf{\Psi}(\mathbf{\Lambda}^{(m)}) \qquad m = 0, 1, 2, \ldots, \qquad (15)$$

where vector $\mathbf{\Lambda}^{(m)} = (\lambda_1^{(m)},\ldots,\lambda_W^{(m)})$`is a result of the $m$-th iteration, and $\mathbf{\Lambda}^{(0)} = (0,0,..,0)$`. Also, $\mathbf{\Lambda}^{(m+1)} \geq \mathbf{\Lambda}^{(m)}$ if $\lambda_i^{(m+1)} \geq \lambda_i^{(m)}$, and $\mathbf{\Lambda}^{(m)} > 0$ if $\lambda_i^{(m)} > 0$ for $i = 1, 2, .., W$.

Theorem. For network load $\lambda_0 < O_{\max}$, the sequence{ $\mathbf{\Lambda}^{(m)}, m \geq 0$ },defined by (15),converges to $\mathbf{\Lambda}^*$, a positive unique solution of system (11).

Proof.

Existence of $\mathbf{\Lambda}^*$. Vector $\mathbf{\Lambda}^{(1)}$ has a positive component for node-i if $p_{0i} > 0$. Vector $\mathbf{\Lambda}^{(2)}$ can have more positive components if there are positive probabilities of transferring a customer from node-i to other nodes. From Proposition 2 and $\mathbf{\Lambda}^{(1)} = \mathbf{\Psi}(\mathbf{\Lambda}^{(0)}) \geq \mathbf{\Lambda}^{(0)}$ follows that the sequence { $\mathbf{\Lambda}^{(m)}$, m=0, 1, 2,...} is a non-decreasing sequence.

Let us show that the sequence (15) is limited in Ω. From Proposition 1 follows that $O(\mathbf{\Lambda})$ (5) is an increasing function of $\mathbf{\Lambda}$, and consequently for $\lambda_0 < O_{\max}$ there is $\mathbf{\Lambda}^* \in \Omega$ that for any $\mathbf{\Lambda} > \mathbf{\Lambda}^*$ ($\mathbf{\Lambda} \in \Omega$)

$$O(\mathbf{\Lambda}) > \lambda_0. \qquad (16)$$

By summing (12) over $j = 1,2,\ldots, W$ we can get

$$\|\mathbf{\Psi}(\mathbf{\Lambda})\| = \lambda_0 - \sum_{i=1}^{W}\lambda_i\pi_i(\lambda_i)\ (1-\sum_{j=1}^{W}p_{ij}) + \|\ \mathbf{\Lambda}\ \|. \quad (17)$$

Applying (5) and (16) to (17) we have

$$\|\ \mathbf{\Lambda}\ \| > \|\mathbf{\Psi}(\mathbf{\Lambda})\| \ \text{ for } \mathbf{\Lambda} > \mathbf{\Lambda}^*\ (\mathbf{\Lambda} \in \Omega). \qquad (18)$$

Let us assume that the sequence { $\mathbf{\Lambda}^{(m)}$, m=0, 1, 2,...} is not limited in Ω. Then there will be a number m, such that $\mathbf{\Lambda}^{(m)} > \mathbf{\Lambda}^*$, and according to (18) $\|\mathbf{\Lambda}^{(m)}\| > \|\mathbf{\Psi}(\mathbf{\Lambda}^{(m)})\|$.

Consequently, $\|\ \mathbf{\Lambda}^{(m+1)}\| = \|\mathbf{\Psi}(\mathbf{\Lambda}^{(m)})\| < \|\mathbf{\Lambda}^{(m)}\|$,

that contradicts the fact that the sequence $\mathbf{\Lambda}^{(m)}$ is a non-decreasing sequence. Thus, a positive vector $\mathbf{\Lambda}^* = \lim_{m\to\infty} \mathbf{\Lambda}^{(m)} < \infty$ is a solution of (11).

Uniqueness of the solution $\mathbf{\Lambda}^*$. Let us assume that there are two different solutions $\mathbf{\Lambda}^* > 0$ and $\mathbf{\Lambda}^{**} > 0$. Then, for the convex domain Ω, we have

$$\|\mathbf{\Lambda}^* - \mathbf{\Lambda}^{**}\| =$$

$$\|\mathbf{\Psi}(\mathbf{\Lambda}^*) - \mathbf{\Psi}(\mathbf{\Lambda}^{**})\| \leq \|\mathbf{\Psi}'(\mathbf{\Lambda})\|\ \|\mathbf{\Lambda}^* - \mathbf{\Lambda}^{**}\|, \quad (19)$$

where $\mathbf{\Lambda}^*, \mathbf{\Lambda}^{**} \in \Omega$, $\mathbf{\Lambda} = \mathbf{\Lambda}^* + \xi(\mathbf{\Lambda}^{**} - \mathbf{\Lambda}^*)$, $0 < \xi < 1$.

From (13) we have $\|\mathbf{\Psi}'(\mathbf{\Lambda})\| = \max_k \sum_{i=1}^{W} \left|\frac{\partial \Psi_i(\mathbf{\Lambda})}{\partial \lambda_k}\right| =$

$\max_k [1 - \omega_k(1 - \sum_{i=1}^{W} p_{ki})]$, where $0 < \omega_k < 1$ (see 14). From

$\sum_{i=1}^{W} p_{ki} < 1$ for $k = 1,2,\ldots,W$ follows that $\|\mathbf{\Psi}'(\mathbf{\Lambda})\| < 1$,

and the inequality (19) can be valid only if $\mathbf{\Lambda}^* = \mathbf{\Lambda}^{**}$. Q.E.D. Computational complexity of (15) is $\sim O(W^2)$.

V. NETWORK PERFORMANCE MEASURES

A. *Nodal measures*

To simplify notation we drop index i for an arbitrary node in the network. Let us consider the following aggregate state for a node

$A(u) = \{\mathbf{n} \in D : \sum_{q=1}^{Q} n_q = u\}$, which comprises all states

with the total population of u customers in the node. With this state we associate two functions:

$$g(u) = \sum_{\mathbf{n} \in A(u)} \prod_{q=1}^{Q} \rho_q^{n_q} \quad \text{and}$$

$$g^{-k}(u) = \sum_{\mathbf{n}_k^0 \in A(u)} \prod_{q=1}^{Q} \rho_q^{n_q}$$

The normalization constant

$$G(N) = \sum_{u=0}^{N} g(u).$$

Distribution of the total number of customers in the node is given by

$$P_u = P_0 \cdot g(u) = g(u) / \sum_{z=0}^{N} g(z) \quad \text{for } 0 \le u \le N.$$

The mean number of customers in the node is

$$\bar{n}(N) = \sum_{u=0}^{N} u P_u .$$

Using Little's Law, the average time a customer spends in the node is

$$\bar{t} = \bar{n}(N) / \lambda\pi(\lambda) \qquad (20)$$

The marginal distribution of the number of customers in the queue-q is

$$P_{n_q}^{(q)} = \rho_q^{n_q} \sum_{u=0}^{N-n_q} g^{-q}(u) / \sum_{z=0}^{N} g(z).$$

The mean number of the queue-q customers is

$$\bar{n}_q = \sum_{n_q=1}^{N} n_q P_{n_q}^{(q)} .$$

The average delay (queue plus server) for a queue-q customer is given by Little's Law

$$\bar{d}_q = \bar{n}_q / \lambda\pi(\lambda)\alpha_q .$$

B. All-network service measures

On the average, λ_0 customers arrive at the network during a unit interval. Therefore, in stationary mode, when $\lambda_0 < O_{\max}$, the network output rate $O(\mathbf{\Lambda}) = \lambda_0$.

During this time interval $\sum_{k=1}^{W} \lambda_k \pi_k(\lambda_k)$ customers, on average, go through the service nodes. Thus, the average number of services received by a customer in the network is

$$\bar{s} = \sum_{k=1}^{W} \lambda_k \pi_k(\lambda_k) / \lambda_0 .$$

The average sojourn time for a customer in the network, including a retrial delay, is

$$\bar{T} = [\lambda_0^{(R)}(1/\mu_0) + \sum_{k=1}^{W} \lambda_k \pi_k(\lambda_k)\bar{t}_k] / \lambda_0 , \qquad (21)$$

where $\bar{t}_k$ is defined in (20) and $\lambda_0^{(R)}$ in (10).

VI. COMPARISON OF ANALYTIC AND SIMULATION RESULTS

In this section, we present some numeric results computed by our analytic method in comparison with simulation. The simulation code is written in C^{++}, and simulates a network processing of ~ 10^6 customers in one run. We experiment with two network topologies: a symmetric complete-graph network and a ring-type network.

The symmetric configuration includes five nodes; each has two identical single servers (two-queue node) and a buffer of size $N = 10$. Traffic arriving to node-i (i =1, 2, .., 5) splits equally between two queues, i.e., $\alpha_{iq} = 0.5$, q = 1, 2. The orbit queue service rate is $\mu_0 = 0.1$, while all other servers in the network have the same service rate $\mu = 1$. The external input flow with rate λ_0 is uniformly distributed between the nodes, i.e., $p_{0i} = 0.2$ (i =1, 2, .., 5). A customer that has completed his service in the node-i is either transferred to the node-j (j =1, 2, .., 5) with probability 0.1 or leaves the network with probability 0.5. Retrials are distributed into the network with probability $\gamma_{0i} = 0.2$ (i =1, 2, .., 5).

TABLE I presents results for λ_0 =2.0, 3.0, 3.6, and 4.0. Columns 3-5 have data for one separate node; column 2 presents the average sojourn time in the network, including retrials. The upper figure in each box has been received by the analytic method. The lower was obtained by simulation.

TABLE I. NETWORK CHARACTERISTICS OF THE SYMMETRIC 5-NODE NETWORK. ANALYTIC RESULTS VERSUS SIMULATION.

	(21)	(9)	(4)	(20)
λ_0	$\bar{T}$	λ_i	λ_i^{out}	$\bar{t}_i$
1	2	3	4	5
2.0	3.335	0.8	0.799	1.663
	3.34	0.8	0.799	1.666
3.0	5.025	1.212	1.198	2.393
	5.226	1.214	1.199	2.5
3.6	7.142	1.512	1.437	3.06
	8.3	1.516	1.439	3.62
4.0	9.914	1.805	1.599	3.67
	13.487	1.842	1.612	5.24

External arrival rates in the range λ_0 = 2.0 – 3.6 moderately load the network. We can observe that for these loads the node input rate is λ_i <1.6, and consequently ρ_{iq} < 0.8. Average sojourn times in network, calculated analytically, are lower than in simulation by 0.15% - 13.9%.

We can conclude that a Poisson assumption for a node input gives reasonable low bounds for this load range. Further increase of source arrival rate brings the network close to congestion, dramatically increasing the difference between analytical result and simulation one.

Another example is a 5-node ring-type network, where all five nodes are identical two-queue nodes, described above. The input flow with rate λ_0 is uniformly distributed between the nodes, i.e., p_{0i} = 0.2 (i =1, 2, .., 5) . After completing his service in node- i , customer is either transferred to node-$(i+1)$ with probability 0.2, or to node -$(i-1)$ with probability 0.2, or exits the network with probability 0.6. Retrials are distributed between nodes with probability γ_{0i} = 0.2 (i =1, 2, ..., 5). For node-1 the "left" neighbor is node-5. For node-5 the "right" neighbor is node-1. We assume p_{ii} = 0, i.e., a node may not route traffic to itself.

The computational results for λ_0 = 3.0, 3.5, 4.0, and 4.5 are shown in TABLE II, which has similar structure as TABLE I. For moderate network load λ_0 = 3.0 – 4.0, the node input rate λ_i < 1.6 and ρ_{iq} < 0.8. Comparison of the analytic results (upper figures in each box) with simulation ones (lower figures) shows that in this load range the analytic method provides acceptable low bound estimates. For instance, the error of calculating the average sojourn times in the network is in the 1.18% - 9.2% range. The network becomes congested under λ_0 = 4.5 and the error is increased to 20.7%. This example demonstrates that our Poissonian hypothesis works even for a weakly connected not congested network.

TABLE II. NETWORK MEASURES OBTAINED ANALYTICALLY AND BY SIMULATION FOR THE RING-TYPE 5-NODE NETWORK.

	(21)	(9)	(4)	(20)
λ_0	$\bar{T}$	λ_i	λ_i^{out}	$\bar{t}_i$
1	2	3	4	5
3.0	3.34	1.003	0.999	1.978
	3.38	1.004	1.001	1.998
3.5	4.019	1.178	1.166	2.3
	4.2	1.179	1.168	2.43
4.0	5.02	1.369	1.332	2.739
	5.531	1.372	1.334	3.03
4.5	6.643	1.607	1.499	3.272
	8.38	1.631	1.52	4.16

VII. CONCLUSION

We have extended the model of an open exponential single-class queuing network with losses due to limited shared waiting spaces in multi-queue M/M/1 nodes [10] to the case of the source-retrials, experienced by blocked customers. The goal of the paper is to show that the model can be solved approximately by an analytical numerical approach. Using the methodology outlined in [10], we have established an approximate numerical method that makes it possible to solve the model analytically. An analytical procedure to evaluate the network throughput that determines a permissible network load was received as well.

The main result of the paper is a method of an approximate analysis of the network model under a moderate load. The core of the approach is solving iteratively a system of non-linear equations for the unknown nodal flow rates. We have rigorously proven that the iterative algorithm converges to a unique solution, which is used to obtain several network and node performance measures.

The model can be used for performance evaluation of computer communication networks with adaptive or alternative routing and source–retransmission of undelivered packets. Also, the paper results can help to analyze different structures of distributed database systems with multiprocessor nodes.

Future work can consider a source-retrial multi-class queuing network with finite shared buffer in multi-queue nodes. The use of Interrupt Poisson Process as a node input might help to conduct an approximate analysis of an even congested network.

ACKNOWLEDGMENT

The author would like to thank anonymous referees for a number of useful comments and suggestions given to the original manuscript.

REFERENCES

[1] G. I. Falin, and J.G.C. Templeton, Retrial queues. Boca Raton, FL: CRC Press, 1997.

[2] J. R. Artalejo, and A. Gomez-Coral, Retrial queueing systems. A computational approach. Berlin: Springer Berlin Heidelberg, 2008.

[3] M. Jain, A. Bhagat, and C. Sherkhar, "Double orbit finite retrial queues with priority customers and service interruptions," Applied Mathematics and Computation, Vol. 253, pp. 324-344, 2015.

[4] M. Irland and G. Pujolle, "Comparison of two packet-retransmission techniques," IEEE Transactions on Information Theory, Vol. IT-26, No. 1, pp. 92-97, 1980.

[5] K. Avrachenkov and U. Yechiali, "Retrial networks with finite buffers and their application to Internet data traffic," Probability in the Engineering and Informational Sciences, Vol. 22, pp. 519-536, 2008.

[6] G. K. Takahara, "Fixed point approximation for retrial networks," Probability in the Engineering and Informational Science, Vol. 10, Issue 2, pp. 243-259, 1996.

[7] J. W. Cohen, "Basic problems of telephone traffic theory and the influence of repeated calls," Philips Telecommunication Review, Vol. 18, pp. 49-100, 1957.

[8] K. Avrachenkov and U. Yechiali, "On tandem blocking queues with a common retrial queue," Computer & Operations Research, Vol. 37, pp. 1174-1180, 2010.

[9] S. Lam, "Store-and-forward buffer requirements in a packet switching network," IEEE Transactions on Communications, Vol. 24, No. 4, pp. 394-403, 1976.

[10] M. Vinarskiy, "A method of approximate analysis of an open exponential queuing network with losses due to finite shared buffers in multi-queue nodes," European Journal of Operational Research, Vol. 258, Issue 1, pp. 207-215, 2017.

[11] W. Aello, A. Kesselman, and Y. Masour, "Competitive buffer management for shared-memory switches," ACM Transactions on Algorithms, Vol. 5, No. 1, pp. 3.1-3.6, 2008.

[12] K. S. Meier-Hellstern, "The analysis of a queue arising in overflow models," IEEE Transactions on Communications, Vol. 37, No. 4, pp. 367-372, 1989.

[13] S. Lam, "Queueing networks with population size constrains," IBM Journal of Research and Development, Vol. 21, No. 4, pp. 370-378, 1977.

[14] P. G. Harrison, "Reversed processes, product form and some non-product forms," Linear Algebra and Its Applications, Vol. 386, pp. 359-381, 2004.

A Simple Framework for Energy Efficiency Evaluation and Hardware Parameter Tuning with Modular Support for Different HPC Platforms

Ondrej Vysocky, Jan Zapletal and Lubomir Riha
IT4Innovations, VSB – Technical University of Ostrava
Ostrava-Poruba, Czech Republic
{ondrej.vysocky|jan.zapletal|lubomir.riha}@vsb.cz

***Abstract*—High Performance Computing (HPC) faces the problem of the potentially excessive energy consumption requirements of the upcoming exascal machines. One of the proposed approaches to reduce energy consumption coming from the software side is dynamic tuning of hardware parameters during the application runtime. In this paper, we tune CPU core and uncore frequencies using Dynamic Voltage and Frequency Scaling (DVFS), and number of active CPU cores by means of OpenMP threads. For our research it is also essential that the HPC cluster contains infrastructure that provides energy consumption measurements. In this paper, we evaluate the energy consumption of an ARM-based platform with lower performance and even lower energy consumption, and two traditional HPC architectures based on x86 CPU architecture - Intel Xeon E5-26xx v3 (codename Haswell) and Intel Xeon Phi (codename KNL). To improve the efficiency and quality of such research we have developed a MERIC library. It enables both resource (time, energy, performance counters) usage monitoring and dynamic tuning of any HPC application that is properly instrumented. This library is designed to contribute minimal overhead to application runtime, and is suitable for analysis and tuning of both simple kernels and complex applications. This paper presents an extension of the library to support new architectures, (i) the low power ARMv8 based Jetson TX1 and (ii) the HPC centric Intel Xeon Phi (KNL) many-core CPU. The evaluation is carried out using a Lattice Boltzmann based benchmark, which shows energy savings on all presented platforms, in particular 20 % on Haswell processors.**

Keywords*—*Energy Efficient Computing; MERIC; HDEEM; RAPL; DVFS.

I. Introduction

High Performance Computing (HPC) is progressing to more and more powerful machines that, with current technology, would consume huge amounts of energy. This becomes one of the most significant constraints to building upcoming machines. For instance, an exascale machine based on Piz Daint (the most powerful European cluster) hardware would consume approximately 90 MW, based on a multiplication of the power of the current system and number of systems we would need to reach the exascale performance.

To reduce the power consumption of modern clusters, from the runtime system point of view it is possible to control selected hardware knobs to fit the needs of running applications. Memory bound (high data bandwidth) kernels have different requirements than compute bound (high CPU throughput) kernels. Within memory bound regions, it is possible to reduce the frequency of the CPU cores to reduce the power without extending the application runtime. In the same fashion, the frequency of the DDR memory controllers, the last level caches, and the DDR memory itself can be similarly reduced for compute bound regions.

For basic applications that generate a similar workload through the entire execution, one can use simple static tuning. For this approach one tunes the selected knobs at the application start, and they remain the same for the entire application runtime. However, more complex applications usually contains several regions with different workloads, and therefore with different optimal settings. These must be dynamically adjusted during the application runtime.

To find optimal settings in terms of energy consumption for particular HPC hardware, it is necessary to measure the consumed energy on different granularity levels. Almost all currently deployed HPC clusters based on Intel Xeon CPUs starting from the Sandy Bridge generation are equipped with Intel Running Average Power Limit (RAPL) counters [1]. The advantage of RAPL is fast access to energy counters with a very low overhead and quite a high sampling frequency of 1kHz. The main disadvantage is that it is able to measure only the energy consumption of the CPU and DDR memory but ignores the energy consumed by the rest of the compute node (main board, fans, storage, network card, etc.). This, called baseline energy consumption, must be accounted for by different means. The most straight forward way is to use a linear model, which predicts its power consumption based on the power consumption of the CPUs and memory.

Other more advanced measurement systems, such as High Definition Energy Efficiency Monitoring (HDEEM) [2], are based on additional hardware attached to the compute node, and provide out of bound energy measurements, which do interfere with running applications and do not introduce any additional overhead. These systems, in addition to the CPU and DDR memory, also measure the energy consumption of the entire compute node and thus provide all the necessary information for finding optimal settings.

Energy efficient high performance computing is an area of interest for several research activities, most commonly applying DVFS or power capping to the whole application run [3][4]. In this case only separate code kernels are extracted from the application and tuned. Complex application tuning is a goal of the Adagio project [5], presenting a scheduling system which changes the hardware configuration with a negligible time penalty based on previous application runs. Dynamic application tuning is the goal of the Horizon 2020 READEX (Runtime Exploitation of Application Dynamism for Energy-efficient eXascale computing) project [6] [7], which develops tools for application dynamic behavior detection, automatic instrumentation, and analysis of available system parameters configuration to attain the minimum energy consumption for the production runs.

Our tool called MERIC uses the same approach, with a focus on manual tuning, and is therefore more flexible for certain tasks. MERIC is a library for efficient manual evaluation of HPC applications' dynamic behavior and manual tuning from the energy savings perspective, applying the idea of dynamic tuning.

The goal of this paper is to present energy measurement and hardware parameters tuning using our MERIC tool on several different hardware platforms (two Intel Xeon E5-26xx v3 (code name Haswell - HSW) processors with different energy measurement systems (RAPL and HDEEM), Intel Xeon Phi (code name Knights Landing - KNL), and an experimental ARM platform). The approach is presented using the Lattice Boltzmann application benchmark.

This paper is organized as follows. Section II describes the MERIC library that was used for the application behavior analysis and runtime tuning. Section III describes the used hardware platforms and their energy measurement interfaces. Following on, Section IV presents experiments we performed on each hardware platform.

II. MERIC

MERIC [8][9] is a C++ dynamic library with a Fortran interface designed to measure resource consumption and runtime of analyzed MPI+OpenMP applications. In addition it can also tune selected hardware (HW) parameters during the application runtime.

MERIC automates hardware performance counters reading, time measurements, and energy consumption measurements for all user annotated regions of the evaluated application. These are called significant regions, and in general the different regions should have different workloads. The main idea of MERIC is that by running the code with different settings of tuning parameters multiple times, one can identify both optimal settings and possible energy savings for each significant region.

The supported system parameters in MERIC are:

- CPU core frequency,
- CPU uncore frequency,
- number of active CPU cores by means of number of OpenMP threads and thread placement, and
- selected application parameters (not used in this paper).

CPU uncore frequency refers to frequency of subsystems in the physical processor package that are shared by multiple processor cores e.g., L3 cache or on-chip ring interconnect. This parameter is not supported on Intel Xeon Phi processors.

The measurement results are analyzed using our second tool called RADAR [10]. This tool generates a detailed LaTeXreport of application behavior for different settings, and generates a final tuning model. The tuning model contains optimal settings for each significant region and it is used by MERIC for final runs of an application to perform dynamic tuning.

III. HPC PLATFORMS

Several current, and potentially future, HPC platforms are able to be tuned and analyzed for energy consumption by the MERIC library. Four of them are used to present the approach of dynamic tuning ofparallel applications.

The Technische Universität Dresden Taurus machine has nodes with Intel Haswell processors (2x Intel Xeon CPU E5-2680v3, 12 cores) [11] from the Bull company, which contain an energy measurement system called HDEEM [2] that has capability to measure energy consumption of the entire compute node with a sampling rate of 1kHz (the measurement error is approximately 2%).

HDEEM provides energy measurements in two different ways. In the first mode, HDEEM works as an energy counter (similar to RAPL), and by reading this counter we measure energy consumed from when HDEEM is initialized. Access to HDEEM measurements is through the C/C++ API. In this mode we read the counter at the start and end of each region. This solution is straightforward, however there is a delay of approximately 4 ms associated with every read from HDEEM. To avoid this delay, we take advantage of the fact that during the measurement HDEEM stores the power samples in its internal memory. The samples are stored without causing any additional overhead to the application runtime because all samples are transferred from HDEEM memory at the end of the application runtime. The energy is subsequently calculated from these samples based on the timestamps that MERIC records during the application runtime. The timestamps are associated with every start and end of significant regions.

Intel RAPL counters [1] are used to extrapolate the energy consumption. Both the RAPL and HDEEM energy measurement systems provide the same sampling frequency of 1 kHz, but the RAPL counters only approximate the energy consumption of the CPUs and RAM DIMMs, and do not take into account the energy consumption of the mainboard and other parts of the compute node. This fact may have major effect on the code analysis. If we were to measure only CPUs and RAM DIMMs without considering consumption of the rest of the node it would result in lower CPU frequencies and a longer runtime. however, the longer runtime leads to higher energy consumption of the entire node due to its baseline. Based on measurements made on the Taurus system, where the same type of hardware is present, the Haswell node baseline (the power consumption of the entire node without the power consumed by the CPUs and memory DIMMs) has been measured as 70 W. We add this constant to each measurement taken by RAPL to calibrate energy measurements.

Both energy measurement systems were compared on the Intel Haswell processor, which allows the CPU uncore frequency to be set in the range of 1.2–3.0 GHz and the CPU core frequency in range of 1.2–2.5 GHz, which we used for UFS and DVFS in our Experiments section. Haswell experiments using RAPL counters were performed on IT4Innovations' Salomon cluster [12].

As a modern Intel platform, Intel Xeon Phi 7210 (KNL) supports energy consumption measurement using RAPL counters. Similarly to the case of Haswell nodes, we had to evaluate a node power baseline for more precise power consumption results. According to our measurements from Intelligent Platform Management Interface (IPMI), when not under a load the node consumes *75* W.

Xeon Phi platforms host GPU cards, and many smaller, less complex and low frequency cores. This is the reason why these cards provides a better FLOPs per Watt ratio than the usual x86 processors [13]. KNL nodes can also be tuned during the application runtime due to the changing number of active OpenMP threads (64 cores each with up to 4 hyper-threads) and a CPU core frequency which can scale from 1.0 GHz to 1.4 GHz. Uncore frequency tuning is not supported on KNL.

For KNL nodes it is possible to setup in a different memory mode, where MCDRAM works as a last-level cache (Cache mode), as an extension of RAM (Flat mode), or partially as a cache and partially as a RAM extension (Hybrid mode). Due to DVFS and energy measurement requirements, we had access to nodes in Cache mode only.

Another tested platform is Jetson/TX1, which is an ARM system (ARM Cortex-A57, 4 cores, 1.3 GHz), which is not a very powerful system, but which can set much lower frequencies than standard HPC systems, consequently allowing ARM systems to consume less energy. This fact makes such platforms interesting for further investigation. In the case of this system, it is not possible to set the uncore frequency, however, the user may change the frequency of the RAM. The minimum CPU core frequency is 0.5 GHz and the maximum is 1.3 GHz. The minimum and maximum RAM frequencies are 40 MHz and 1.6 GHz respectively.

TABLE I. JETSON/TX1 ENERGY MEASUREMENT INTERFACE AND ITS EFFECT ON THE CPU LOAD

frequency [Hz]	CPU load
10	2%
50	4%
100	8%
200	14%
500	23%
1000	30%

This system was selected from the available Barcelona Supercomputing Center ARM prototype systems under the Mont-Blanc project [14] because it is the only one that allows DVFS and supports energy measurements. To gather the power data from the board, the Texas Instruments INA3221 is featured on the board [15]. It measures the per node energy consumption and stores sample values in a file. It is possible to take approximately hundreds of samples per second, however the measurement runs on the CPU. Table I shows how the CPU is effected due to different energy measurement sampling frequencies, measured via the htop process-manager.

IV. EXPERIMENTS

In the following section we compare presented hardware platforms using the Lattice Boltzmann benchmark, which is a computational fluid dynamics application that describes flows in two or three dimensions.

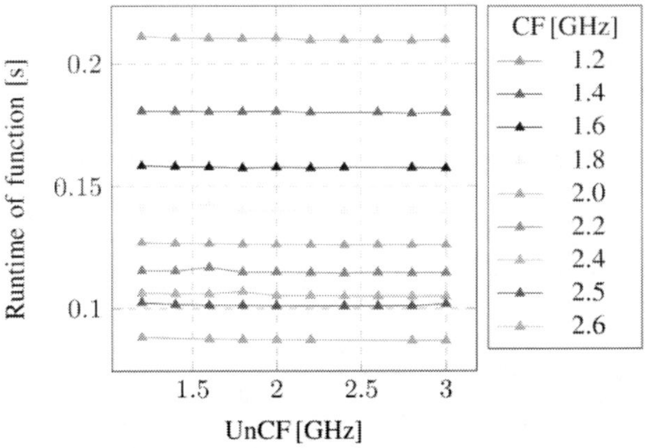

Figure 1: Collide region runtime when different CPU core and uncore frequencies are applied on a Haswell node.

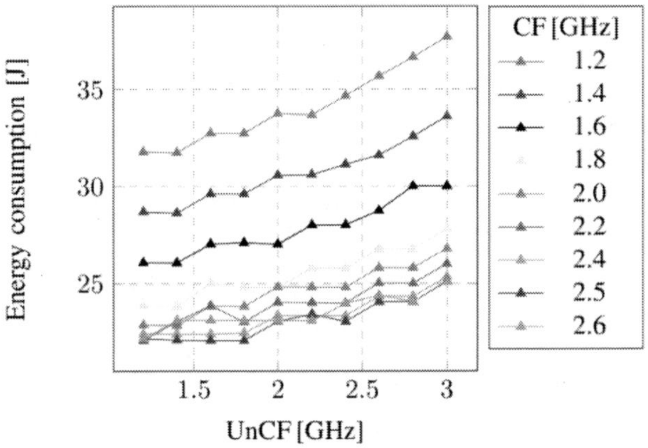

Figure 2: Collide region energy consumption when different CPU core and uncore frequencies are applied on a Haswell node.

The most significant parts of the code are functions called Collide and Propagate. Figure 1 shows the Collide region runtime for various CPU core and uncore frequencies on an Intel Xeon CPU (Haswell). The Collide region performs all the mathematical steps, so it is a typical compute-bound region, and its runtime is not effected by the uncore frequency. Figure 2 shows that on the other hand, the energy consumption is affected by increasing the uncore frequency, and that by reducing it to its minimum we save energy.

conversely, the Propagate region demonstrates very different behavior. It consists of a large number of sparse memory accesses, so it is highly affected by the uncore frequency, while core frequency has minimal impact on its runtime, as show in Figure 3. Also Figure 4 shows that the CPU core frequency can

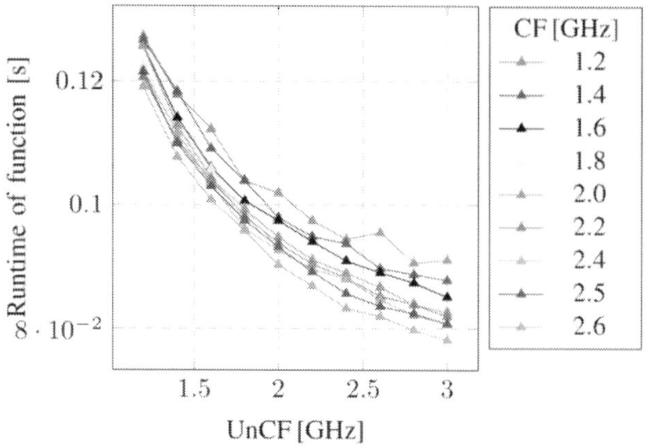

Figure 3: Propagate region runtime when different CPU core and uncore frequencies are applied on a Haswell node.

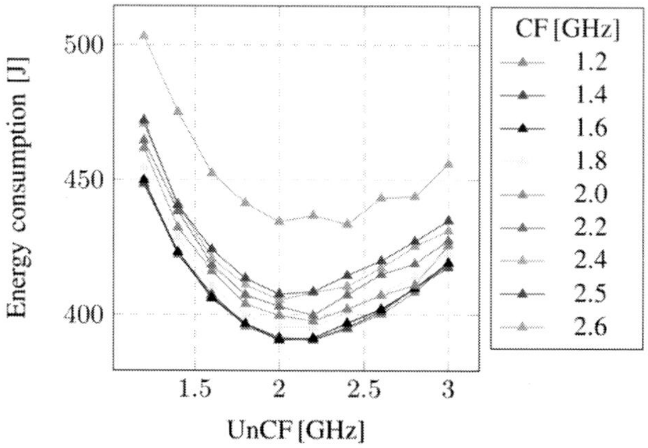

Figure 4: Propagate region energy consumption when different CPU core and uncore frequencies are applied on a Haswell node.

be reduced, but only to a specific minimum, since afterwards the energy consumption starts to grow again.

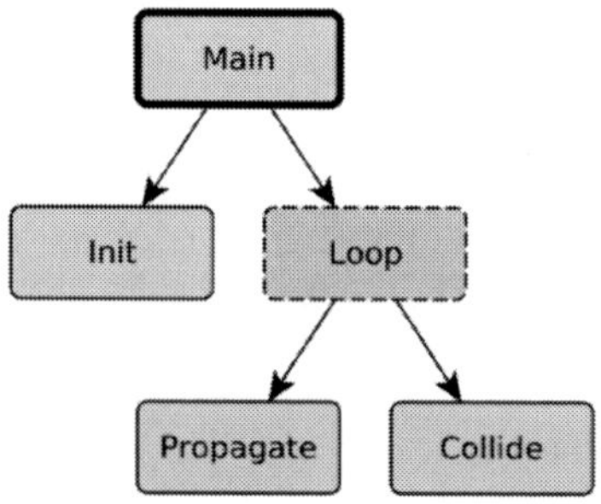

Figure 5: Diagram of significant regions in the LBM benchmark.

These two regions take most of the time of the main loop, however, an initialization of the application itself also takes several seconds, depending on the problem size, and we should not ignore this region. In this simple benchmark, we inserted four regions as illustrated in Figure 5. Please note that Loop region is not evaluated as it only repeatedly calls the Propagate and Collide regions.

TABLE II. LBM APPLICATION REGIONS' OPTIMAL CONFIGURATIONS FOR THE ANALYZED PLATFORMS

Region	**Parameter**	**HSW** HDEEM	**HSW** RAPL	**KNL**	**JTX**
Main	threads [-]	24	24	256	4
	CF [GHz]	2.5	2.5	1.4	1.33
	UCF [GHz]	2.2	2.2	–	–
	RAMF [GHz]	–	–	–	1.1
Init	threads [-]	–	–	–	–
	CF [GHz]	2.6	2.6	1.4	1.33
	UCF [GHz]	1.4	1.6	–	–
	RAMF [GHz]	–	–	–	0.41
Propagate	threads [-]	6	6	128	4
	CF [GHz]	1.6	1.6	1.0	1.22
	UCF [GHz]	2.2	2.4	–	–
	RAMF [GHz]	–	–	–	1.6
Collide	threads [-]	24	24	256	4
	CF [GHz]	2.5	2.5	1.2	1.33
	UCF [GHz]	1.6	1.4	–	–
	RAMF [GHz]	–	–	–	0.41

A. *Application Analysis*

The application analysis runs the benchmark in the following configurations:

- Intel Xeon Haswell CPU (HSW) - CPU core frequency (1.2 – 2.6 GHz, step 0.2 GHz), CPU uncore frequency (1.2 to 3.0 GHZ, step 0.2 GHz), number of OpenMP threads (2 – 24 threads, step 2 threads);
- Intel Xeon Phi (KNL) - CPU core frequency (1.0 – 1.4 GHz, step 0.1 GHz), number of OpenMP threads (16, 32, 64, 128,192, 256 threads);
- Jetson TX1 - CPU core frequency (0.5 – 1.3 GHz, variable step), RAM frequency (0.04 to 1.6 GHZ, variable step), number of OpenMP threads (1 – 4 threads, step 1 thread).

First, we explore the analysis done on Intel Xeon Haswell processors, using different energy measurement systems. Table II presents the optimal configuration for the inserted regions. Despite the inaccuracy of the RAPL counters, the optimal configuration of the regions is very similar (the optimal configurations differs in one step of the analysis). The differences are caused by several factors: (i) small differences might be caused due to running the analysis on a different node; (ii) the proximity of the measured values; (iii) the baseline estimation for RAPL counters.

By evaluating the optimum configuration for each significant region while running the application with a domain size of *512x4096* for one hundred iterations, the tuned application has an approximately 1.5 % longer runtime, but consumes 19.8 % less energy.

Figure 6 shows the application behavior (energy consumption of the Main region) when running on Jetson/TX1 using different CPU core and RAM frequencies. The smallest possible RAM frequencies have a massive impact on application

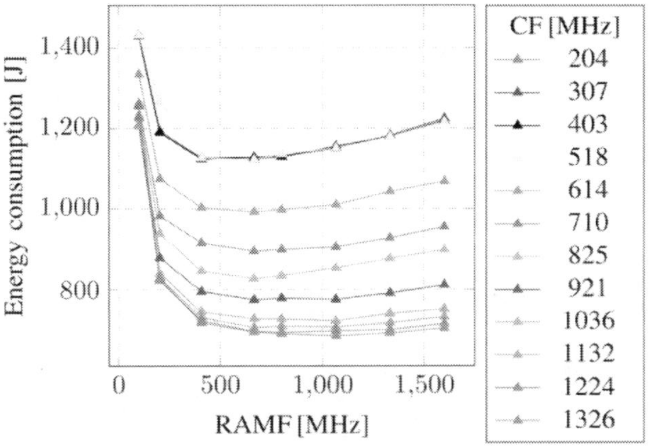

Figure 6: Jetson/TX1 application analysis comparing the energy consumption when applying various available CPU core and RAM frequencies.

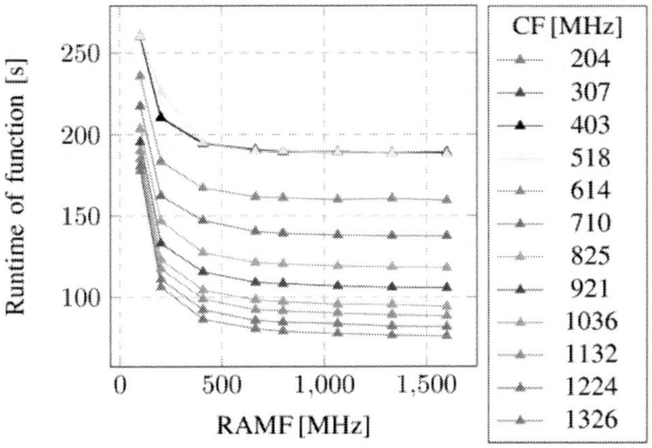

Figure 7: Jetson/TX1 application analysis comparing application runtime when applying various available CPU core and RAM frequencies.

runtime, as can be seen in Figure 7, which results in significantly higher energy consumption. In this case the graph of the application energy consumption follows the graph of application runtime. The minimum consumed energy was in the configuration 1065.6 MHz RAMF and 1326.00 MHz CF, when the application consumed 684.53 J.

From the analysis, see Table II, we can see the different behavior of th Propagate (optimum at 1600 MHz RAMF and 1224 MHz CF) and Collide (optimum at 408 MHz RAMF and 1326 MHz CF) regions. However the difference in RAM frequency does not translate into significant energy savings because the CPU core frequencies are quite similar for both regions.

When comparing tuned and non-tuned runs on Jetson the time remains the same while energy consumption drops about 4 %. When comparing to the same test case executed on Haswell CPUs where the tuned application finishes in 234 s and consumes 1992 J, the Haswell solved the same problem 10 times faster but consumed 2.3 times more energy than Jetson.

We evaluated the same test case on the Intel Xeon Phi 7210 (KNL), but since the test size was selected to run on Jetson/TX1, the test was too small for KNL node. In the *512x4096* domain size configuration, the Propagate and Collide regions take about 50 milliseconds only, which results very frequent frequency switching.

The overhead of switching CPU core frequencies on KNL limits its usage for such short regions. The Haswell processor can change the CPU core frequencies in about10 microseconds, while KNL nodes requires 20 milliseconds if it is done in the OMP parallel region and each thread is switching the frequency of its core. In case the master thread does the switching for all cores, it takes more than 50 milliseconds when using cpufreq library [16]. There are libraries providing slightly faster DVFS/UFS than cpufreq, such as the x86_adapt library [17], but these unfortunately currently do not support KNL.

Dealing with such overheads forces us to specify much higher restrictions for minimum region size. We have scaled the Lattice domain size to find the minimum problem size, which will provide some energy savings. When running the LBM simulation on a *4096x8192* domain, each Propagate and Collide region took 274.47 ms and 358.46 ms respectively. From this configuration we can see only a three percent longer runtime and one percent overall energy savings when running 100 iterations. Extending the region's size would continue the reduction of the DVFS overhead and increase the energy savings.

On KNL the sequential Init region becomes much more important because of the low single core performance of KNL. When running the application for 100 iterations on a *512x4096* domain on Haswell, this region takes less than 5 % of the application runtime. When running the same test case on KNL the initialization takes over 40 % of the application runtime. For a domain size of *4096x8192* elements, the initialization part takes longer than the Loop region with 100 iterations. Of course this ratio will differ as the number of iterations increases.

TABLE III. TABLE OF PRESENTED RESULTS COMPARING ENERGY SAVINGS FOR EACH PLATFORM WHEN RUNNING THE LBM BENCHMARK FOR 100 ITERATIONS

platform	default		static savings		dynamic savings	
domain	time	energy	time	energy	time	energy
HSW - S	24 s	5.7 kJ	-11.6%	7.8%	-1.5%	19.8%
JTX - S	233 s	2.1 kJ	-2.4%	2.6 %	-0.1%	4.0%
KNL - S	9 s	1.9 kJ	0%	0%	-2.8%	-3.6%
KNL - L	152 s	32.2 kJ	0%	0%	-3.0%	1.4%

Table III shows how much energy it is possible to save if one hardware configuration is set for the whole application run (static savings). This table shows the results for two different domain sizes - large (L) domain size represents a domain of 4096x8192 elements, the small (S) domain has 512x4096 elements. Despite having two very different regions in the application, on Haswell and Jetson/TX1 it is possible to save 7.8 % and 2.6 % energy respectively. This savings are reached due to CPU uncore frequency (RAM frequency in the case of Jetson/TX1) reduction (HSW: 2.6 GHz; JTX: 1065 MHz), which explains why there are no static savings for KNL. Selected optimal static configuration is friendly for the Collide region, but extends the runtime of the Propagate region. When applying optimal configuration dynamically for each region (dynamic tuning) the application runtime, compared to non-tuned run, extends slightly, but energy savings further improves from static tuning.

V. Conclusion and Future Work

The MERIC library is a lightweight tool for the evaluation of resource consumption and dynamic hardware parameters tuning. The library is focused on the tuning of complex applications without rewriting the application itself. It is continually extended to support different and experimental platforms. Two Intel Xeon CPU E5-26xx v3 (codename Haswell) based machines with RAPL and HDEEM energy measurement systems, one Intel Xeon Phi (codename KNL) system with RAPL counters, and finally a Jetson/TX1 with an INA3221 system have been presented and compared using the Lattice Boltzmann benchmark.

Tuning achieved up to 20 % energy savings with a 1 % longer runtime for Haswell nodes. On the Jetson and KNL nodes there are several restrictions that limit reachable gains. We attained about 4 % energy savings without any runtime penalty in case of the Jetson TX1 system. For KNL it was possible to reach savings only if the problem size had been scaled, and regions' sizes extended sufficiently to overcome the problem of system slow frequency switching.

The ARM platforms become more and more interesting for future HPC systems builders, because of their low energy consumption. The possibility to tune within a wide range of frequencies seems interesting in the case of Jetson/TX1. Despite the limited performance of its CPU cores, it was able to provide the simulation result, and consumed a significantly smaller amount of energy than a usual HPC node powered with two Intel Xeon CPUs.

Many more energy efficient platforms are coming to the market, especially new ARM and IBM systems, as well as GPU cards, and we would like to extend the MERIC library and provide support for their hardware tuning.

Acknowledgment

This work was supported by The Ministry of Education, Youth and Sports from the Large Infrastructures for Research, Experimental Development and Innovations project IT4Innovations National Supercomputing Center LM2015070.

This work was supported by the READEX project - the European Union's Horizon 2020 research and innovation programme under grant agreement No. 671657.

This work was partially supported by the SGC grant No. SP2018/134 "Development of tools for energy-efficient HPC applications", VSB - Technical University of Ostrava, Czech Republic.

This work was supported by Barcelona Supercomputing Center under the grants 288777, 610402 and 671697.

References

[1] M. Hähnel, B. Döbel, M. Völp, and H. Härtig, "Measuring energy consumption for short code paths using rapl," *SIGMETRICS Perform. Eval. Rev.*, vol. 40, no. 3, pp. 13–17, Jan. 2012. [Online]. Available: http://doi.acm.org/10.1145/2425248.2425252

[2] D. Hackenberg, T. Ilsche, J. Schuchart, R. Schne, W. E. Nagel, M. Simon, and Y. Georgiou, "HDEEM: High definition energy efficiency monitoring," in *2014 Energy Efficient Supercomputing Workshop*, Nov 2014, pp. 1–10.

[3] A. Haidar, H. Jagode, P. Vaccaro, A. YarKhan, S. Tomov, and J. Dongarra, "Investigating power capping toward energy-efficient scientific applications," *Concurrency and Computation: Practice and Experience*, p. e4485. [Online]. Available: https://onlinelibrary.wiley.com/doi/abs/10.1002/cpe.4485

[4] J. Eastep, S. Sylvester, C. Cantalupo, B. Geltz, F. Ardanaz, A. Al-Rawi, K. Livingston, F. Keceli, M. Maiterth, and S. Jana, "Global extensible open power manager: A vehicle for hpc community collaboration on co-designed energy management solutions," in *ISC*. Cham: Springer International Publishing, 2017, pp. 394–412.

[5] B. Rountree, D. K. Lowenthal, B. R. de Supinski, M. Schulz, V. W. Freeh, and T. K. Bletsch, "Adagio: making dvs practical for complex hpc applications," ser. ICS '09. New York, NY, USA: ACM, 2009, pp. 460–469. [Online]. Available: http://doi.acm.org/10.1145/1542275.1542340

[6] Y. Oleynik, M. Gerndt, J. Schuchart, P. G. Kjeldsberg, and W. E. Nagel, "Run-time exploitation of application dynamism for energy-efficient exascale computing (READEX)," in *Computational Science and Engineering (CSE), 2015 IEEE 18th International Conference on*, C. Plessl, D. El Baz, G. Cong, J. M. P. Cardoso, L. Veiga, and T. Rauber, Eds. Piscataway: IEEE, Oct 2015, pp. 347–350.

[7] J. Schuchart, M. Gerndt, P. G. Kjeldsberg, M. Lysaght, D. Horák, L. Říha, A. Gocht, M. Sourouri, M. Kumaraswamy, A. Chowdhury, M. Jahre, K. Diethelm, O. Bouizi, U. S. Mian, J. Kružík, R. Sojka, M. Beseda, V. Kannan, Z. Bendifallah, D. Hackenberg, and W. E. Nagel, "The READEX formalism for automatic tuning for energy efficiency," *Computing*, vol. 99, no. 8, pp. 727–745, 2017. [Online]. Available: https://doi.org/10.1007/s00607-016-0532-7

[8] IT4Innovations. MERIC library. URL: https://code.it4i.cz/vys0053/meric [accessed: 2018-06-25].

[9] O. Vysocky, M. Beseda, L. Riha, J. Zapletal, V. Nikl, M. Lysaght, and V. Kannan, "Evaluation of the HPC applications dynamic behavior in terms of energy consumption," in *Proceedings of the Fifth International Conference on Parallel, Distributed, Grid and Cloud Computing for Engineering*, pp. 1–19, paper 3, 2017. doi:10.4203/ccp.111.3.

[10] IT4Innovations. READEX RADAR library. URL: https://code.it4i.cz/bes0030/readex-radar [accessed: 2018-06-25].

[11] Technische Universitat Dresden. System Taurus. URL: https://doc.zih.tu-dresden.de/hpc-wiki/bin/view/Compendium/SystemTaurus [accessed: 2018-06-25].

[12] IT4Innovations National Supercomputing Centre, IT4I. Salomon supercomputer. URL: https://docs.it4i.cz/salomon/introduction/ [accessed: 2018-06-25].

[13] T. Dong, V. Dobrev, T. Kolev, R. Rieben, S. Tomov, and J. Dongarra, "A step towards energy efficient computing: Redesigning a hydrodynamic application on cpu-gpu," in *2014 IEEE 28th International Parallel and Distributed Processing Symposium*, May 2014, pp. 972–981.

[14] Mont-Blanc project. Mont-Blanc project mini-clusters. URL: http://montblanc-project.eu/prototypes [accessed: 2018-06-25].

[15] Barcelona Supercomputing Center. Power Monitoring on mini-clusters. URL: https://wiki.hca.bsc.es/dokuwiki/wiki/prototype/power_monitor [accessed: 2018-06-25].

[16] E. Calore, A. Gabbana, S. F. Schifano, and R. Tripiccione, "Software and dvfs tuning for performance and energy-efficiency on intel knl processors," *Journal of Low Power Electronics and Applications*, vol. 8, no. 2, pp. 1–11, 2018. [Online]. Available: http://www.mdpi.com/2079-9268/8/2/18

[17] R. Schoene. x86_adapt. Techniche Universitat Dresden. URL: https://doc.zih.tu-dresden.de/hpc-wiki/bin/view/Compendium/X86Adapt [accessed: 2018-06-25].

Performance Optimization of D3Q19 Lattice Boltzmann Kernels on Intel® KNL

Ivan Girotto*‡§, Sebastiano Fabio Schifano†, Enrico Calore†, Gianluca Di Staso‡ and Federico Toschi‡

* The Abdus Salam, International Centre for Theoretical Physics
† University of Ferrara and INFN Ferrara
‡ Eindhoven University of Technology
§ University of Modena and Reggio Emilia
E-mail: igirotto@ictp.it, schifano@fe.infn.it, enrico.calore@fe.infn.it, g.di.staso@tue.nl, f.toschi@tue.nl

Abstract—**This work discusses and assesses the impact of fundamental code optimization steps performed to maximize computing performances and memory throughput on Intel® Knights Landing (KNL) processor for Lattice Boltzmann (LB) applications. The benefits of using different memory data layouts is presented in regards to the most computationally intensive kernels of such applications, reporting performance results measured for the LBE3D code developed at the Applied Physics Department of the Eindhoven University of Technology, and run on a single KNL node for a common flow simulation case. We finally analyze and discuss the impact of different memory layouts on energy efficiency.**

Index Terms—**LBE3D; KNL; Optimization; Energy Efficiency; Data Memory Layout; Vectorization; Performance Analysis.**

I. Introduction

The combination of multi-threaded programming and vectorization, combined with efficient use of different levels of memory hierarchy, are still considered to be the most relevant solution to achieve high computing performances on latest generations x86-64 processors. However, the majority of legacy scientific codes are not yet capable to exploit all these features, and optimized memory data layouts and access patterns, together with efficient use of a large number of threads and data vectorization, are necessary to obtain high computing performances.

The Lattice Boltzmann Method [1] (LBM) is widely used in computational fluid-dynamics to describe behavior of fluid flows, and nowadays is commonly applied in several science and engineering fields to accurately model single and multi-phase flows, also using irregular boundary conditions. Furthermore, applications based on LBM are also employed to perform large scale simulations to study the dynamics and the behavior of fluid and gases, requiring a huge amount of computational resources. However, while these applications are renown to deliver good scaling performances on distributed systems enabling simulation of physical phenomena at high-resolution, it is not easy to achieve high computing efficiency even at level of single node. In fact, most of applications based on LBM are not engineered and optimized for modern CPUs based on multi-core architecture and using large vector unit, where data organisation of application domain plays a key role for enabling high computing efficiency.

In this work, we focus on the LBE3D code based on D3Q19 LBM model, and assess the impact on computing performances of several code optimization steps to maximize both the number of flops and the memory throughput on modern Intel® based many-core systems. In particular, we use several data layouts to store the data domain of the application, with the aim to find out a single memory layout that fits the computing requirements of several kernel routines of the code.

Performances in term of both computing and energy consumption of LBM applications have been studied in several works for different architectures [2]–[4]. Here, we follow a similar approach with the main difference that the analysis reported refers to a real case application for a 3-dimensional lattice.

The remainder of this paper is organized as follow: in Section II, we introduce the main features of the KNL processor, in Section III, we briefly describe the LBE3D code and the data layouts aimed to improve performances of LBM based applications, in Section IV, we present the results obtained measuring the LBE3D code performances on the KNL processors while in Section V, a short analysis on energy efficiency is reported.

II. The KNL processor

The results presented in the following sections are all obtained on a 64-cores Intel ® Xeon Phi™ CPU 7230 processor, commonly referred as KNL, running at 1.30 GHz and delivering a theoretical peak performance of about 3 TFlop/s in double precision. The KNL processor is equipped with 6 Double Data Rate fourth-generation (DDR4) channels, supporting 98 GB of synchronous Dynamic Random-Access Memory (DRAM) with a peak raw bandwidth of 115.2 GB/s and four high-speed memory banks based on the Multi-Channel DRAM (MCDRAM) that provides 16 GB of memory, capable to deliver an aggregate bandwidth of more than 450 GB/s. In this work, we only consider the Quadrant cluster configuration in which the 64-cores available are divided in four quadrants, each directly connected to one MCDRAM bank. MCDRAM on a KNL can be configured at boot time in Flat, Cache or Hybrid mode. The Flat mode defines the whole MCDRAM as addressable memory allowing explicit data allocation, whereas Cache mode uses the MCDRAM as a last-level cache. In this work, we used Intel® library for Message Passing Interface (MPI) to compile the LBE3D application. Vectorization is enabled at compile level using the -xMIC-AVX512 Intel® compiler option. Multi-thread version of LBE3D is implemented

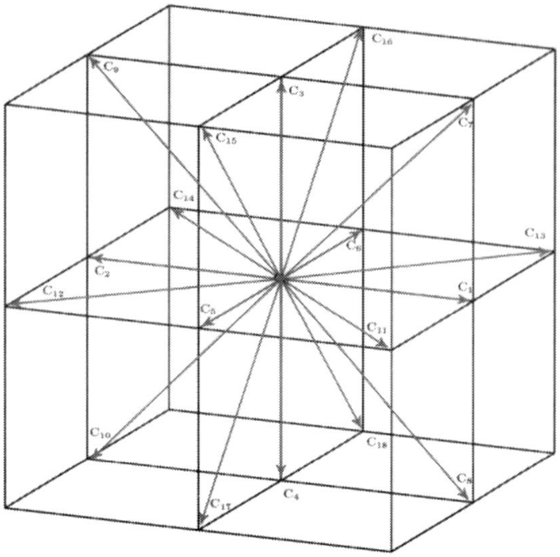

Figure 1. Schematic representation of the D3Q19 lattice employed in this work.

using OpenMP and enabled at compile time. Threads affinity at run time is obtained with "KMP_AFFINITY=compact" and "I_MPI_PIN_DOMAIN=socket" environment variables. Memory allocation for all results related to the KNL configured in Flat mode is made by using the `numactl -m 1 mpirun ./lbe3d` command.

III. LBE3D AND DATA LAYOUTS

The LBM is based on the synthetic dynamics of populations arranged at the edges of a discrete lattice. It is discrete in time, space and momenta, offering a large amount of easily identifiable parallelism while making it an ideal tool for investigating performances of modern systems for high-performance computing [5]–[7]. At each time step, populations are first moved from lattice-site to lattice-site applying the propagate operator, and then are modified through a collisional operator changing their values according to the local equilibrium condition. The computing pattern for the collision (`collide`) and the consequent propagation (`propagate`) within the lattice grid are renown main bottlenecks for the LB class of applications.

With this work, we transferred previous experiences on code optimization for LB class of applications implementing new data layouts on the LBE3D code, a LBM based application featuring a standard single relaxation time with the Bhatnagar-Gross-Krook (BGK) collision operator [8], which builds on top of a generic compile/profiling library (ftmake), currently maintained at the Eindhoven University of Technology, The Netherlands. More in particular, the LBE3D code implements a numerical scheme based on the LBM [9] and it has been used to perform simulations under a broad range of flow and fluid conditions [10]–[13].

Here, we focus on the D3Q19 LB stencil, a 3-dimensional model with a set of 19 population elements corresponding to (pseudo-)particles moving one lattice point away along all 19 possible directions. A schematic representation of the stencil pattern is shown in Figure 1, where the arrows represent the direction along which populations sitting at a site node are allowed to stream. All presented performance measurements are referred to a simple channel flow set-up as shown in Figure 2. A fluid between two parallel solid walls is put into motion by a homogeneous body force, and no-slip boundary conditions are applied at these walls, while periodic boundary conditions are applied along the two other directions.

Figure 2. Velocity field along the forcing direction. Snapshot taken once the flow field reached the final steady state.

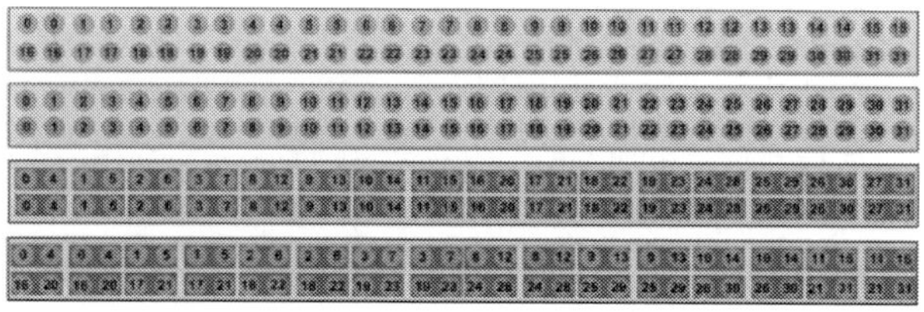

Figure 3. Top to bottom, AoS, SoA, CSoA and CAoSoA data memory layouts for a 4 x 8 lattice with two populations (red and blue) per site.

Many stencil based applications, including LBM, are commonly implemented using either Array of Structures (AoS) or Structure of Arrays (SoA) data layouts. In the AoS approach, originally used in the LBE3D code too, population elements of each lattice site are stored contiguously in memory. Therefore, the AoS structure is constructed as a 3-dimensional lattice where each element is composed by N population values (NPOP). On the other hand, LB based applications adopting the SoA schema allocate the 3-dimensional lattice as a collection of NPOP arrays, each storing for every site a single element population value. However, none of those two data layouts have been demonstrated to be ideal for LB based applications since, while the AoS delivers better performances for the `collide` kernel, it lacks in memory bandwidth if compared with SoA when considering the `propagate` kernel.

Alternate data layouts aim to improve the overall performances of LB based applications, and in Figure 3 we show a graphical representation for a sample lattice of 4 x 8 using two populations per site (memory addresses increase left-to-right top-to-bottom). In summary, beside the AoS and SoA layout, we have two new layouts called CSoA and CAoSoA. The CSoA layout is an extension of the SoA where VL lattice-site data at distance L/VL (L dimension of major order store) are clustered in consecutive elements for each population array, with VL equal to the number of double precision elements that can be stored in the vector register available on the given architecture. This layout keeps the data properly aligned in memory and allows to vectorize the steps of `propagate` kernel. The CAoSoA structure is a mix between CSoA and AoS, and allows to exploit the benefit of the VL clusterization of lattice sites element as introduced by the CSoA schema but with the benefit of higher locality in regards to the populations. For this reason, this layout may deliver better overall performances for the `collide` kernel. In Figure 3, each dark grey-box is a cluster with VL=2 for both the CSoA and the CAoSoA data layouts.

IV. Analysis of Results

In this Section, we measure the impact of the different memory layouts in terms of computing while an analysis in term of energy consumption is provided in the following paragraph. We first focus and analyze performance for the `propagate` and `collide` kernels, and then we assess the impact on the whole LBE3D code.

As mentioned earlier, LBM is characterised by a phase of propagate, where populations move from lattice-site to lattice-site, describing the flows momentum. Kernels implementing this phase are, in particular, memory bounded because the movement is practically implemented as the copy of a single data (double precision floating point number) from one location to another location in memory. Therefore, a key aspect to achieve maximum speed is to describe this operation with a memory access pattern that can exploit the maximum memory bandwidth. Clustered data layouts allow to vectorize such operation, whether data are aligned in memory, as the compiler replaces the scalar operation of copy with a copy operation on registers capable of multiple elements of the same kind (vector registers). In Figure 4, we report the measured performances of memory bandwidth obtained by the `propagate` kernel on a KNL node configured in Flat mode. The CSoA version allows to achieve almost 350 GB/s memory with a significant improvement in performance if compared with the canonical AoS or SoA approaches. We can confirm that also for the cases of 3-dimensional lattices the CSoA version allows for the `propagate` kernel to achieve the highest value of memory bandwidth if compared with other analysed data layouts. It is relevant to underline how in most cases the memory bandwidth saturates at 64 threads (a single hardware thread per core).

The measured memory bandwidth drops if considering larger lattices with a data domain unable to fit in the 16 GB/s of the MCDRAM. In Figure 5, data are obtained with the KNL configured in Cache mode and the real peak performance achieved by the CSoA data layout is of about 80 GB/s, with a factor of 4x reduction if compared with the memory bandwidth obtained when data fit into the MCDRAM. Moreover, the intensive use of the DRAM memory squeezes the performance gap among the various data layouts such that CSoA becomes only 10% better of the SoA and comparable with the CAoSoA versions.

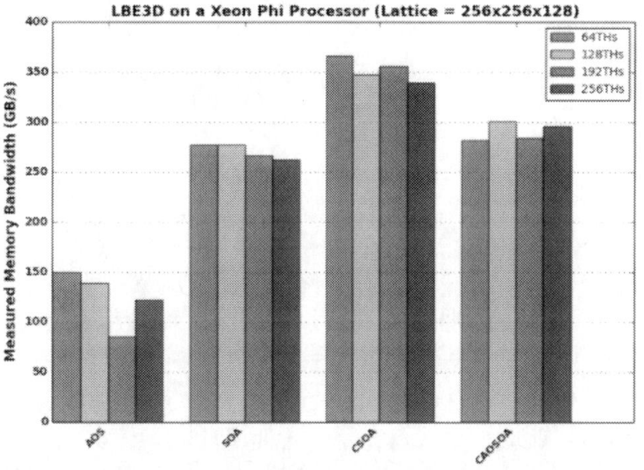

Figure 4. Measured memory bandwidth for the `propagate` kernel using different data layouts: AoS, SoA, CSoA and CAoSA. KNL is configured in flat mode.

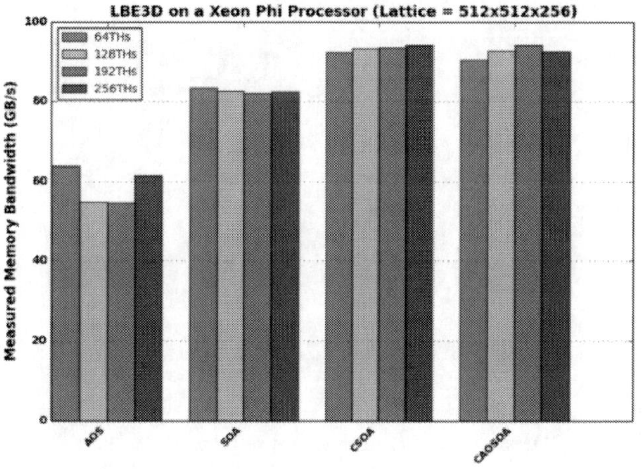

Figure 5. Measured memory bandwidth for the `propagate` kernel using different data layouts: AoS, SoA, CSoA and CAoSA. KNL is configured in cache mode.

The other important phase of LBM is the collision phase. It is implemented as the `collide` kernel which is generally considered compute bounded because all discretised quantities such as forces, velocities and densities are per site computed with high data locality. For most of those quantities the lattice elements are read from the input lattice and written to the output lattice contiguously, but for the computation of the density, and velocity, which requires accessing all population elements for each site. While this is a cache friendly operation for the AoS scheme, due to data locality (all populations elements are stored contiguously), it is not for data layouts where per-site population are scattered in memory, such as SoA and CSoA. However, as per the CSoA version the speedup achieved by vectorized operations on clustered data helps to overrun this problem. The mixed schema of the CAoSoA is expected to take advantage of accessing contiguous population elements while working on clustered data.

In Figure 6, the measured value of peak performance is

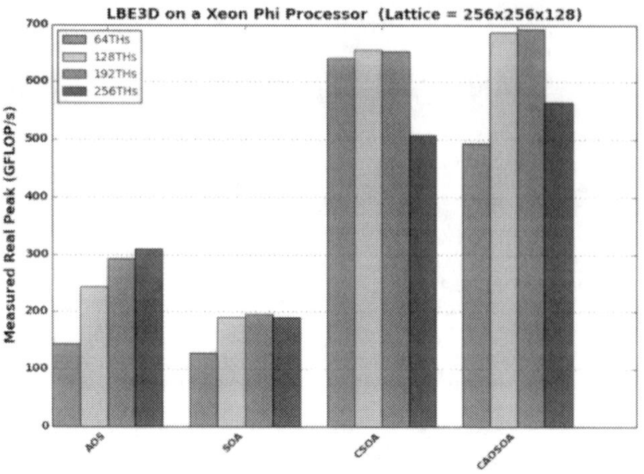

Figure 6. Measured real peak of performances for the `collide` kernel using different data layouts: AoS, SoA, CSoA and CAoSA. The KNL is configured in Flat mode

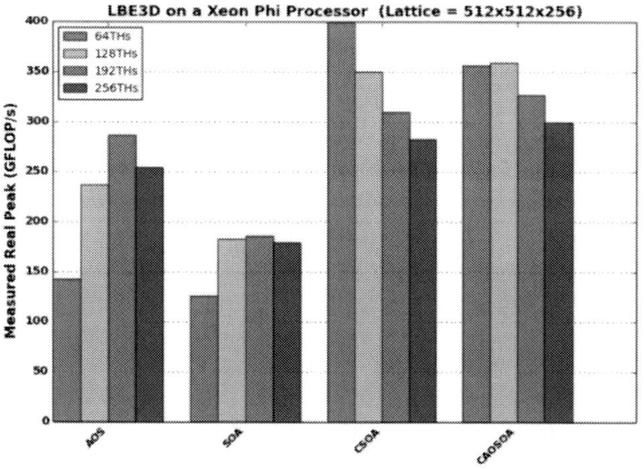

Figure 7. Measured real peak of performances for the `collide` kernel using different data layouts: AoS, SoA, CSoA and CAoSA. The KNL is configured in Cache mode

reported. In flat mode for a medium size grid of 256x256x128 we measure a peak performance of about 700 GFLOP/s corresponding to around the 25% of the nominal peak: approximately half of the value reported on the Nov 2018 list of the TOP500 for KNL based architectures running the High Performance Computing Linpack Benchmark. CSoA and CAoSoA are confirmed to outperform canonical AoS and SoA data layouts by a factor between 2x to 3x. However, when increasing the lattice size while switching to the Cache mode configuration, the performance gap between the various data layouts drops significantly also in the case of the `collide` kernel. As we report in Figure 7, when intensively using DRAM the real performance peak is reduced by a average factor 2x if compared with the same kernel running on KNL in Flat mode, and the gaps between the different data layouts drops between 1.5x to 2.5x.

In the following we present the impact of the different data layouts in regards to the LBE3D application. We concentrate on performances of the main LB loop (Figure 8), computationally the most significant part of the LBE3D application. Indeed, initialization and finalization phases, as well as the time spent on I/O operations are disregarded because becoming irrelevant at the increasing of the number of time steps (in production). In the particular case of the the I/O, it remains irrelevant as long as the frequency of I/O operations is kept low in regards to the number of LB loops (user driven).

Other than the `propagate` and the `collide` kernels also boundaries update is considered as well as the update of the sites near to the walls (see par. 4). We also include the analysis of performances for the fused version of the code. As illustrated in Figure 8 by fused we mean a version of the LBE3D were the `propagate` and the `collide` kernels are nested within the same loop that parses all the populations of the 3-dimensional lattice. In the case of 3-dimensional lattices the number of elements per dimension is limited because considering regular lattices the memory requirement grows exponentially at the increasing of the number of elements per dimension. For instance a lattice dimensions of 512^3 requires 20GB of memory which goes much beyond the memory available on the KNL's MCDRAM. At the same time, reducing the number of elements per dimension includes the risk of unbalance at the increasing of the number of threads while the vectorization benefits of irregular grids larger on the most inner dimension. To reduce the problem of threads imbalance we also introduced the OpenMP `collapse` clause distributing threads workload among the two outermost dimensions of nested loops over a 3d-lattice for all significant sections of the LBE3D code. However, this only minimally reduced the effect of imbalance when increasing the number of threads.

```
for all time step do
    < Set boundary conditions >
    for all lattice site do
        < Move >
    for all lattice site do
        < Collide_Fused >
    end for
end for
```

```
for all time step do
    < Set boundary conditions >
    for all lattice site do
        < Move_Collide_Fused>
    end for
end for
```

Figure 8. On the left, a pseudo-code description of the main loop of LB based application. On the right, a representation of the fused version of the two main kernels.

In Figure 9, performance results for the LBE3D case are reported. It is evident the benefit of using the clustered versions CSoA or CAoSoA if compared with more canonical AoS or SoA data layout. We have measured this impact to be a factor of 2x to 3x depending by the lattice dimension with the KNL configured in Flat mode. Achieved vectorization by the fused version of LBE3D is shown in Table I where we report the Vector Processing Unit (VPU) activity as the measured ratio of the two Vtune's counters UOPS_RETIRED.SCALAR_SIMD and UOPS_RETIRED.PACKED_SIMD. The final value is given by the ratio between the number of vector operations the core performed (PACKAED_SIMD) to the sum of all operations (SCALAR_SIMD and PACKED_SIMD) as properly described in [14].

TABLE I. VPU USAGE MEASURED BY THE INTEL® VTUNE FOR FUSED LBE3D

data layouts	*Vector VPU Intensity*
AoS	20%
SoA	20%
CSoA	100%
CAoSoA	100%

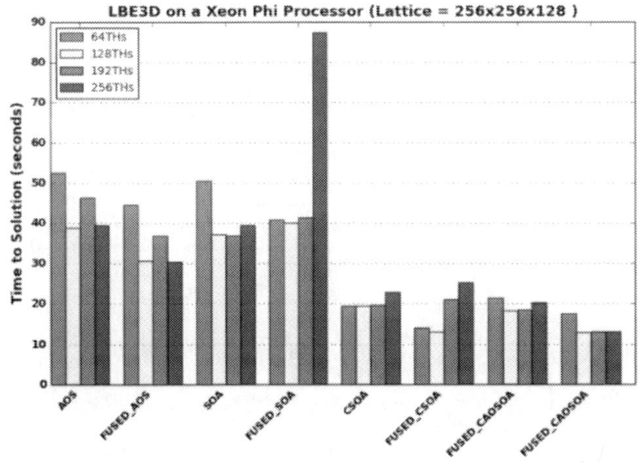

Figure 9. Time to solution for 1000 time steps of the LB main loop for the LBE3D application. Performances are reported across the multiple data layout presented, at the increasing of the number of hardware threads active per core.

Increasing the number of threads beyond 2 hardware threads per core does not provide any performance improvement, actually Figure 9 reports that with the KNL configured in Flat mode the best results are achieved using 2 hardware threads per core among all versions. In general, beyond the 2 hardware threads per core there are some fluctuations within the 20% of the total time of the main LBE3D loop (see Figure 8) but there is an unexpected degradation of performances, almost by a factor 2x, for both the fused SoA and CSoA versions at 256 threads. By deeper analyzing this phenomena with Vtune we saw that the peak is associated to a strong increase of misses at Level-2 (L2) of the translation lookaside buffer (TLB), measured monitoring the counter MEM_OUPS_RETIRED.DTLB_MISS_LOADS (see [14] for better details). At the same time, a deeper profiling has shown that for this particular cases the most time consuming function becomes the routine kmp_flag_64::wait, from the limiomp5.so library which includes the Intel® implementation of OpenMP. Despite we still cannot explain this high number of TLB misses for this particular case, we can state how this configuration drastically slows down due to a problem of threads unbalancing that coincides with a peak of the number of L2 TLB misses.

The benefit of the fused version is generally 1.5x with respect to the canonical version which uses two separate kernels for `propagate` and `collide`. In Figure 10, we report the profiling breakdown for 2 hardware threads per core (128 threads in total). The profiling chart shows the impact of the various data layouts for the `propagate` and `collide` kernel in regards to the whole LB main loop. The impact of the fused version of the kernel is also well in evidence.

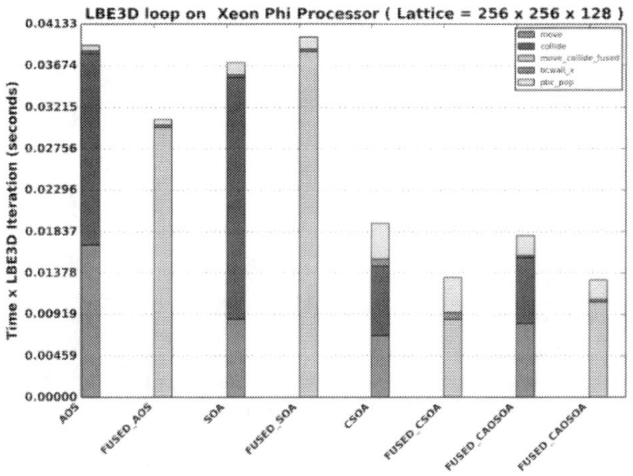

Figure 10. Profiling breakdown for a single time step of the LB main loop for the LBE3D application. Data are reported using the OpenMP version of the LBE3D application using 2 hardware thread per core.

V. Energy Efficiency

We now consider energy efficiency for the LBE3D across the multiple data layouts presented. We use data from the Running Average Power Limit (RAPL) register counters available in the KNL read through the custom library developed in [15]. In Figure 11, we show the measured values of energy consumption (Joule) for the LBE3D application respectively for the processor and the off-chip DRAM memory.

The DRAM energy consumption is lower as the KNL is configured in Flat mode and during the simulation data are all stored into the MCDRAM. Indeed, energy consumption for the DRAM memory only registers the value in the state of idle while for the MCDRAM is accounted within the CPU (on cheap memory).

What is relevant to notice is that despite the CSoA and CAoSoA data layouts are expected to stress the CPU system more than the AoS and SoA (higher utilization of the VPU), we can assume the absorbed power remains approximately constant when considering different data layouts. Indeed, it is evident how the energy consumption remains mostly proportional to the time to solution such that Figures 11 and 9 are comparable and showing a similar trend: usage of the CSoA data layout brings a factor from 2x to 3x advantage both in term of time to solution, and energy to solution.

VI. Conclusion

In this contribution, we have presented the impact on computing performances and energy consumption of different data layouts for the case of the LBE3D code.

Best improvements are given by the newly introduced data layouts (CSoA and CAoSoA) on the KNL, when the data domain fits the MCDRAM memory capability of 16 GB. In this case, the LBE3D application shows best performances setting 2 hardware threads per core (128 threads in total), while exhibits a problem of load unbalancing when increasing the number of hardware threads per core beyond 2. Considering the whole main LB loop in terms of time to solution, the

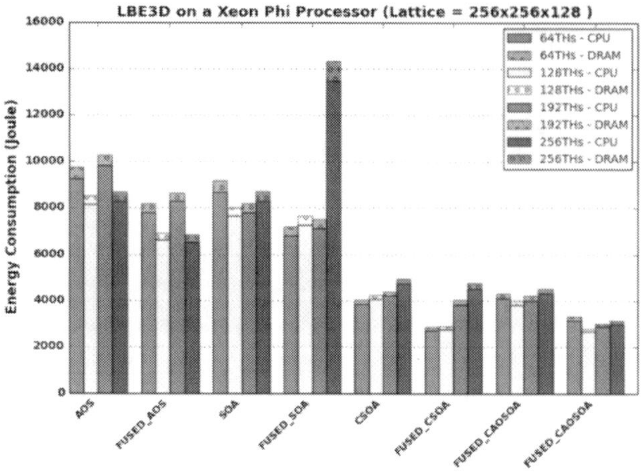

Figure 11. Energy consumption profiling of the LBE3D application.

CSoA and the CAoSoA data layouts are comparable offering an overall better performance corresponding to approximately 2-3x faster compared to the other layout schemes: AoS and SoA. In particular, the CSoA shows a peak performance of about 700 GFlop/s for the `collide` kernel, and 350 GB/s in terms of memory bandwidth for the `propagate` kernel. Larger lattices that do not fit the MCDRAM requires access to the DRAM memory which in Cache mode provide an average time to solution lower by approximately a factor 2x. This bottleneck put at the same level the performances exhibit by all version of the code.

Analysis on the LBE3D in regards to energy efficiency shows that the both CSoA and CAoSoA data layouts are more efficient because delivering faster time to solution, although a slightly higher average power drain is measured due to a more intense utilization of the on-chip system.

The optimization steps presented here for the case of the LBE3D are quite general and can also be applied to other LB production codes. Moreover, we expect that similar performance improvements can also be achieved on other kind of processor based on large vector registers. In fact, the optimizations shown are mainly targeted to make efficient use of VPU capable to perform high number of operations per clock cycle.

In future works, we will keep on investigating how the proposed data layouts perform on current and next generation of computer architectures for high-performance computing, including accelerators based platforms.

Acknowledgment

We would like to thank CINECA, INFN and The University of Ferrara for access to their HPC systems.

References

[1] S. Succi, *The Lattice Boltzmann Equation: For Fluid Dynamics and Beyond*. Clarendon Press, 2001, ISBN: 978-0-19-850398-9.

[2] E. Calore, N. Demo, S. F. Schifano, and R. Tripiccione, "Experience on Vectorizing Lattice Boltzmann Kernels for Multi- and Many-Core Architectures," in *Parallel Processing and Applied Mathematics: 11th International Conference, PPAM 2015, Krakow, Poland, September 6-9, 2015. Revised Selected Papers, Part I*, ser. Lecture Notes in Computer Science. Cham: Springer International Publishing, 2016, pp. 53–62. doi: 10.1007/978-3-319-32149-3_6

[3] E. Calore, A. Gabbana, S. F. Schifano, and R. Tripiccione, "Early experience on using knights landing processors for lattice boltzmann applications," in *Parallel Processing and Applied Mathematics: 12th International Conference, PPAM 2017, Lublin, Poland, September 10-13, 2017*, ser. Lecture Notes in Computer Science, vol. 1077, 2018, pp. 1–12. doi: 10.1007/978-3-319-78024-5_45

[4] E. Calore, A. Gabbana, J. Kraus, S. F. Schifano, and R. Tripiccione, "Performance and portability of accelerated lattice Boltzmann applications with OpenACC," *Concurrency and Computation: Practice and Experience*, vol. 28, no. 12, pp. 3485–3502, 2016. doi: 10.1002/cpe.3862

[5] S. Williams, J. Carter, L. Oliker, J. Shalf, and K. Yelick, "Optimization of a Lattice Boltzmann computation on stateof-the-art multicore platforms," *Journal of Parallel and Distributed Computing*, vol. 69, pp. 762–777, 2009. doi: 10.1016/j.jpdc.2009.04.002

[6] S. Williams, J. Carter, L. Oliker, J. Shalf, and K. A. Yelick, "Lattice Boltzmann simulation optimization on leading multicore platforms," *2008 IEEE International Symposium on Parallel and Distributed Processing*, pp. 1–14, 2008. doi: 10.1109/IPDPS.2008.4536295

[7] M. Bernaschi, M. Fatica, S. Melchionna, S. Succi, and E. Kaxiras, "A flexible high-performance lattice Boltzmann gpu code for the simulations of fluid flows in complex geometries," *Concurrency Computat.: Pract. Exper.*, pp. 22: 1–14, 2009. doi: 10.1002/cpe.1466

[8] P. L. Bhatnagar, E. P. Gross, and M. Krook, "A model for collision processes in gases. i. small amplitude processes in charged and neutral one-component systems," *Phys. Rev.*, vol. 94, pp. 511–525, 1954. doi: 10.1103/PhysRev.94.511

[9] R. Benzi, S. Succi, and M. Vergassola, "The lattice Boltzmann equation: theory and applications," *Physics Reports*, vol. 222, no. 3, pp. 145 – 197, 1992. doi: 10.1016/0370-1573(92)90090-M

[10] P. Perlekar, R. Benzi, H. J. H. Clercx, D. R. Nelson, and F. Toschi, "Spinodal decomposition in homogeneous and isotropic turbulence," *Phys. Rev. Lett.*, vol. 112, p. 014502, Jan 2014. doi: 10.1103/PhysRevLett.112.014502

[11] A. Scagliarini, H. Einarsson, A. Gylfason, and F. Toschi, "Law of the wall in an unstably stratified turbulent channel flow," *Journal of Fluid Mechanics*, vol. 781, p. R5, 2015, doi: 10.1017/jfm.2015.498.

[12] G. Di Staso, S. Srivastava, E. Arlemark, H. Clercx, and F. Toschi, "Hybrid lattice Boltzmann-direct simulation Monte Carlo approach for flows in three-dimensional geometries," *Computers & Fluids*, 2018. doi: 10.1016/j.compfluid.2018.03.043

[13] A. Gupta, H. Clercx, and F. Toschi, "Simulation of finite-size particles in turbulent flows using the lattice Boltzmann method," *Communications in Computational Physics*, vol. 23, no. 3, pp. 665–684, 2018. doi: 10.4208/cicp.OA-2016-0268

[14] J. Jeffers, J. Reinders, and A. Sodani, *Intel Xeon Phi Processor High Performance Programming*. Morgan Kaufmann, Jun. 2016, ISBN: 978-0-12-809194-4.

[15] E. Calore, A. Gabbana, S. F. Schifano, and R. Tripiccione, "Evaluation of dvfs techniques on modern hpc processors and accelerators for energy-aware applications," *Concurrency and Computation: Practice and Experience*, vol. 29, no. 12, pp. 1–19, 2017. doi: 10.1002/cpe.4143

Energy Efficiency of Epiphany Many-Core Architecture for Parallel Molecular Dynamics Calculations

Vsevolod Nikolskii and Vladimir Stegailov
International Laboratory for Supercomputer Atomistic Modelling and Multi-scale Analysis
National Research University Higher School of Economics
Moscow, Russia
E-mail: {vnikolskiy, v.stegailov}@hse.ru

***Abstract*—The paper considers the performance and energy consumption of Parallella board with Epiphany coprocessor for molecular dynamics simulation. The coprocessor has cacheless many-core architecture, which is a promising energy efficient technology for the evolution of modern supercomputers. The paper describes the development and verification of molecular dynamics simulation program for the new platform. It reveals the capabilities of effective parallelization of the code on currently available system taking into account the future development. Comparison of the energy consumption with a modern general-purpose processor Cortex-A53 shows the advantage of the Parallella platform, while there are still opportunities to improve the software.**

***Keywords*–PGAS; OpenSHMEM; atomistic modelling; Lennard-Jones; n-body problem; power consumption.**

I. Introduction

Molecular Dynamics (MD) is an extremely powerful mathematical and computational tool of modern science. MD models are used in materials science, chemistry, biology, physics and many interdisciplinary fields. Users of the method perform researches to refine the models, to achieve a better fit to experimental data, to expand the limits of applicability of the method, and to create new empirical interaction potentials. However, this paper does not concern these topics directly, it is devoted to the computational aspects of the molecular dynamics method.

Since MD is a very computationally demanding problem and it accounts for a large fraction of the computational time on the supercomputers all over the world, the issues of effective implementation and parallelization techniques of the method are well studied. Nevertheless, these issues are closely related to the particular considered computer architecture.

The possibilities of using MD calculations to solve real problems are significantly limited by the achievements of the modern computer industry. To solve a number of urgent problems, at least the exaflop level of computing power is required, the achievement of which is associated with many difficulties.

After many years of extensive growth, the dominant computer architecture has come close to its limits, and the further development of the industry lies in the use of new architectures. The many-core mass-parallel processor architecture is considered as a promising technology. Among modern devices, Epiphany is almost the only available for a wide range of researchers example of mass-parallel processor architecture and deserves close attention [1].

The rest of this paper is organized as follows: Section II is a review of related work. In Section III we describe hardware and software system, used in this paper. Section IV briefly describes the test simulation problem. In Section V we consider the adaption of MD algorithm for parallel processor architecture Epiphany. Over the naive implementation, we describe a method for reducing the memory exchanges between processors in a parallel program. Power of the board running MD simulation is measured using digital watt-meter in Section VI. The results are compared with modern general-purpose Central Processing Unit (CPU), that have compared power. Finally, Section VII contains the conclusion.

II. Related Work

The balance of programming complexity for data-parallel accelerators was discussed by Lee et al. [2]. In the recent review [3], the key aspects of accelerator-based systems performance modelling were considered. Wu et al. revealed the properties of MD codes on multi- and many core processors [4]. Paper [5] present the results of experiments with parallel algorithms (including MD) on Tilera's TilePro64, that shows the advantage of cashless mode.

The recent work [6] is devoted to the development of general-purpose high-performance computing libraries for the Epiphany architecture. Ross and Richie discussed a threaded Message Passing Interface (MPI) model and its implementation for Epiphany [7]. The design of the OpenMP 4.0 infrastructure for the Parallella board was presented in [8].

Sukhinov and Ostrobrod [9] reported a successful implementation of an applied face-detection algorithm for the Epiphany-III coprocessor. The paper [10] discusses the use of the Parallella board with E16G3 for solving the problem of computational fluid dynamics. A simple test program was implemented, performance was measured and compared with a modern server processor and graphics accelerator. At a low overall performance, the Parallella platform showed high energy efficiency comparable to a graphics accelerator. In the paper, it was shown that the small amount of memory available on the computing elements is a serious limitation for the algorithm. Thus, the results obtained in the work are characteristic of a particular class of algorithms, and can not be directly generalized to the molecular dynamics.

III. Epiphany Architecture and Programming Model

In this work, we use the prototype board Parallella (Figure 1). It includes a dual-core ARM host CPU, FPGA (Field-Programmable Gate Array) and a 16-core Epiphany-III coprocessor (E16G301) and 1 GB of memory. There are several

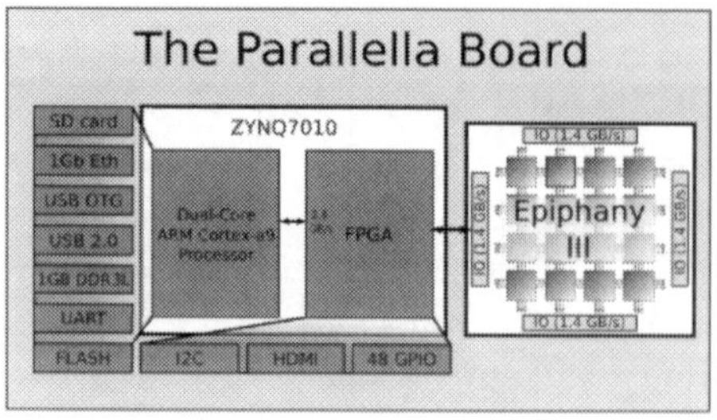

Figure 1. The scheme of the Parallella board.

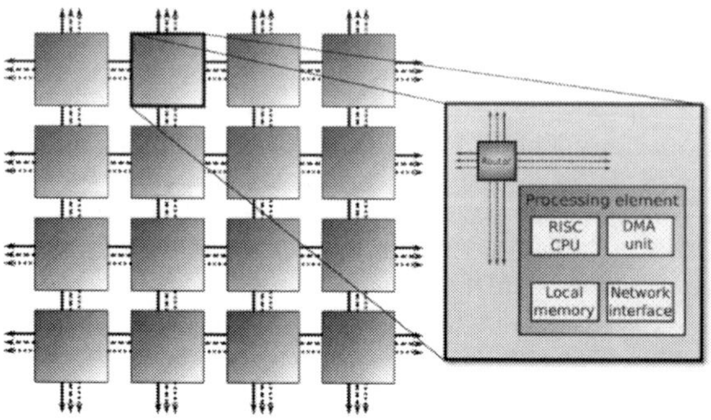

Figure 2. The Epiphany chip architecture scheme.

interfaces: Gigabit Ethernet, Micro-SD storage, 48 General-Purpose Input/Output (GPIO) pins, High Definition Multimedia Interface (HDMI) and Universal Serial Bus (USB). The host runs an Ubuntu Linux modification (so-called Parubuntu Linux). The Epiphany architecture [11] is a distributed shared memory architecture comprised of an array of Reduced Instruction Set Computer (RISC) processors communicating via a low-latency mesh Network on Chip (NoC), see Figure 2. The eMesh NoC consists of three separate and orthogonal mesh structures, each serving different types of transaction traffic.

1) The cMesh is used for write transactions to on-chip mesh-nodes. It has a maximum bandwidth of 4.8 GB/s up, and 4.8 GB/s down in each of the four routing directions. Write transactions move through the network with a latency of 1.5 clock cycles per routing hop. A transaction traversing from the left edge to right edge of a 64-core chip would thus take 12 clock cycles.
2) The rMesh is used for all read transactions. Read transactions do not contain any data, but travel across the rMesh until the destination node is reached. Here, a write transaction is initiated to transport the data back to the requesting node. The rMesh can issue one read transaction every 8 clock cycles, resulting in 1/8th of the maximum cMesh bandwidth.
3) The xMesh is used for write transactions destined for off-chip resources and for passing through transactions destined for another chip in a multi-chip configuration. It is split in a North-to-South and an East-to-West network. The bandwidth of the xMesh is matched to the off-chip links of the architecture.

Each node in the processor array is a complete RISC processor capable of running an operating system with small amount of fast local memory (32 KB).

Epiphany uses a flat cacheless memory model. All amount of the distributed memory is readable and writable by all processors in the system. The edges of the 2D array can be connected to non-Epiphany interface modules, such as memory modules, FIFOs, I/O link ports, or standard buses. The array of processors with 32-bit address map can be scaled up to 4095 cores on a single chip. The existing prototype Epiphany-V reaches the value of 1024 cores on a single chip [12]. Epiphany-IV (2011) with 64 cores is able to demonstrate 70 GFlops/W processing efficiency at the core supply level through such architectural properties as the absence of cache. According to Vocke, E16G301 peak power efficiency of 32 GFlops/W can be attained at 400 MHz clock frequency [13], while on the Parallella board the Epiphany co-processor runs at a fixed frequency of 600 MHz.

In this work, the OpenSHMEM for Epiphany is used for the parallel algorithm development [14][15]. This is an open source OpenSHMEM 1.4 implementation that can be built using Epiphany eSDK.

OpenSHMEM is responsible for data exchange between Processing Element (PE) and implements the parallel programming model named "Partitioned Global Address Space" (PGAS). All the memory on the processing elements is addressable, but it is divided into logical sections and allows one to consider the use of data locality. This model perfectly matches the architecture of Epiphany. The technology of Remote Direct Memory Access (RDMA) to is used. The main programming idea is to create a universal function that can process memory areas from specified computational elements.

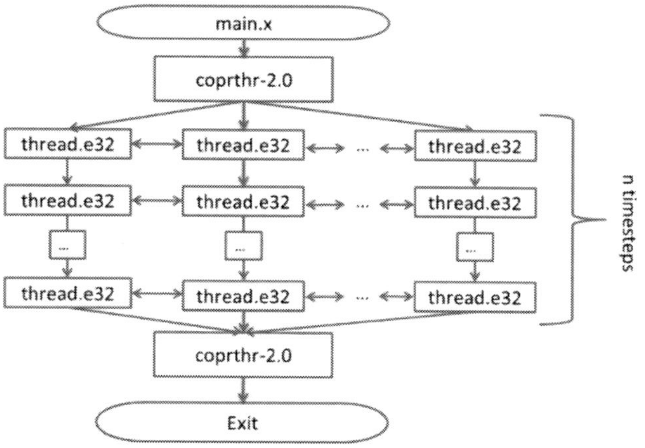

Figure 3. The scheme of the threaded host-device (CPU - Epiphany) program for the Parallela board.

Library and toolchain COPRTHR-2.0 are responsible for the loading and start of the program kernel. It loads the compiled code into PEs under the control of a lightweight OS and launches it (Figure 3). Also, through the functions of this library, the initial data is transferred from the main memory of the board. Using the utility from the COPRTHR toolkit one can analyze the memory allocation in the compiled code. An essential limitation is that the compiled code takes up to 77% of the memory of PEs, syscore and fragmentation drains up to 5% of memory, so free memory is estimated at just 6608 bytes for code with manual loop unrolling and slightly more without that optimization.

IV. Molecular Dynamics Model

The dynamics of N interacting particles is described by the system of Newton's equations of motion. Force $\mathbf{F}_i$, acting on a particle is defined by the potential function U, which determines the physical properties of the system. In this work, we use the Lennard-Jones potential, which represents the generic interaction of neutral atoms:

$$U(r) = 4\varepsilon\left[\left(\frac{\sigma}{r}\right)^{12} - \left(\frac{\sigma}{r}\right)^{6}\right]. \quad (1)$$

In computer simulations, the Lennard-Jones potential can be considered equal to zero for sufficiently long distances (e.g., $r \geq 2.5\sigma$). We use such a truncated potential in this work.

The integration of equations of motion is performed by the velocity Verlet scheme. This scheme is well studied, the optimality of the scheme for molecular-dynamics simulations was shown [16][17].

V. Implementation

A. Program Structure

The conceptual scheme of an MD simulation program is presented on Figure 4. The Verlet scheme is separated in two steps: `Verlet Initial Integrate` and `Verlet Final Integrate`. Between these steps the forces are updated. This is the most intensive part of the algorithm (it costs about 80% of the total computational time).

```
Initial Setup
Periodic Boundary Conditions
Compute Forces
loop over N time steps:
    Verlet Initial Integrate
    Periodic Boundary Conditions
    Clear Forces
    Compute Forces
    Verlet Final Integrate
                (a)

*Initial Setup
Periodic Boundary Conditions
*Compute Forces
loop over N time steps:
  Verlet Initial Integrate
  Periodic Boundary Conditions
  *Particles exchange
  Clear Forces
  *Compute Forces
  Verlet Final Integrate
                (b)
```

Figure 4. The pseudocode of the main loop of the MD program: (a) the atom decomposition parallelization; (b) domain decomposition the parallelization.

The difference between two algorithms on Figure 4 is in the approaches to parallelism. In the details, all functions are different in these two cases, but the key algorithmic differences are in the steps "Initial Setup", "Compute Force" and "Particles exchange" (highlighted by the asterisk).

The current state of an MD model is represented as two arrays of structures. Since Epiphany is a cacheless processor, it does not matter whether one uses an array of structures or a structure of arrays — that was confirmed by the experiment.

The first structure contains three coordinates (a three-dimensional vector) and the ID of a particle, which are needed to compute the interactions. The second structure contains 3 velocities and 3 forces, that are necessary for the evolution of the system. In single precision, it gives 40 bytes per particle. The memory management routines are atypical on Epiphany [14]. With only 6608 bytes of free local memory on PEs (see Section III), the simulation is limited by just ~ 140 particles per PE.

```
// Number of particles is predefined and the same on each
   processing element
const n = Total num. of particles / num. of PEs;
forall processing elements of Epiphany do in parallel
    my_ca = array of n particles coordinates vectors from this PE;
    my_fa = array of n particles forces vectors from this PE;
    forall PE of Epiphany do
        Select PE;
        remote_ca = RDMA to coordinates vectors on selected PE;
        for i = 0 to n do
            r1 = my_ca[i];
            foreach r2 in remote_ca do
                distance = |r1 - r2|;
                if distance <= rc^2 then
                    f = PairForce(distance);
                    my_fa[i] += f · (r1 - r2);
                end
            end
        end
    end
end
```

Figure 5. The parallel force computation loop in the case of atom decomposition approach.

```
forall processing elements of Epiphany do in parallel
    // Num. of particles varies on PEs and changes over time
    n = num. of particles on this PE;
    my_ca = array of particles coordinates vectors from this PE;
    my_fa = array of particles forces vectors from this PE;
    forall PE neighboring to this PE do
        Select PE;
        remote_n = number of particles on selected PE;
        remote_ca = RDMA to coordinates vectors on selected PE;
        for i = 0 to length(my_ca) do
            r1 = my_ca[i];
            foreach r2 in remote_ca do
                distance = |r1 - r2|;
                if distance <= rc^2 then
                    f = PairForce(distance);
                    my_fa[i] += f · (r1 - r2);
                end
            end
        end
    end
end
```

Figure 6. The parallel force computation loop in the case of domain decomposition approach.

During the "Initial Setup" step (before the main loop) the MD data is loaded from the main global memory to the local memory of each core of Epiphany. In the case of atom decomposition approach, data for all the particles in the MD model are equally divided between the local core memory blocks and remain there until the end of the calculation. In the case of domain decomposition approach, each particle takes place in the memory of a core according to its coordinate in the MD simulation box. To maintain this state, a "Particles exchange" communication is performed on each time step. The force computation is adapted to the parallelization approach in both cases (see Figure 5 and Figure 6).

B. Parallelism

As it was mentioned above, the force computation loop takes about 80 % of the total time to solution, thus the most of the effort is devoted to accelerating this part of the MD algorithm. Fortunately, the natural parallelism in MD is that the force calculations and velocity/position updates can be done simultaneously for all atoms [19]. To do this, the calculated equations must be distributed among the processors. It is achieved in two popular ways, both of which are discussed in more details below.

The analysis of parallelism is limited by the following conditions:

1) The small amount of memory on a single core. We can not test a whole medium size problem on a single core of Epiphany, the data must be "spread out" throughout the entire computational field to solve the problem.
2) Only 16 cores are available the Epiphany-III chip that is used in this work.

It will be shown below that under such conditions the issue of parallelism in our case is closely related to the algorithms of finding all atom pairs.

1) Atom Decomposition: The particles are distributed among the cores, regardless of their geometric positions in the model. Every core gets a subgroup of atoms, and processor computes forces on its atoms no matter where they move in the course of the MD simulation. At Figure 7 each box represent the whole computational domain in the memory of a core. The particles that are stored in the local memory of some core are shown as filled circles. Particles that are accessed by the remote core via the network-on-chip interconnect are shown as open circles. The potential cutoff radius is depicted around the same particle on both cores. At every time step, "all-to-all" data exchanges are performed to search and receive coordinates of neighbor particles because interacting particles (i.e., located closely enough in the simulation box at this time step) can be found on any other core. This communication provides not a significant load for the 16-cores Epiphany chip with very fast and low-latency NoC, but massive and frequent "all-to-all" communications are a limiting factor for scalable algorithms. Thus, they must be eliminated.

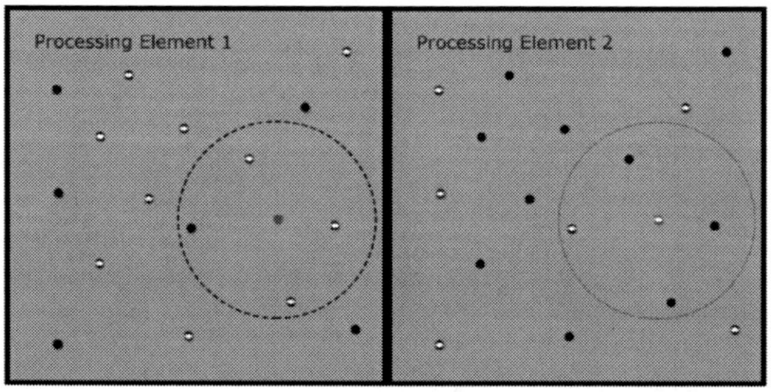

Figure 7. The atom decomposition scheme: an example for the case of two cores.

This approach is quite easy to implement on Epiphany with shared memory and hardware RDMA feature. While one has to store identical copies of atoms information on all cores in a distributed memory system, information replication is not required while using shared memory. On each time step, the atom information from other processors is obtained by direct memory access in the force computation loop.

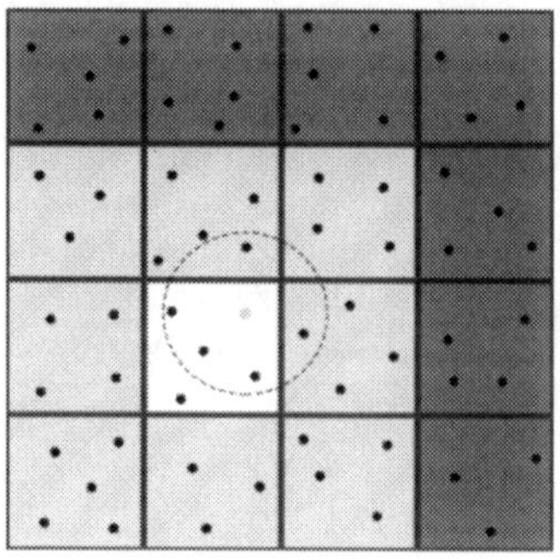

Figure 8. The domain decomposition scheme.

2) Domain Decomposition: The MD simulation box is divided into blocks and each block is assigned to one of the processor's cores. All particles from a certain block are stored in the memory of the corresponding core. As a particle moves through the MD simulation box, it passes to another core. It is done in the "Particles exchange" part on each time step that is presented on Figure 4 and discussed in previous Subsection V-A. To calculate the interactions for particles on each core, it is sufficient to make exchanges, not with all cores, but to communicate only with neighboring cores to cover the cut-off radius of the potential. The idea is shown at Figure 8: the white square is an area dedicated to a single core. The light-gray squares represent the adjacent cores that contain the particles that can be located close enough to interact with particles on the core considered. The particles in the dark-gray area are too far from the considered domain to contribute to the interparticle interactions. The circle represents a cut-off radius of the potential.

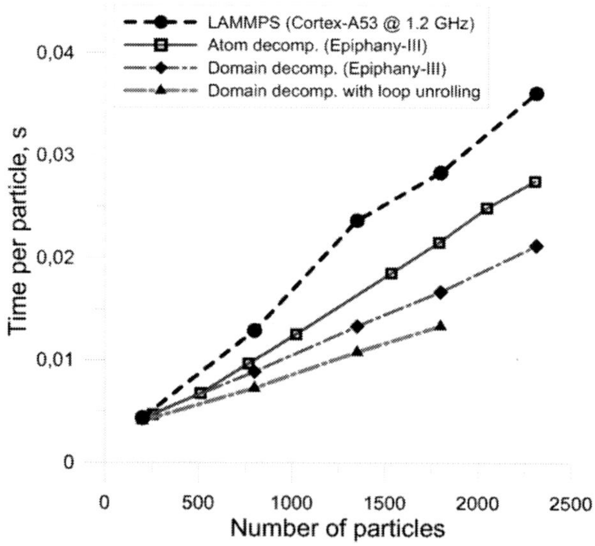

Figure 9. The time-to-solution per particle plotted versus the number of particles in the model.

The benchmarking of two decomposition techniques and their comparison with popular MD code LAMMPS [19] are represented on Figure 9, which depict the results for atom decomposition and domain decomposition run on Parallella with Epiphany-III chip and the performance of LAMMPS package on a single core of ARMv8 Cortex-A53 core. The test model was configured for constant volume that minimizes the difference between the cut-off radius r_c and the domain decomposition block edge length d. The number of atoms was varied by the change of density. The MD package LAMMPS was run on the single core of ARMv8 Cortex-A53 processor in double precision. It keeps all data in the main memory and thus has no parallelization overhead. On the other hand, Parallella has higher peak performance and Epiphany-III uses single precision floating point arithmetic, so LAMMPS timings should be compared taking into account the differences of the peak performance. Loop unrolling is very beneficial for acceleration of computation on Epiphany cores, however in this case more local memory on each core is needed for the code itself and the maximum number of particles in the MD model becomes lower.

The peak floating point performance of Epiphany (in single precision) is 19.2 GFlops that is 4 times higher than the peak floating point performance (in double precision) of one Cortex-A53 core considered. Our MD algorithm in single precision on Epiphany is 2 times faster on Epiphany than the similar algorithm in LAMMPS running on a Cortex-A53 core. The non-ideal scaling with respect to the peak floating point performance [18] can be explained by the memory access limitation on the Epiphany architecture.

C. *Interference of Parallelism and Complexity Reduction*

There are two most common approaches to reduce the N^2 complexity of N-body problems with short-range potentials: the Verlet neighbor list method and the cell lists method. In modern MD packages, the combination of these two methods is used usually to achieve better performance. Neighbor lists require a huge amount of extra memory, thus they are not applicable on Epiphany due to strict memory limitations. Cell lists are implemented for the Epiphany MD code in the framework of this study. For the atom decomposition parallelization method, the use of the cell lists for particles on all cores simultaneously is not effective due to the low number of particles on separate cores.

There is a reasonable relation between the parameters of the LJ potential, the cut-off radius and the density of particles in the MD model. The number of particles that fits into the memory of a single core is also given. In this way, the range of the most used block edge lengths (d) in the domain decomposition method is determined.

In the case of $d \gg r_c$, it is effective to implement separate complexity reduction algorithm. In the case of Epiphany, d is relatively close to r_c, and the division of particles into the cells is naturally maintained by the domain decomposition algorithm. If we implement both domain decomposition and cell linked-list algorithms, we have to pay a full cost for the latter in terms of computer time, while it does not bring much time-saving.

Without additional cell lists on every time step, a core just gets the information only from itself and from nearest cores (e.g., for 2D projection there are 8 neighbor cores, Figure 8).

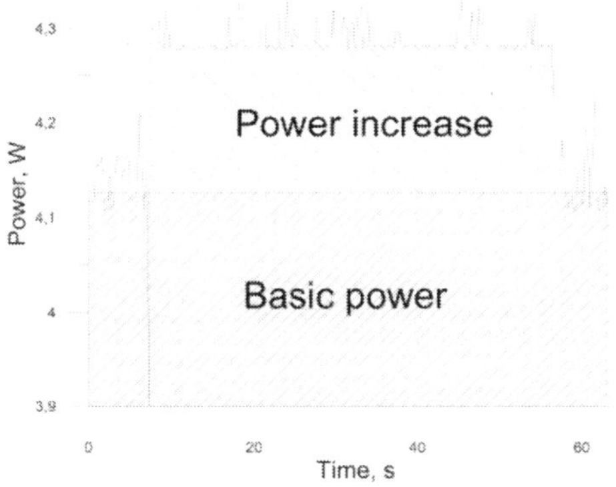

Figure 10. Energy consumption timeline.

In this way, instead of computation of $N * N$ pair forces, we reduce this number to $N * (N * 9/16)$. However, it still has non-linear complexity, that is shown of Figure 9. But for the given configuration, it is more effective than the classic close-to-linear algorithm with a much higher time-to-solution.

D. *Verification*

The verification of our prototype program is one of the important steps in the development. We used several criteria: conservation of total energy, comparison of the potential energy time evolution with *a priory* correct program results (we use the popular package LAMMPS [19]), and direct comparison of the resulting coordinates or velocities of atoms with the coordinates or velocities, calculated by the reference program with the same initial conditions and the same time step.

By default, LAMMPS performs the calculation in double precision floating-point arithmetic, while Parallella with Epiphany-III supports only single precision hardware accelerated arithmetic. Hardware double precision is implemented in the newer models of Epiphany only. Single precision MD is implemented in most packages (e.g., LAMMPS, GROMACS, HOOMD). Single precision is sufficient for MD simulations. It is especially useful for calculations on desktop-level GPUs, which have limited double-precision performance. That is why the Epiphany-III chip limitation of floating point operations in single precision only is not crucial for the MD algorithm.

VI. Energy Efficiency

To measure energy consumption, we use a high-precision digital watt-meter ODROID Smart Power. It draws an energy consumption profile with 10 Hz sample rate when the program starts. As an opponent of the Parallella, we chose the popular platform Raspberry Pi 3, since it can be supplied and measured using the same device. Peak performance of one core of Raspberry Pi 3 processor Cortex-a53 is 4 times lower than peak performance of 16 cores of Epiphany-III. Let us note that Raspberry Pi 3 is manufactured using 40 nm technology, while Epiphany-III is made using 65 nm technology. We can assume that the implementation of the same architecture in a more modern technical process can bring an additional advantage. In Figure 10 presents the energy profile when the program is started on Parallella, that can be used for direct calculation of energy-to-solution [20]. It is possible to separate

TABLE I. ENERGY CONSUMPTION VALUES.

	Time, s	*Total Energy, J*	*Energy Increase, J*
Parallella	24	100.7	3.8
Raspberry Pi 3	51	183.6	40.8

the background energy consumption, which mainly falls on the CPU and interfaces, from the consumption of Epiphany, which is of primary interest to us. According to our measurements, when Epiphany is under load, the power consumption increases by only 0.2 Watt. The obtained results can be used to estimate power consumption of hardware systems, running real-life supercomputing programs.

VII. CONCLUSION AND FUTURE WORK

We described the OpenSHMEM implementation for the Epiphany architecture of the domain-decomposition parallelization for a generic molecular dynamics algorithm with the short-ranged Lennard-Jones potential. The correctness of the new algorithm was verified by the comparison with the same model calculation with LAMMPS. The difference between the resulting trajectories corresponds to the machine precision. It was shown that manual loop unrolling speeds up algorithm significantly. The comparison with LAMMPS running on a single ARMv8 Cortex-A53 core shows that the algorithm for Epiphany running on all 16 cores is 2 times faster, while there remain opportunities for improving the algorithm. The comparison of total energy consumption shows that Parallella board is $\sim$2 times more energy efficient that Raspberry Pi 3 in terms of total energy-to-solution. The isolated consumption of Epiphany-III chip is $\sim$11 times less, than the consumption of modern and effective processor Arm Cortex-A53.

ACKNOWLEDGMENT

The study was funded by RFBR according to the research project No. 18-37-00487 and supported within the framework of the Basic Research Program at the National Research University Higher School of Economics (HSE) and within the framework of a subsidy by the Russian Academic Excellence Project 5-100.

REFERENCES

[1] W. D. Gropp, "MPI+X for extreme scale computing," in 12th International Conference on Parallel Processing and Applied Mathematics, 2017, pp. 1-38. [Online]. Available: https://www.ppam.pl/docs/presentations/Gropp_PPAM2017.pdf [accessed: 2018-06-27].

[2] Y. Lee *et al.*, "Exploring the tradeoffs between programmability and efficiency in data-parallel accelerators," SIGARCH Comput. Archit. News, vol. 39, no. 3, Jun. 2011, pp. 129–140. doi:10.1145/2024723.2000080.

[3] U. Lopez-Novoa, A. Mendiburu, and J. Miguel-Alonso, "A survey of performance modeling and simulation techniques for accelerator-based computing," IEEE Transactions on Parallel and Distributed Systems, vol. 26, no. 1, Jan 2015, pp. 272–281.

[4] Q. Wu, C. Yang, T. Tang, and L. Xiao, "MIC acceleration of short-range molecular dynamics simulations," in Proceedings of the First International Workshop on Code OptimiSation for Multi and Many Cores, ser. COSMIC '13. New York, NY, USA: ACM, 2013, pp. 2:1–2:8. doi:10.1145/2446920.2446922.

[5] V. Chandru and F. Mueller, "Hybrid MPI/OpenMP programming on the Tilera manycore architecture," 2016 International Conference on High Performance Computing & Simulation (HPCS), Innsbruck, 2016, pp. 326-333. doi: 10.1109/HPCSim.2016.7568353

[6] M. Tasende, "Generation of the single precision BLAS library for the Parallella platform, with Epiphany co-processor acceleration, using the BLIS framework," in 2016 IEEE 14th Intl Conf on Dependable, Autonomic and Secure Computing, 14th Intl Conf on Pervasive Intelligence and Computing, 2nd Intl Conf on Big Data Intelligence and Computing and Cyber Science and Technology Congress, Aug 2016, pp. 894–897.

[7] J. A. Ross, D. A. Richie, S. J. Park, and D. R. Shires, "Parallel programming model for the Epiphany many-core coprocessor using threaded MPI," Microprocessors and Microsystems, vol. 43, no. Supplement C, 2016, pp. 95–103, many-Core System-on-Chip: Architectures and Applications (PDP 15).

[8] S. N. Agathos, A. Papadogiannakis, and V. V. Dimakopoulos, "Targeting the Parallella," in Proceedings Euro-Par 2015: Parallel Processing: 21st International Conference on Parallel and Distributed Computing, Vienna, Austria, August 24–28, 2015, pp. 662–674. doi:10.1007/978-3-662-48096-0_51.

[9] A. Sukhinov and G. Ostrobrod, "Efficient face detection on epiphany multicore processor", Computational Mathematics and Information Technologies, vol. 1, no. 1, 2017, pp. 113–127.

[10] S. Raase and T. Nordström, "On the use of a many-core processor for computational fluid dynamics simulations," Procedia Computer Science, vol. 51, no. Supplement C, 2015, pp. 1403–1412, Int. Conf. On Computational Science, ICCS 2015. doi:10.1016/j.procs.2015.05.348

[11] A. Olofsson, T. Nordström, and Z. Ul-Abdin, "Kickstarting high-performance energy-efficient manycore architectures with Epiphany," in 48th Asilomar Conference on Signals, Systems and Computers, pp. 1719–1726, 2014. doi:10.1109/ACSSC.2014.7094761

[12] A. Olofsson, "Epiphany-V: A 1024 processor 64-bit RISC System-On-Chip," pp. 1–15, 2016, [Online]. Available: https://arxiv.org/pdf/1610.01832.pdf [accessed: 2018-06-27].

[13] T. Vocke, "An evaluation of the Adapteva Epiphany many-core architecture," Master's thesis, University of Twente/Thales, Aug 2015. [Online]. Available: http://essay.utwente.nl/68024/1/vocke_MA_EEMCS.pdf [accessed: 2018-06-27]

[14] J. A. Ross and D. A. Richie, "Implementing openshmem for the Adapteva Epiphany RISC array processor," Procedia Computer Science, vol. 80, Supplement C, 2016, pp. 2353–2356, International Conference on Computational Science (ICCS 2016), 6-8 June 2016, San Diego, California, USA.

[15] J. Ross and D. Richie, "An OpenSHMEM implementation for the Adapteva Epiphany coprocessor," in OpenSHMEM and Related Technologies. Enhancing OpenSHMEM for Hybrid Environments, Springer International Publishing, 2016, pp. 146–159.

[16] M. López-Marcos, J. Sanz-Serna, and J. Díaz, "Are Gauss-Legendre methods useful in molecular dynamics?" Journal of Computational and Applied Mathematics, vol. 67, no. 1, 1996, pp. 173–179.

[17] M. A. López-Marcos, J. M. Sanz-Serna, and R. D. Skeel, "Explicit symplectic integrators using Hessian-vector products," SIAM Journal on Scientific Computing, vol. 18, no. 1, 1997, pp. 223–238. doi:10.1137/S1064827595288085.

[18] V. P. Nikolskiy and V. V. Stegailov, "Floating-point performance of ARM cores and their efficiency in classical molecular dynamics," J. Phys.: Conf. Ser., vol. 681, pp. 012049, 2016. doi:10.1088/1742-6596/681/1/012049.

[19] S. Plimpton, "Fast parallel algorithms for short-range molecular dynamics," J Comp Phys, vol. 117, 1995, pp. 1–19. [Online]. Available: http://lammps.sandia.gov [accessed: 2018-06-27].

[20] E. Calore, S. F. Schifano and R. Tripiccione, "Energy-Performance Tradeoffs for HPC Applications on Low Power Processors," In Euro-Par 2015: Parallel Processing Workshops, Proceedings of the Euro-Par 2015 International Workshops, Vienna, Austria, 24–25 August 2015. Springer: Berlin, Germany, 2015. pp. 737–748.

Optimal Hardware Parameters Prediction for Best Energy-to-Solution of Sparse Matrix Operations Using Machine Learning Techniques

Vojtech Nikl*, Ondrej Vysocky†, Lubomir Riha† and Jan Zapletal†
*IT4Innovations Centre of Excellence, Brno University of Technology, Brno, Czech Republic
inikl@fit.vutbr.cz
†IT4Innovations, VŠB – Technical University of Ostrava, Ostrava-Poruba, Czech Republic
{ondrej.vysocky|lubomir.riha|jan.zapletal}@vsb.cz

***Abstract*—Combinations of 3 hardware parameters (number of threads, core and uncore frequency) were tested for 4 sparse matrix algorithms (matrix-matrix addition, matrix-matrix multiplication and matrix-vector multiplication in 2 formats) on a set of over 2,000 matrices for the purpose of identifying the best energy-to-solution setting for each matrix and sparse matrix operation combination. On this set of data, the possibility of optimal hardware settings prediction based on the properties of each matrix were analysed using neural networks, support vector machines and fast decision tree learners. All 3 classes of algorithms have been proven to be a very effective instrument in a lot of areas including prediction and classification. In neural networks, the input neurons represented properties of a given matrix, output neurons represented the optimal hardware parameters. Network properties (hidden neuron layers, neurons per layer, learning coefficient and training cycles) impact on the prediction accuracy were analysed and the results showed that a network with 30 hidden neurons produced results close to the best achievable. The prediction accuracy of all neural networks ranged from 20–95%, with roughly 70% being the average. Support vector machines were accurate in 60–65% of cases and Fast decision tree learners provided the least accurate predictions, 50–55%.**

***Keywords*—Sparse matrices, neural network, support vector machine, fast decision tree learner, weka, energy efficiency, prediction**

I. Introduction

A sparse matrix is a matrix in which most of the elements are equal to zero. Some common applications are partial differential equations, numerical analysis and linear algebraic operations. Sparse matrices can represent real-world problems ranging from microscopic systems [1] up to whole galaxies [2].

Sparse operations are characterised by low arithmetic intensity, resulting in a challenging memory-bound problem, where underclocking the processor or limiting the number of compute threads can reduce the memory congestion and have a minimal impact on the performance itself.

The goal is to find the optimal hardware setup to save the most energy for each specific set of input parameters. One way is to manually measure all combinations of the hardware parameters and choose the optimal one. However, that quickly becomes inconvenient for increasing number of matrices. This approach is also called Hyper-Parameter Optimisation (HPO).

Bergsta et. al. [3] presented two popular HPO algorithms, neural and deep belief networks with the Gaussian Process approach and the Tree-structured Parzen Estimator approach, and showed that the results obtained from running an image classification problem with 32 hyper-parameters are human and brute force random search competitive, with an average error being just under 15%.

Bergsta et. al. [4] also put an emphasis on the initial hyper-parameter layout. Grid and random layouts were compared on a neural network case study. It showed that random experiments were more efficient than the grid ones for the hyper-parameter optimisation in the case of the most learning algorithms on several data sets. The main reason is that not all hyper-parameters are equally important to tune.

Stamoulis et. al. [5] focused on the hyper-parameter optimisation of neural networks in the direction of power and memory constrains on GTX 1070 and Tegra X1 [6] GPUs from Nvidia. The framework used Bayesian optimisation model and overall the enhancements allowed for up to 57.2× more function evaluations, which yielded significant accuracy improvements by up to 67.6%.

Smithson et. al. [7] showed an approach for reducing the state space of the neural network properties by using another neural network, which reduced this state space by hyper-parameter optimisations. In the end, a Pareto-optimal set of networks was created. Compared to manually designed networks from literature, this technique produced results with nearly identical performance while reducing the associated costs by a factor of 3.

Auto-weka [8] is a JAVA library and a machine learning platform. Auto-sklearn [9] is its sister package written in Python. These frameworks offer a set of popular learners and algorithms for problems where it is hard to identify the best approach. It automatically searches through the joint space of Weka's learning algorithms and their respective hyper-parameter settings to maximise performance, using a state-of-the-art Bayesian optimisation method.

The current state-of-the-art in the hyper-parameters optimisation approaches, outlined in previous paragraphs, show that machine learning techniques, neural networks especially, provide a powerful tool for solving these tasks. This paper, however, presents a unique challenge from the area of sparse matrix operations. Based on the properties of a given matrix, the goal is to successfully predict the optimal hardware parameters in terms of the best energy-to-solution and also the energy consumption itself. This paper focuses mainly on neural networks and their performance tuning as well as comparing them to the support vector machines and fast decision tree learners, provided and recommended by the Weka library for this class of problems.

II. Setup

In this section, all hardware and software used, their versions, settings, properties, algorithms etc. are described. All source codes were compiled with the combination of *Intel Compiler 2017*, `-O3 -xHost` flags and *Intel MKL 2017*to perform the sparse calculations, which were provided as modules on the cluster.

A. Sparse Algorithms

4 sparse algorithms were analysed:

- matrix-matrix addition in CSR format (SpMMadd)
- matrix-matrix multiplication in CSR format (SpMMmult)
- matrix-vector multiplication in CSR format (SpMVmultCSR)
- matrix-vector multiplication in IJV (i.e. COO) format (SpMVmultIJV)

IJV format stores data as a set of coordinates and is more suitable for the matrix-vector multiplication than CSR. The matrix-matrix addition and multiplication adds or multiplies a given matrix with itself (transposed if necessary), respectively, matrix-vector multiplication multiplies a given matrix with its first row as a vector.

B. Matrices

All sparse matrices were sourced from the SuiteSparse Matrix collection [10] [11] in the *Matrix Market File* (.mtx) format. The collection contains 2757 matrices ranging from a single up to almost 2 billion nonzero elements. Due to the resource and allocation limitations of the cluster, only a randomly chosen subset of matrices was used for each sparse operation (1755 for SpMMadd, 1627 for SpMMmult, 2493 for SpMVmultCSR, 2605 for SpMVmultIJV).

C. Neural Network and Weka

The Genann library [12] was used to implement the multilayer fully-connected feedforward neural networks with a sigmoid activation function and the back-propagation learning.

Each network had 226 input neurons representing the parameters of a matrix. The numerical parameters were *Rows*, *Columns*, *Nonzero ratio* and *Symmetry percentage*, each occupying one input neuron. The values of these parameters were normalised to $[0, 1]$ range by the *min-max* normalisation as

$$X_{norm} = \frac{X - X_{min}}{X_{max} - X_{min}} \tag{1}$$

The categorical parameters, normalised using the *one-hot* encoding [13], are *Group* (143 variants), *Kind* (65 variants), Type (12 variants) and *SPD* (symmetric positive definite, 1 variant). Each variant was represented by its own input activating neuron.

Four output neurons represented *Number of threads*, *Core frequency*, *Uncore frequency* (separate L3 cache frequency introduced by Intel in the Haswell architecture) and *Energy*.

Editable analysed parameters are hidden neuron layers (1–5), the number of neurons per hidden layer (10–250), learning coefficients (0.1–0.99), the number of learning cycles (i.e. epochs) (1, 10, 100, 1000) and the training set sizes (10–90% of total data, the rest formed testing data).

For algorithms provided by the Weka library - support vector machines for regression, referred to as *SMOreg*, and fast decision learning trees, referred to as *REPtree*, the csv files with all the input vectors (matrix properties) and experimentally measured data were converted to the *arff* format. The parameters of both of these algorithms were set to default values recommended by the authors.

D. Hardware

All experiments were run on the Taurus supercomputer [14], where each node consists of 2× Intel Xeon E5-2680v3 (12 cores) processors and 64–256 GB RAM. The benchmarked core and uncore frequencies were 1.2, 1.5, 1.8, 2.1 and 2.5 GHz, and additionally 3.0 GHz for the uncore. The numbers of threads tested covered 2, 4, 6, 8 and 12. Ideally, the whole Cartesian product of these parameters should be measured, however, that would inadequatly increase the search space without the benefit of much improved results. The workload was duplicated to both sockets, because sparse routines scale very poorly to a higher number of threads and across NUMA regions and duplicating the calculations gives more accurate energy measurements. The energy consumption difference running the same algorithm and hardware settings among the nodes is roughly ±5% on average.

E. Benchmarking

During the initial experimental data collection phase, each sparse operation for each matrix and each combination of HW settings was run twice to warm up the caches, the measured hot run was repeated to run at least 5 times and for at least 1 second. The energy and time measurement as well as the dynamic hardware parameter settings were done using the *MERIC* library [15] [16], which uses *HDEEM* [17] for high frequency energy measurements. For each sparse matrix, all tests were executed on the same node to reduce the initial I/O overhead, but different matrices run in parallel on randomly allocated nodes.

III. Experimental results

The impact on prediction accuracy was individually evaluated for each dynamic neural network parameter. The accuracy is expressed as the Euclidean norm in a 4-dimensional space of error values as

$$Error\ distance = \sqrt{Err_t^2 + Err_c^2 + Err_u^2 + Err_e^2} \tag{2}$$

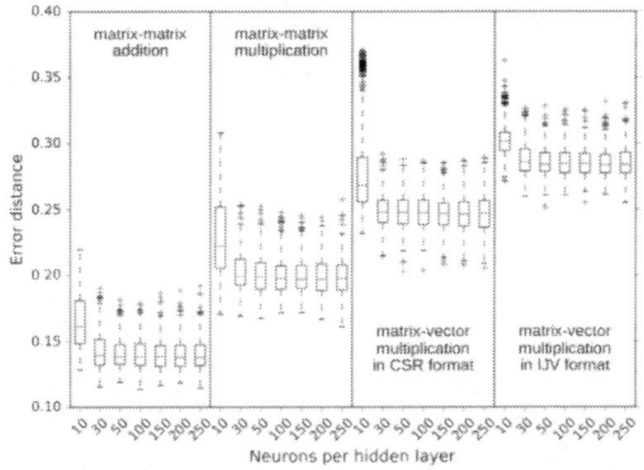

Figure 1: Impact of number of neurons on prediction accuracy of NN.

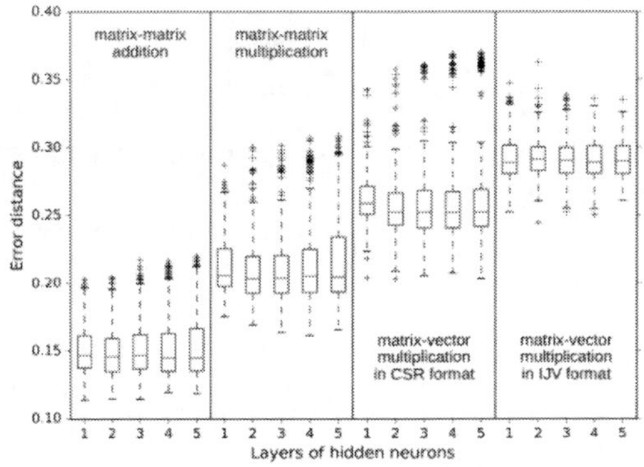

Figure 2: Impact of neuron layers on prediction accuracy of NN.

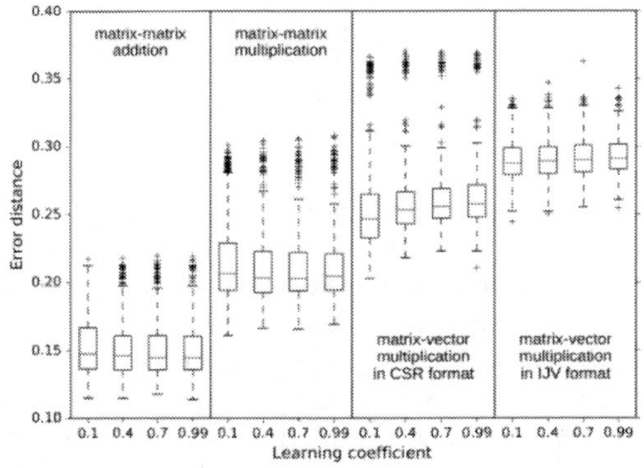

Figure 3: Impact of learning coefficients on prediction accuracy of NN.

where $Err_t = P_t - M_t$, $Err_c = P_c - M_c$, $Err_u = P_u - M_u$, $Err_e = P_e - M_e$, P_t is predicted number of threads, M_t is measured number of threads, P_c is predicted core frequency, M_c is measured core frequency, P_u is predicted uncore frequency, M_u is measured uncore frequency, P_e is predicted relative energy savings and M_e is measured relative energy savings. P values were predicted by a neural network on the output neurons, M values were experimentally measured on the cluster. All predicted and measured values were normalised.

For the following Figs. 1, 2, 3 and 4, only 1 000 epoch runs were plotted to ensure fully trained networks except for the SpMVmultIJV, where more than 100 training cycles led to overtraining. More than 1 000 epochs (not shown in the plots) did not improve the error distance. Every box of each boxplot represents all variants of neurons, layers, learning coefs. and training set sizes. One of these attributes is always set on the X axis of each chart.

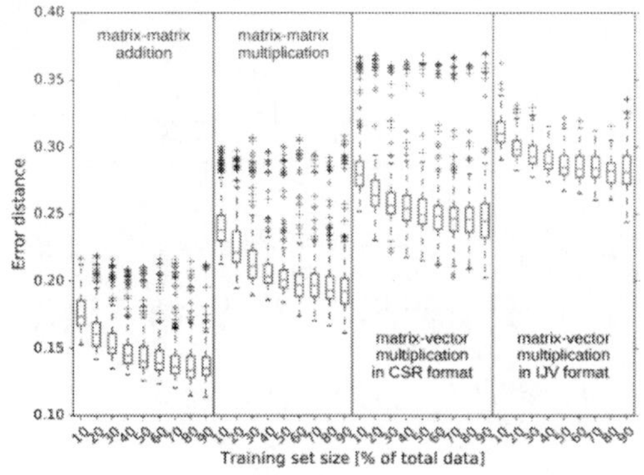

Figure 4: Impact of training on prediction accuracy of NN.

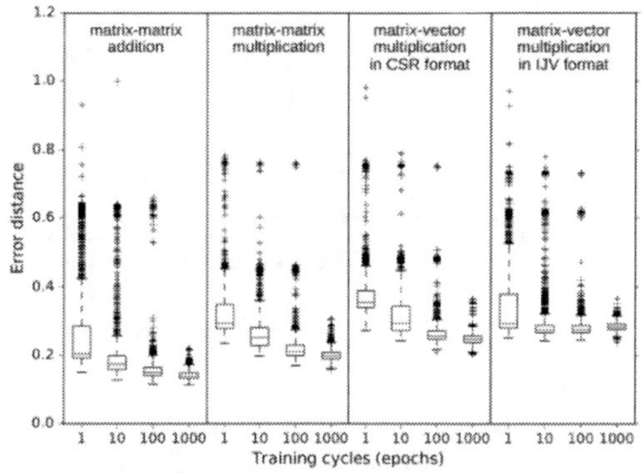

Figure 5: Impact of the training cycles on prediction accuracy of NN.

Fig. 1 shows that about 30 hidden neurons is enough to represent the relation between the input and output data. The number of hidden layers (see Fig. 2) was not detrimental to the results and 1–2 layers produced best mean results. The learning coefficient (see Fig. 3) did not have a big impact either, the best value depends on the algorithm. The number of training cycles (see Fig. 5) was an important factor in ensuring the network has converged to an optimal state.

The most important attribute turned up to be the training set size. It is much less time and resource-consuming to train a bigger network rather than enlarging the training set, which always improved the prediction quite significantly (see Fig. 4).

Since the network training takes a negligible amount of time compared to the sparse calculations on average matrices,

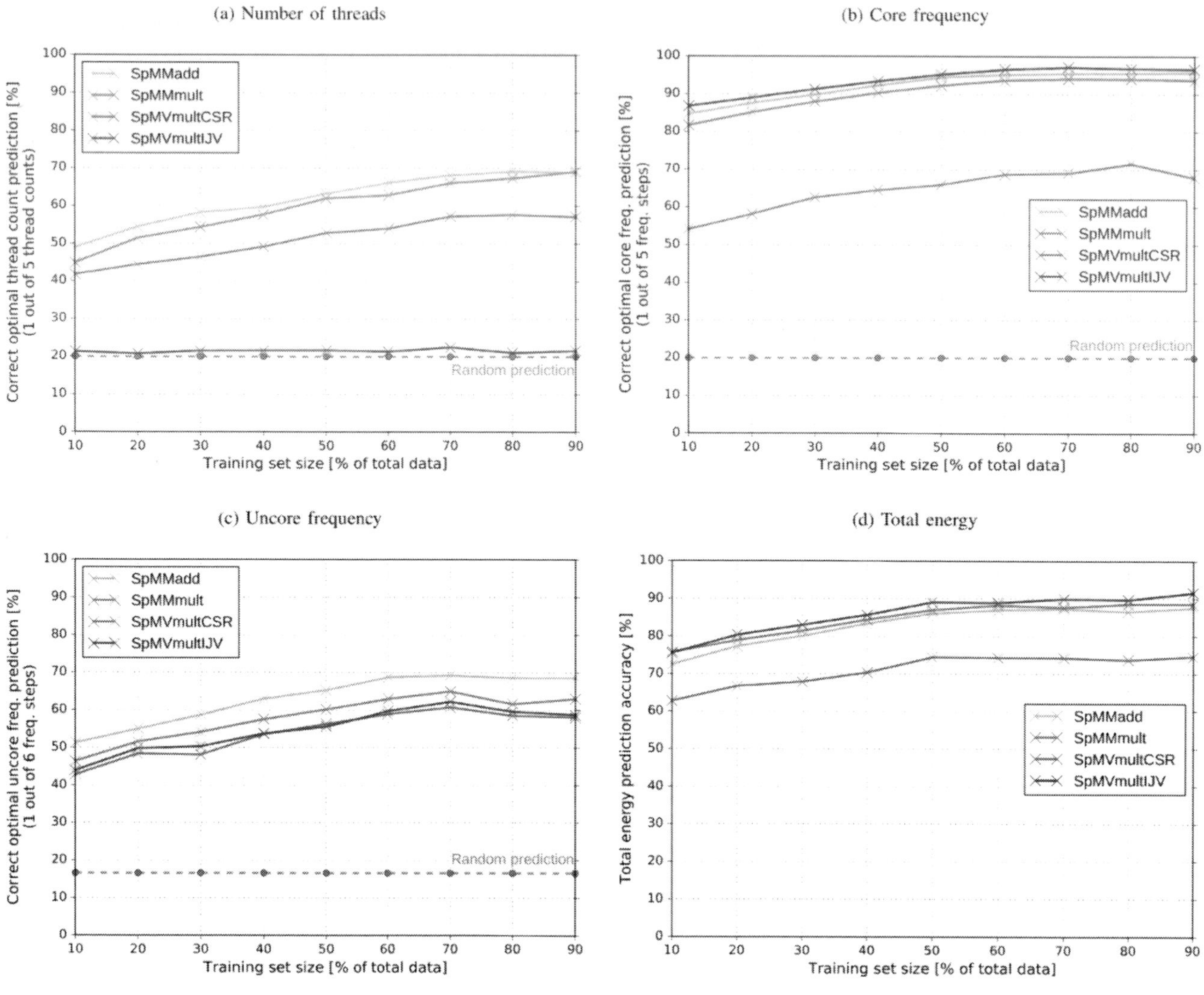

Figure 6: Prediction accuracy of the values back to absolute discrete values.

the best network was chosen for each sparse algorithm (see Table I) and the effect of a training set size on prediction accuracy is more closely analysed in Fig. 6. The Y axis represents the percentage of correctly predicted values after rounding each one to the closest discrete value experimentally measured on the cluster. For example, if 6 is the optimal number of threads and the neural network predicted any value within the $[5, 7)$ range, the prediction was considered correct. The same applies to the core and uncore frequencies. The total energy plot represents the average accuracy of predicted Joules compared to measured Joules.

Note that increasing the number of layers and neurons over 30 has negligible impact on optimal values, so if the neural network learning effort was also considered important, a neural network with 1 layer of 30 hidden neurons provided similarly good results in this case.

The thread count prediction accuracy ranges from 40 to 70% except for the SpMVmultIJV algorithm, which has a success rate of a random prediction. The main reason is that no thread count provided unambiguously best energy savings, more than one setting was often very close to the optimal one, so the neural network had more trouble learning the best value. The same behaviour was observed with the uncore frequency. The distribution for threads and uncore freq. was scattered across the whole spectrum of values, on the other hand, the optimal

TABLE I. BEST NEURAL NETWORK SETTINGS.

Algorithm	Neurons	Layers	Learning coef.	Epochs
SpMMadd	100	1	0.99	1 000
SpMMmult	250	4	0.1	1 000
SpMVmultCSR	50	5	0.1	1 000
SpMVmultIJV	50	2	0.1	100

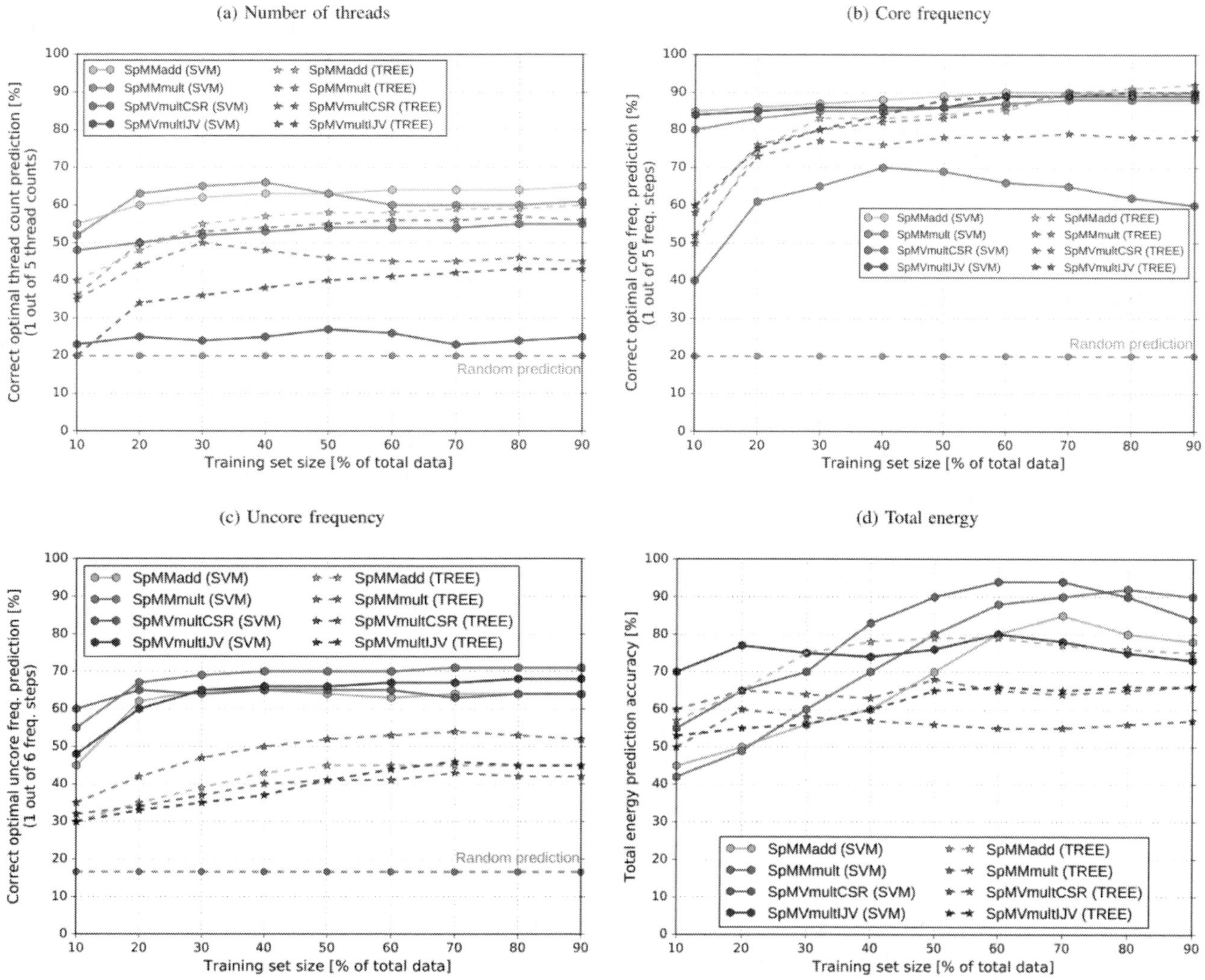

Figure 7: Prediction accuracy of Support Vector Machine (SVM in the legends) and Fast decision tree learners (TREE in the legends).

core frequency was 2.5 GHz in about 90% of the runs and quite rarely 2.1 GHz or even lower, so the prediction was quite simple, except for the SPMVmultCSR, where the values are more distributed into the lower frequencies around 1.5 GHz. Energy was also predicted quite precisely with up to 90% accuracy.

Fig. 7 similarly shows the prediction accuracy using support vector machines (SVM) and fast decision tree learners (TREE). SVM provide results similar to neural networks, on average the precision is 5–10% worse. The worst results are achieved in the same spots, predicting the number of threads of the SPMVmultIJV algorithm and the core frequency of the SPMVmultCSR, which only strenghten the argument that the current data configuration is hard to predict. However, TREE provides noticeably better results in these area and was able to find some additional dependencies. On average, SVM is about 5–10% more accurate than TREE and neural networks are 5–10% more accurate than SVM.

IV. Conclusion

The ability of neural networks, support vector machines and fast decision tree learners to predict the energy requirements and optimal hardware parameters (number of threads and core and uncore frequencies) for the best energy-to-solution of sparse matrix operations was evaluated. The experiments showed that 1 hidden layer of 30 neurons, 1000 learning cycles and almost any learning coefficient were able to produce results close the best achievable. The prediction accuracy depends on the algorithm and the predicted parameter, and for neural networks can reach up to 95%, with 60-70% being the average for most combinations. Support vector machines were 5–10% less accurate in their prediction compared to neural networks, and struggled on similar problems. Fast decision tree learners were 5–10% less accurate than SVMs, however, they proved to be useful in specific areas. The tree structure might be more appropriate in certain situations. Overall, all algorithms proved to be a useful tool in the area of energy efficiency.

ACKNOWLEDGMENT

This work was supported by the READEX project - the European Union's Horizon 2020 research and innovation programme under grant agreement No. 671657.

This work was supported by The Ministry of Education, Youth and Sports from the Large Infrastructures for Research, Experimental Development and Innovations project 'IT4Innovations National Supercomputing Center - LM2015070'.

This work was supported by the FIT-S-17-3994 Advanced parallel and embedded computer systems project.

REFERENCES

[1] A. von Gladi, M. Ahlborg, T. Knopp, and T. M. Buzug, "Compressed sensing of the system matrix and sparse reconstruction of the particle concentration in magnetic particle imaging," *IEEE Transactions on Magnetics*, vol. 51, no. 2, pp. 1–4, Feb 2015.

[2] U. Becciani, E. Sciacca, M. Bandieramonte, A. Vecchiato, B. Bucciarelli, and M. G. Lattanzi, "Solving a very large-scale sparse linear system with a parallel algorithm in the gaia mission," in *2014 International Conference on High Performance Computing Simulation (HPCS)*, July 2014, pp. 104–111.

[3] J. S. Bergstra, R. Bardenet, Y. Bengio, and B. Kégl, "Algorithms for hyper-parameter optimization," in *Advances in Neural Information Processing Systems 24*, J. Shawe-Taylor, R. S. Zemel, P. L. Bartlett, F. Pereira, and K. Q. Weinberger, Eds. Curran Associates, Inc., 2011, pp. 2546–2554. [Online]. Available: http://papers.nips.cc/paper/4443-algorithms-for-hyper-parameter-optimization.pdf

[4] J. Bergstra and Y. Bengio, "Random search for hyper-parameter optimization," *J. Mach. Learn. Res.*, vol. 13, no. 1, pp. 281–305, Feb. 2012. [Online]. Available: http://dl.acm.org/citation.cfm?id=2503308.2188395

[5] D. Stamoulis, E. Cai, D. Juan, and D. Marculescu, "Hyperpower: Power- and memory-constrained hyper-parameter optimization for neural networks," *CoRR*, vol. abs/1712.02446, 2017. [Online]. Available: http://arxiv.org/abs/1712.02446

[6] NVIDIA. Tegra X1 processor. URL: http://www.nvidia.com/object/tegra-x1-processor.html [accessed: 2018-07-10].

[7] S. C. Smithson, G. Yang, W. J. Gross, and B. H. Meyer, "Neural networks designing neural networks: Multi-objective hyper-parameter optimization," in *2016 IEEE/ACM International Conference on Computer-Aided Design (ICCAD)*, Nov 2016, pp. 1–8.

[8] L. Kotthoff, C. Thornton, H. Hoos, F. Hutter, and K. Leyton-Brown, "Auto-weka 2.0: Automatic model selection and hyperparameter optimization in weka," vol. 18, pp. 1–5, 03 2017.

[9] M. Feurer, A. Klein, K. Eggensperger, J. Springenberg, M. Blum, and F. Hutter, "Efficient and robust automated machine learning," in *Advances in Neural Information Processing Systems 28*, C. Cortes, N. D. Lawrence, D. D. Lee, M. Sugiyama, and R. Garnett, Eds. Curran Associates, Inc., 2015, pp. 2962–2970. [Online]. Available: http://papers.nips.cc/paper/5872-efficient-and-robust-automated-machine-learning.pdf

[10] T. A. University. SuiteSparse Matrix Collection. URL: https://sparse.tamu.edu/ [accessed: 2018-07-10].

[11] T. A. Davis and Y. Hu, "The University of Florida Sparse Matrix Collection," *ACM Trans. Math. Softw.*, vol. 38, no. 1, pp. 1:1–1:25, Dec. 2011. [Online]. Available: http://doi.acm.org/10.1145/2049662.2049663

[12] Genann. Genann repository. URL: https://github.com/codeplea/genann [accessed: 2018-07-10].

[13] A. Gulli and S. Pal, *Deep Learning with Keras*. Packt Publishing, 2017. [Online]. Available: https://books.google.cz/books?id=20EwDwAAQBAJ

[14] Technische Universitat Dresden. System Taurus. URL: https://doc.zih.tu-dresden.de/hpc-wiki/bin/view/Compendium/SystemTaurus [accessed: 2018-06-25].

[15] O. Vysocky, M. Beseda, L. Riha, J. Zapletal, V. Nikl, M. Lysaght, and V. Kannan, "Evaluation of the HPC applications dynamic behavior in terms of energy consumption," in *Proceedings of the Fifth International Conference on Parallel, Distributed, Grid and Cloud Computing for Engineering*, paper 3, 2017. doi:10.4203/ccp.111.3.

[16] P. Ivanyi, B. H. V. Topping, and G. Varady, Eds., *Proceedings of the Fifth International Conference on Parallel, Distributed, Grid and Cloud Computing for Engineering*. Civil-Comp Press, Stirlingshire, UK.

[17] D. Hackenberg, T. Ilsche, J. Schuchart, R. Schne, W. E. Nagel, M. Simon, and Y. Georgiou, "HDEEM: High definition energy efficiency monitoring," in *2014 Energy Efficient Supercomputing Workshop*, Nov 2014, pp. 1–10.

Collaborative Software Development: Who Owns Copyrights?

Iryna Lishchuk
Institut für Rechtsinformatik, Leibniz Universität Hannover
L3S Research Center
Hannover, Germany
email: iryna.lishchuk@iri.uni-hannover.de

Abstract—**This paper investigates the nature of collaborative research projects in terms of software copyright and data ownership. It discusses and seeks to answer such questions as: Who owns copyright in collaborative software development? If several partners contribute into the software toolkit, how do they share copyright? If data driven software is developed and trained against personal data, does it affect copyright ownership? How the data providers and developers share the rights? The legal analysis is conducted against research action undertaken in the medical research project HarmonicSS, supported by case studies from open source projects.**

Keywords-copyright ownership; data sharing; data driven software; sharing of rights.

I. Introduction

In research projects, software developments are normally a result of collaborative work. Sooner or later, a question: "Who owns copyright?" arises. Is it a software developer who carried out the work that owns software copyright or is it a partner institution? May a software developer decide on release of his software developments open source? When a number of partners develop a software work jointly or contribute individual modules, how do the partners share their rights? The matter of copyright ownership is important for exploitation. First, it is the holder of copyright, who has the right to exploit the work. Second, it is also the right holder, who has the power to decide the licensing strategy.

The matter becomes even more complicated when data driven software is developed in collaboration with data providers. In this situation, apart from software developers also the data providers come into play. The logic question arises: if software is developed against the data and rights in data belong to the data providers, who owns rights in data driven software: data providers or developers? An associated concern on part of data providers is whether their data rights are affected by the software development process.

The author considered the licensing implications of "open source" software elsewhere [1]. The critical issues behind data sharing have also been well articulated [2]. The focus of this paper is on the sharing and management of copyrights and data ownership in collaborative research projects. The research project HarmonicSS is a good example for this.

HarmonicSS is a large-scale ICT medical research project in the domain of personalized medicine [3]. Full title is "*HARMONIzation and integrative analysis of regional, national and international Cohorts on primary Sjögren's Syndrome (pSS) towards improved stratification, treatment and health policy making disease*". The HarmonicSS vision is to create and maintain a platform with open standards and tools entrusted to address the unmet needs in primary Sjogren Syndrome (pSS) and designed to enable secure storage, governance, analytics, access control and controlled sharing of information at multiple levels. The research work is done in collaboration and a number of project results are developed by multiple institutions, including technical experts and clinical partners. An example is Patient selection tool for multinational clinical trials. The tool is aimed to select patients from the integrative cohort eligible for multinational clinical trials for new pSS treatments. The technical background is composed by a Service Oriented Architecture (SOA) and open source tools and models developed in the PONTE project: Efficient Patient Recruitment for Innovative Clinical Trials of Existing Drugs to other Indications [4]. The models include: Clinical Trial Protocol Authoring Tool, Eligibility Criteria Model, Set of mechanisms and models linking to healthcare patient data sources for clinical research querying, Decision Support during study design and patient selection, etc. Apart from the data protection issues, which such collaborative medical research calls into play, the issues of data ownership and software copyright are not less essential. Several factors matter here, namely: Who owns copyright if several contributors are involved? How co-owners share the copyright? How the works developed in collaboration can be exploited and what are the pre-requisites for that? Are there any implications produced by data driven software development for the rights in data? Who owns the results? The legal implications behind the copyright and data ownership issues and potential options how such issues may be resolved we consider next.

The rest of this paper is organized as follows. The doctrine of first ownership in copyright is discussed in Section II. The nature of software development projects in terms of copyright is considered in Section III. Section IV elaborates on data rights. The management of copyrights by contractual means are discussed in Section V. Conclusions finalize the paper.

II. First Ownership

This Section elaborates on the principle of first ownership in copyright both from legal background and practical implications.

A. Legal Background

This study relates to the field of copyright law and examines the legal relations in collaborative software development across jurisdictions. However, the cross-border nature of collaborative software development does not change the legal background much. The copyright law is at much extent harmonized across jurisdictions. The main legal instruments of copyright law, such as the Berne Convention, the WIPO Copyright Treaty and the TRIPS Agreement introduce the minimum standard of copyright that shall be implemented by all Member States to the WTO and the Berne Union. The high-level study of copyright law suffices to examine issues discussed in this paper. The focus is made on harmonization of copyright in the EU, particular in the field of software copyright, such as introduced by the Directive 2009/24/EC on the legal protection of computer programs (Software Directive) [7].

To start with, it may be beneficial to note that all open source licenses, both as proprietary licenses, start with copyright notice, namely the declaration about who owns copyright. The copyright mark © denominates who holds software copyright in a program and has the right to dictate software distribution or licensing in one or another way. The copyright line, as integrated into the Apache License [5] looks as follows:

"Copyright [yyyy] [name of copyright owner]"

However, it is a typical situation in software development that the programmer who writes the code is the author of a program, but not necessarily the copyright holder. The code means a source code, written in one or another programming language; whereas software licensed "open source" must include source code, and must allow distribution in source code as well as compiled form.

According to the rule of first ownership in copyright, "*the first owner of copyright in a work is usually the author of the work*" [6]. It means, copyright in a work inherits the creator of a work, i.e. the author – a natural person. The same principle applies in software copyright. According to Article 2 (1) Software Directive:

"*The author of a computer program shall be the natural person or group of natural persons who has created the program or, where the legislation of the Member State permits, the legal person designated as the rightholder by that legislation.*"

However, under the work-for-hire doctrine, copyright in a work, created by an employee in course of employment, passes to the employer. This principle has also been anchored in software copyright and is reflected in Article 2 (3) Software Directive:

"*Where a computer program is created by an employee in the execution of his duties or following the instructions given by his employer, the employer exclusively shall be entitled to exercise all economic rights in the program so created, unless otherwise provided by contract.*"

In this constellation, namely where a computer program is created by a developer under employment, the developer bears moral rights in a program he creates, such as the right to be named as the author, whereas the employer inherits the economic rights. The moral and economic rights constitute full-fledged copyright. The moral rights are inalienable by nature and reserved by the author at any time. The moral rights are recognized by Article 6bis (1) Berne Convention:

"*Independently of the author's economic rights, and even after the transfer of the said rights, the author shall have the right to claim authorship of the work and to object to any distortion, mutilation or other modification of, or other derogatory action in relation to, the said work, which would be prejudicial to his honor or reputation.*" [8]

The economic rights encompass entitlements to the commercial exploitation of a work. The basic economic rights include the right to distribution, reproduction, modification and making available to the public [8].

In application to collaborative software development, this principle means the following. When a software developer writes a program for the project in the status of an employee, then, in the absence of an agreement, the employer, namely the partner institution holds software copyright. Consequently, it is the partner institution that has the legal position of the right holder and has the power to decide on the licensing strategy (be it open source or proprietary).

In a situation, where a programmer writes a program acting as a freelancer or subcontractor, then according to the rule of first ownership in copyright, it is the software developer who owns copyright and holds all moral and economic rights in a program, unless contractually agreed otherwise [6]. The difference between a freelancer and employee is that a freelancer sells his services to the employer without a long-standing commitment. By contrast, an employed developer commits to provide software development services to the employer under certain conditions for a specific period of time in return for remuneration. For example, the parties (the customer and developer) may agree that all economic rights in a program are assigned to the customer. This being the case, the customer is entitled to decide on the licensing software "open source". By contrast, if only use-license is negotiated, allowing the customer to run the program for his needs, the economic rights stay by the developer.

At the same time, provided a programmer writes the code and/or contributes into an open source project in his spare time, the rule of first ownership in copyright applies and it is the programmer who owns both moral and economic rights in the program he creates [7].

B. Practical Implications

In fact, the issue of copyright ownership plays an important role in software exploitation. As the case law shows, the ignorance and/or disregard to the issue of copyright ownership, namely who holds copyright in a code: employer, software project or the developer often leads to copyright litigation. It may be observed, that often in cases where popular IT companies litigate over a piece of software, which company B allegedly copied from company A, the dispute often arises from the fact that company B hired a developer X from company A, who wrote the piece of code at issue and integrated that piece of code into a software product of company B.

One example is the case Oracle America, Inc., v Google Inc. [9], tried by the U.S. courts from 2012 through 2016. In principle, the case concerned copyrightability of Java APIs, namely whether the Java APIs are protected by copyright. In brief, the copyright in Java APIs was recognized in the appellate instance [10], followed by the Google fair use defence and petition to the U.S. Supreme Court to review the case. Finally, the dispute was decided in favor of Google with verdict recognizing Google re-implementation of Java APIs as fair use [11].

Apart from the API copyrightability issue, there was also a small piece of code, which Orcanle claimed was replicated from Java into Android verbatim. And that piece of code made its way into Android in the result of Google hiring software engineer from Sun.

Dr. Joshua Bloch worked at Sun as a distinguished engineer specializing in Java from August 1996 through July 2004. While at Sun, Dr. Bloch wrote the nine line code called "rangeCheck". It performed a function to check the range of values before sorting the list. This function was put into a file, "Arrays.java", which was part of the class library for the 37 API packages at issue. In 2004, Dr. Bloch came to work to Google. In his spare time, he continued working on Java, and around 2007 wrote the files "Timsort.java" and "ComparableTimsort". These files also contained the same "rangeCheck" function that he wrote while at Oracle before. Dr. Bloch contributed his Timsort file to OpenJDK and Sun included Timsort as part of Java J2SE 5.0 release. In 2009, while working on Google Android project, Dr. Bloch contributed Timsort and Comparable Timsort to the Android platform. And this is how the nine line „rangeCheck" happened to be in Android and this was how the infringement happened to occur [9].

When discovered, the „rangeCheck" was removed from the Android edition. Because „rangeCheck" was nine lines appearing in a class of 3,179 lines of code, it was found as "an innocent and inconsequential instance of copying in the context of a massive number of lines of code" [9]. This example demonstrates how the constellation and the legal relations, in which the programmer has written the code, may affect copyright ownership and produce some legal implications.

III. Nature of Software Development in Terms of Copyright

This Section considers the works of collaborative software development in terms of copyright: joint works, composite works and derivative works.

A. *Collaborative Nature of Software Projects*

The collaborative nature of software development process brings another copyright relevant issue into play, namely: "How all the contributors share copyright?"

As noted above, software development projects are normally collaborative projects, which receive contributions from a number of software developers, who often work and contribute their bits of code independently [12]. As a rule, such collaboration results in a software product combined from inputs of various contributors. Thus, a large number of people may be involved in initial development, but even more can work on revised versions and updates [6]. As one author commented: "*Given the growing expanse of users working collaboratively, today's Linux is less a seamless piece of coding than a tapestry of hundreds of hackers' contributions.*" [13].

However, in legal terms, a ´derivative work´, a ´work of joint ownership´ and a ´composite work´ shall be distinguished. The legal consequences that these three formats produce vary.

B. *Joint Work*

The legal nature of a joint work reflects the idea of co-authorship [12]. The UK Copyright Act CDPA 1988, Section 10 (1), defines a work of joint ownership as "*a work produced by the collaboration of two or more distinct authors in which the contribution of each author is not distinct from that of the other author or authors*" [14]. The main characteristic of a joint work is that contributions are not separable, are not distinct from each other and do not constitute separate works in themselves and cannot be protected in their own right. Another essential factor, which marks a joint work, is intent of the contributors for their inputs "*be merged into inseparable or interdependent parts of a unitary whole*." [12]. In other words, if the contributors into a collaborative software development pursue the goal that their inputs merge into inseparable or interdependent parts of a whole, such collaborative project can qualify as a joint work [12].

Article 2 (2) Software Directive says: "*In respect of a computer program created by a group of natural persons jointly, the exclusive rights shall be owned jointly*" [7]. In principle, and unless agreed otherwise, contributors act as co-owners and enjoy equal rights to license the whole work on a non-exclusive basis subject to accounting obligations [12]. By that, neither contributor holds exclusive rights on his own, but can enforce the copyright [12]. On the other hand, the exploitation of a joint work requires consent of all contributors. If, for instance, one contributor refuses to cooperate with the others and disagrees with the licensing strategy the attempts to exploit such software product stand under the risk of being challenged as copyright infringement [6]. A possible alternative is to rewrite or remove the part of disagreeing party.

In free and open source (FOSS) projects, this issue is settled in a way that all bits are being contributed under the same or compatible license.

C. Derivative Work

Derivative is another type of collaborative work. In general terms, a derivative work builds upon a pre-existing work, creates a new, separate work, includes portions of a prior work and receives an individual copyright [12]. In legal terms, the development of a derivative work on top of a prior work requires authorization of the original right holder to modify his program and develop derivative works. The right to modification belongs to exclusive rights of a right holder, as defined by Article 4 (1) (b) Software Directive: "*the translation, adaptation, arrangement and any other alteration of a computer program and the reproduction of the results thereof, without prejudice to the rights of the person who alters the program;" [7].*

In contrast to joint ownership, the creator of a derivative work inherits a copyright in it: *"The party executing the new work holds the copyright in the new elements in its own right and a right to control the whole as a unified, copyrightable product." [12].*

Although, there is an independent copyright in a derivative work, it extends only to the portions derived from the original work and does not affect or prejudice the original copyright. A contributor, who builds on top of a prior work and creates his own derivative, may mark his copyright, for example as follows:

"Copyright © 2018 Project Development Who Made Changes"

The copyright line is normally followed by license notice.

D. Composite Work

A "composite work", also called "collective work" or "compilation", is distinct from the above types. A characteristic element of a composite work is that it is combined from elements that constitute independent and individual works in themselves. An example of a composite work can be a software package combined from a number of programs or modules each separately owned [6]. In contrast to joint works, the parties to a composite work "*do not intend that their contributions be merged to the point of being indistinguishable.*" [12]. Thus, the same program or module can be integrated into different composite works, whereas copyright in such module remains by the contributor.

The exploitation of composite works has some legal peculiarities. In principle, where a software project or package has a number of contributors and/or is made up of a number of individual programs or modules, the exploitation of such product as a whole would normally require consent of all contributors. In other words, if any of the contributors would seek to exploit the product as a unit whereas some contributors would disagree, a disagreeing party or parties may claim copyright infringement. The solutions for handling the situation might be (a) to remove the contribution of the disagreeing party (as Google removed "rangeCheck" from Android); (b) to rewrite a piece of software at issue [6]; or (c) to advance and settle potential IP issues by an agreement.

IV. DATA RIGHTS

Another issue closely associated with the development of data driven software concerns the data rights. This issue is particularly relevant when the data used to train the software is personal health data. The privacy considerations behind the data sharing for medical research deserve a profound elaboration elsewhere and go beyond the scope of this paper [16]. At the same time, the proprietary issues behind the data sharing are relevant for the management of intellectual property rights (IPR) and merit a deeper look here.

As an example of data driven software a Salivary Gland Ultrasonography image segmentation, developed in the HarmonicSS project may be used. The tool is designed for automatic ultrasonography image segmentation for the identification of large salivary glands. Salivary gland ultrasonography (SGUS) is considered as a valuable tool for the assessment of major salivary gland involvement in primary Sjögren's syndrome. The tool will operate against image processing techniques for automatic intensity and texture features extraction for segmenting the large salivary glands. The techniques will be validated by comparing the automatically segmented large salivary glands with those manually annotated by the experts. Usability will be assessed with Software Usability Scale (SUS) and Technology Acceptance Model (TAM) [3]. In the development process, the tool is supposed to be trained, and further validated against the real patient data.

Following the Commission Recommendation on the management of intellectual property in knowledge transfer activities and Code of Practice for universities and other public research organisations [17], the data, which the clinical partner institutions process before starting the project and agree to share for the project research, qualifies as background. The clinical data providers are supposed to hold all necessary rights in the clinical data they contribute. By contributing the data to the project, the data providers also agree (and shall have the legal capacity) to grant access rights to such data as technical partners may request for implementation of the project. And this is the mechanism, how the clinical data enters into the project and may be used for research.

Against this background, the developers of a SGUS image segmentation tool shall seek the access rights to the clinical data they need to train the tool and, if granted, may use the clinical data under the use rights. At a stage when the SGUS tool is developed, the question of copyright ownership arises. An associated issue is how copyright ownership interrelates with the rights in clinical data. In this respect, following the Commission Recommendation, the ownership of results shall stay with the party that has generated it [17]. In application to the SGUS tool, it means, the software copyright in the SGUS tool shall stay with the developers. As regards the correlation of copyrights with the data rights, the Commission Recommendation provides: *"The ownership of background should not be affected by the project"*. What follows is that the rights which data providers hold in clinical data stay by the data providers and are not affected by the copyright, which software developers inherit in the SGUS tool.

V. Contractual Management of IP Rights

Last, but not least, the European Commission when guiding research projects funded by the Commission calls for the management of Intellectual Property (IP) rights preferably at the outset of the project. Accordingly, the Principles regarding collaborative and contract research, established by the European Commission [17], provide *"IP-related issues should be clarified at management level and as early as possible in the research project, ideally before it starts. IP-related issues include allocation of the ownership of intellectual property which is generated in the framework of the project…"* Although, a general rule is that results generated in a collaborative research project should stay with the party that produced the results, the ownership *"can be allocated to the different parties on the basis of a contractual agreement, adequately reflecting the parties' respective interests, tasks and financial or other contributions to the project"* [17].

This approach, namely management of IP rights by an agreement has been adopted by the research project HarmonicSS. The management of IP rights in the project is specifically addressed by an IPR agreement. IPR agreement lays down principles of research, regulates the allocation of rights in data and research results and governs the issue of composite ownership in combined works. The matters of individual and joint ownership are already covered by the contractual framework of the project.

In particular, the IPR agreement defines the concept of composite work, allocates the ownership to contributing partners according to the contribution of each and binds the parties who contribute into composite works and wish to exploit composite works as a whole to agree on the ownership shares, allocation and exercise of rights, sharing of revenues, protection measures and the division of related cost in advance. In the same vein, such issues as the terms of licensing software from collaborative development shall be addressed by the agreement. For instance, an option of dual licensing may be considered, such as: licensing "open source" for research, and proprietary licensing into commercial exploitation. The variable licensing schema is followed by many commercial software providers. One example is Microsoft, offering open programs and commercial licensing agreements [18].

In summary, integral licensing is important for any collaborative software development project, since licensing is the key to successful software exploitation and bringing software right to the right sectors of the market. Such integral licensing may be reached by an agreement between the project participants deciding to license project outcomes under the one licensing schema.

VI. Conclusion

This paper investigates the issues of copyright and data ownership in collaborative software projects in application to data driven software. The outcome is the result of legal research conducted in ICT research projects with focus on technical matter but is not technical in itself. The conclusions made in the course of this study follow:

1) Ownership of copyright: Essentially, the legal relations surrounding the creation of a software product are define the ownership of copyright. A developer is a copyright holder if he wrote a program in his capacity as a natural person, for instance, contributed into an open source project in his spare time. By contrast, if a developer contributes a code into a collaborative research project on behalf of the partner institution, the partner institution acts as copyright owner, unless agreed otherwise.

2) Sharing of copyrights: As a rule, in a collaborative software development with multiple contributions, contributors share copyrights. However, the exploitation of collaborative works depends on the type of contributions, and underlying terms. In principle, exploitation of composite works requires consensus of all contributors and is normally managed by an agreement.

3) Data rights: The rights is data, which the clinical data providers agree to share to the project, stay by the data providers. The data rights are not affected by the results generated by processing the data. The rights in data driven results, such as data driven software modules, pass to the developing parties. The rights in the results are without prejudice to the data rights.

4) Management of IP rights: The exclusive economic rights in software are alienable by nature and can be regulated by contractual schemes. The allocation of copyright shares, the exercise of rights among the contributors, the licensing strategy and division of revenues, if applicable, can be governed by an agreement laying down the terms, under which participants agree to contribute.

Acknowledgment

This project has received funding from the European's Union Horizon 2020 Research and Innovation Programme under Grant Agreement No 731944 and from the the Swiss State Secretariat for Education, Research and Innovation SERI under grant agreement 16.0210.

References

[1] I. Lishchuk, "Open Source Software and Some Licensing Implications to Consider", International Journal On Advances in Systems and Measurements, v 9 n 3&4, pp. 266-275, 2016.

[2] D. Longo, and J. Drazen, "Data Sharing", Editorials, NEJM 374;3; 21 June 2016.

[3] HarmonicSS, the Project. [online]. [Accessed: 8 June 2018]. Available from: http://harmonicss.eu/.

[4] PONTE, Efficient Patient Recruitment for Innovative Clinical Trials of Existing Drugs to other Indications, Project ID: 247945, funded under: FP7-ICT.

[5] Apache License, Version 2.0. [online]. [Accessed: 8 June 2018]. Available from: http://opensource.org/licenses/Apache-2.0.

[6] C. Reed, and J. Angel, Computer Law: The Law and Regulation of Computer Technology, 6. Edition, Oxford University Press, 2007.

[7] Directive 2009/24/EC of 23 April 2009 on the legal protection of computer programs, OJEU, L 111/16, 5.5.2009.

[8] Berne Convention for the Protection of Literary and Artistic Works, adopted in 1886.

[9] U.S. District Court for the Northern District of California, Ruling of 31 May 2012, Case C 10-03561 WHA, Oracle America, Inc., v. Google Inc.

[10] U.S. Court of Appeals for the Federal Circuit, Ruling of 09 May 2014, Oracle America, Inc., v. Google Inc., Appeals from the United States District Court for the Northern District of California in No. 10-CV-3561.

[11] J. Mullin, "Google beats Oracle—Android makes "fair use" of Java APIs," Ars Technica, 26 May 2016 [online]. [Accessed: 8 June 2018]. Available from: http://arstechnica.com/tech-policy/2016/05/google-wins-trial-against-oracle-as-jury-finds-android-is-fair-use/.

[12] R. Nimmer, Legal Issues in Open Source and Free Software Distribution, adapted from Chapter 11 in Raymond T. Nimmer, The Law of Computer Technology, 1997, 2005 Supp.

[13] D. McGowan, Legal Implications of Open-Source Software, 2001 U. Ill. L. Rev. 241, 268, 274 (2001); Greg R. Vetter, The Collaborative Integrity of Open Source Software, 2004 Utah L. Rev. 563.

[14] UK, Copyright, Designs and Patents Act 1988.

[15] Software Freedom Law Center, Maintaining Permissive-Licensed Files in a GPL-Licensed Project: Guidelines for Developers, 2007. [online]. [Accessed: 8 June 2018]. Available from: www.softwarefreedom.org.

[16] M. Stauch, The Draft Data Protection Regulation and the Secondary Use of Patient Data for Research: Projects amd Concerns. Journal of professional Negligence, 29:72, 2013.

[17] Commission Recommendation on the management of intellectual property in knowledge transfer activities and Code of Practice for universities and other public research organisations, 10.4.2008, C(2008)1329.

[18] Microsoft, Licensing programs. [online]. [Accessed: 8 June 2018]. Available from: https://www.microsoft.com/en-us/Licensing/licensing-programs/licensing-programs.aspx.

A Theoretical Concept: Towards Mathematical Declarations of Code Intentions

Athanasios Tsitsipas, Lutz Schubert
Institute of Information Resource Management
University of Ulm
Ulm, Germany
e-mail: {athanasios.tsitsipas, lutz.schubert}@uni-ulm.de

Abstract—**"The whole is more than the sum of its parts" (Aristotle). Current imperative languages do not allow a program to be simply broken up (decomposition) or to merge several parts of a program, but demand appropriate knowledge and manual effort. The idea behind is to transfer methods from mathematical combinatorics to standard programming models to enable the distribution of a task across multiple heterogeneous resources. This approach allows distributed, heterogeneous resources to be treated as an integrated platform, with no hassle of adaptation for the developer. In this paper we propose and discuss a theoretical framework, with which the correctness of the code can be guaranteed with automated (de-)composition and adaptation. This will lay the groundwork for new programming methods that will allow code to be more fully understood, analysed and modified. This is relevant for all areas that develop and use software.**

Keywords–Software Engineering; (De-)composition; Group Theory.

I. Introduction

The world functions like a well-tweaked clock; it constantly moves and changes as we struggle to keep pace with it. We represent our world mathematically in order to explain, predict and reason with it - in other words, to scientifically deal with it. We base on theorems, axioms and lemmas that will eventually enable us to break down a problem into simpler steps, commonly understandable. Everything flows (Heraclitus) in the world of Information Technology(IT) with new types of resources and applications arriving on a daily basis, making it hard to keep pace. Software Engineering is still based on the principles of Alan Turing, and we are still developing hardware-specific programs. However, as more manufacturers specialize in Integrated Circuits for Dedicated Devices, variations in platforms have increased. Thus, different compilers become necessary, *e.g.*, convert C / C ++ into code optimized for the respective platform. This process is time consuming and requires that the code itself should be adapted to the target platform. Our goal is to create a theoretical framework that establishes concepts and methodologies, harnessing the power of mathematics as means to control, analyse and reason over the dynamic elements of a modern IT environment. We believe that we can define a program once and execute it on and across multiple environments, with no exertion of adaptability for specific resource types and environments. We should be able to add, subtract or alternate functions and/or features in an IT environment on demand, without having to worry explicitly about correctness and feasibility.

Within this short paper we will first examine the background information in related areas of software engineering (section II). In section III we outline the approach, where we propose a theoretical framework that describes the dependencies that arise in the decomposition and merging of subtasks from a mathematical point of view and thereby ensures the correctness of the resulting tasks. We conclude (section IV) with a short summary and future work.

II. Background

In current software development, the following things cannot be done properly with standard programming models: correctness of code (de)composition, multipurpose deployment, and easy execution. Currently, code (de)composition can only be achieved using well-defined patterns, which implicitly constrain execution to pre-defined use cases, logic and situations (infrastructures). This is because a compiler cannot understand a program automatically (so-called Halting problem). Nevertheless, we need to be able to automatically change the algorithmic logic when combining or separating functionalities, as well as, when using new resources. The functional behaviour needs to remain the same even though we change the algorithm (the logic). By using predefined code patterns, such as executing loops sequentially, or using map-reduce. This can partially be achieved by the compiler, if sufficient information is given (*i.e.*, if it fits a certain pattern), but not generally in a well-defined fashion. By applying group theory to combine logical elements, we could in principle develop a generic method for algorithmic (de)composition and adaptation, thus not solving, but certainly reducing the Halting problem considerably.

We change the way of standard programming with a mathematical description that abstracts from the algorithmic intention of the code, and not use programming models to only parallelise it (*i.e.*, Skeleton, TBB, Cilk). In order to utilize arbitrary resources in changing environments, we have to be able to break up (decompose) a function into a combination of functions, aligned to the available resources. Something similar has been attempted with the General Problem Solver [1] and is proven to be NP-hard. The General Problem Solver tried to find an optimal path over an infinite graph, whereas the group theory defines the combinatorial behaviour that in itself can generate a graph (and hence path) through a complex function (much like solving an equation can be represented by graphs).

Non-functional properties of execution (such as performance) depend on the available resources, which may change unpredictably. However, if we can express the non-functional properties as a projection of the function, then any decomposition of the functional declaration will be applicable to its projected functions too, and therefore to the non-functional properties. Since execution characteristics (non-functional properties) will change with the resources used, we need to exploit the behavioural patterns for code execution in alignment with the resource characteristics to find the best match between intended properties and the way this pattern executes on said resource. In our proposal, we exploit the (de)composition capabilities of mathematics, *i.e.*, that the same function can be expressed as different compositions of functions - this decouples the algorithmic (de)composition complexity from the actual functional intention and can be solved through a set of reference transformation rules, as demonstrated in POLCA [2]–[6].

III. Principal Approach

Concepts from the realm of mathematics in abstract algebra, and more specifically from group theory form the basis for the proposed work. The theory of groups occupies a central position in mathematics to delineate and control the space occupied by any polynomial function. The definition of the group is a well-formulated method in mathematics and can be applied in many domains, including arithmetic, geometry, but even beyond in biology, chemistry, physics [7]. A group is a set of elements, equipped with an operation $\star$ that comply with certain algebraic laws (associativity). If we combine two elements in a group (add two integers), the result is also in the group. Mathematical groups are not constrained to simple elements (such as numbers), but can be applied to complex objects. In the context of this work, we will try to transfer these concepts to programming languages, making computable functions complex objects that can serve as elements in a group. Note that this goes beyond the standard algorithmic definition of a function. By trying to perceive the infrastructure and the applications as a mathematical equation, we consider them in sets and combinations of elements.

We impose approaches that were developed as early as the 1960s, but were not pursued because of their difficulties in implementation: the mathematical declaration of the problem instead of the imperative-algorithmic one. What is special about the mathematical versus the algorithmic declaration is that the same problem can be solved in different ways, namely (1) by **mathematical transformation**

$$a^2 + 2ab + b^2 = (a+b)^2 = (b+a)^2 = (a+b)(b+a) \quad (1)$$

and, (2) by **converting the formula into various algorithmic forms**:

```
double binom(double a, double b)
    return (a*a+2*a*b+b*b);
or return (exp(a,2)+exp(b,2)+2*a*b);
```

Thus, the mathematical declaration is a superordinate definition of the overall behavior of the application, which can be broken down and distributed into different subtasks. Moreover, by using the transformations of the group, the correctness of the solution is always guaranteed, *i.e.*, in the given case by the commutativity, associativity and distributivity of + and * over $\mathbb{R}$ in the above examples. The relevant point is that this applies to every mathematical group, regardless of the definition of the operation and the space (as long as they satisfy the basic conditions) [3], [8].

The composition and in particular decomposition of code in Software Engineering is an NP-hard task. The challenge here is how to apply concepts from group theory to software engineering to enable the distribution of functions across multiple heterogeneous resources. Such an approach has never really been attempted before and though the principle may seem obvious, there are no well-defined methods yet and the consequences of any such approach must still be explored: Due to the inherent complexity of the problem there is an increased risk that the methodology may be applicable only under limited conditions. However, it will open discussions and will be an intriguing topic and of relevance for scientific research and industrial purposes.

IV. Conclusion and Future Work

With the proposed idea, it will be possible to deal better with complex applications that utilize multiple resources, which is currently possible only with a tremendous amount of effort. While programming and adapting programs is still a hard task, we envision a programming model where a functional abstraction through intentions of code will be realised, thus enabling us to overcome the problems arising from (de)composition of algorithmic logic (Halting Problem). As future steps, by developing new compilation methods and a novel code declaration to analyse, rearrange and manage software and finally ensure correctness, we will initiate new discussions for a path to rethink the way of programming. One major challenge faced by the idea consists in the potential combinatorial explosion: by applying group theory, a code can be arbitrarily combined and segmented leading to a potential infinite number of solutions (or rather: equivalent functions). To counter this, new methods to constrain and guide the search space will have to be examined, relating to current compiler techniques.

References

[1] A. Newell, J. C. Shaw, and H. A. Simon, "Report on a general problem solving program," in *IFIP congress*, vol. 256, 1959, p. 64.

[2] The mathematics behind polca. http://polca-project.eu/downloads/presentations/33-math-behind-polca/file. Accessed: 2018-04-01.

[3] J. Kuper, L. Schubert, K. Kempf, C. Glass, D. R. Bonilla, and M. Carro, "Program transformations in the polca project," in *Design, Automation & Test in Europe Conference & Exhibition (DATE)*. IEEE, 2016, pp. 882–887.

[4] S. Tamarit, J. Mariño-Carballo, G. Vigueras, and M. Carro, "Towards a semantics-aware transformation toolchain for heterogeneous systems," in *Program Transformation for Programmability in Heterogeneous Architecture Workshop (PROHA)*, 2016.

[5] D. R. Bonilla, C. W. Glass, and J. Kuper, "Optimized polynomial evaluation with semantic annotations," in *Program Transformation for Programmability in Heterogeneous Architecture Workshop (PROHA)*, 2016.

[6] S. Tamarit, G. Vigueras, M. Carro, and J. Marino, "A haskell implementation of a rule-based program transformation for c programs," in *International Symposium on Practical Aspects of Declarative Languages*. Springer, 2015, pp. 105–114.

[7] E. P. Wigner, "The unreasonable effectiveness of mathematics in the natural sciences," in *Mathematics and Science*. World Scientific, 1990, pp. 291–306.

[8] L. Schubert, J. Kuper, and J. Gracia, "Polca–a programming model for large scale, strongly heterogeneous infrastructures," *Parallel Computing: Accelerating Computational Science and Engineering (CSE)*, vol. 25, p. 43, 2014.

A Parallel Hardware Architecture for Fork-Join Parallel Applications

Atakan Doğan, İsmail San
Department of Electrical and Electronics Engineering
Anadolu University
Eskişehir, Turkey
email: atdogan@anadolu.edu.tr, email: isan@anadolu.edu.tr

Kemal Ebcioğlu
Global Supercomputing Corporation
Yorktown Heights, NY, USA
email: kemal.ebcioglu@acm.org

***Abstract*—In order to facilitate the implementation on hardware and improve the performance of a class of fork-join applications that can be modeled by an OpenMP program, a parallel hardware architecture with a specialized memory hierarchy is proposed. Furthermore, three different case studies are provided to show how this model can be employed for the hardware acceleration of such applications.**

Keywords-parallel applications; parallel hardware; hardware thread; caches; NoCs.

I. INTRODUCTION

The OpenMP Application Programming Interface is a well-established standard for parallel programming on shared-memory multiprocessors. OpenMP has adopted the fork-join model of parallel execution. According to this model, an OpenMP program begins as a single thread of execution, called an initial thread. When any thread encounters an OpenMP parallel construct, a team of master and slave threads (this is the fork) is created to execute the code enclosed by the construct. At the end of the construct, only the master thread continues, while all slave threads terminate (this is the join) [1].

In the literature, there are several studies that attempt to generate a parallel hardware from OpenMP applications [2]-[7]. A few High Level Synthesis (HLS) tools, such as Xilinx's SDAccel [8], have support to produce parallel hardware from OpenCL. Finally, fork-join like hardware constructs that are automatically generated from sequential code using compiler dependence analysis is described in [9].

The most recent and similar study in the literature is presented by [9]. However, [9] does not clearly specify how it copes with at least the following issues: (i) How does it achieve an implicit barrier among threads at the end of a parallel region? (ii) How does it perform reduction on hardware? (iii) Is multiple level of fork-join parallelism possible? The parallel hardware architecture model proposed here will be proved to have an answer for these questions that are needed for the acceleration of OpenMP applications.

The rest of the paper is organized as follows: Section II introduces the proposed parallel hardware architecture. Section III shows how this architecture provides support for the fork-join applications using three different case studies. Finally, Section IV concludes the paper.

II. PARALLEL HARDWARE ARCHITECTURE

Motivated by these and other related studies, a generic parallel hardware architecture that can be configured by an OpenMP program for a class of fork-join parallel applications is proposed in this study and illustrated in Figure 1.

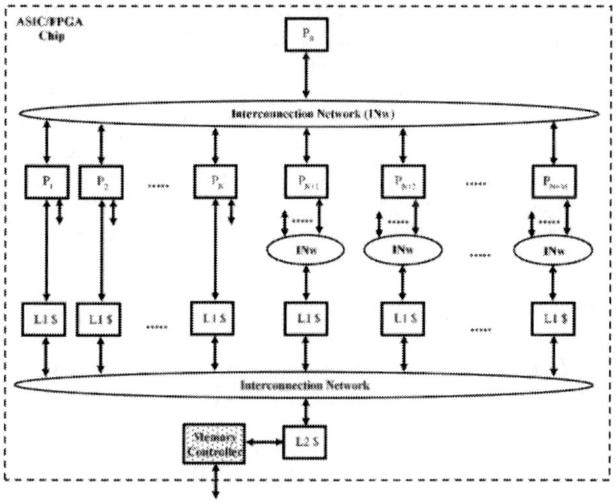

Figure 1. A parallel hardware architecture for parallel applications.

Inside an FPGA (Field Programmable Gate Array) or ASIC (Application Specific Integrated Circuit) chip in Figure 1, there are a few types of components, which include hardware threads, L1 caches (L1 $), single L2 cache (L2 $), and interconnection networks (INw). Each component communicates with messages through its sending FIFO (First-In First-Out) and receiving FIFO interfaces, where an arrow in Figure 1 represents such a bidirectional message communication interface.

A. *Hardware Threads*

A hardware thread component is a finite state machine that performs either coordination (P_0 in Figure 1) or computation (P_i, $i>0$).

P_0 is the master hardware thread that coordinates/synchronizes the execution of a parallel application among the slave hardware threads. That is, P_0

spawns (forks) new slave threads by sending a start request to each of these slave threads; a barrier synchronization (join) among slave threads is completed once P_0 receives a finish response from each of them.

P_i, 1≤*i*≤N+M, are a team of slave hardware threads that really implement the execution of parallel application as follows:

- Waiting for a start request from its parent thread P_0.
- After receiving a start request, working on the task while sending memory load/store requests to L1 cache units. Note that the task, for example, corresponds to the computation due to of #pragma omp parallel for {...}.
- Upon completing the computation, sending a finish response to P_0.

B. Memory Hierarchy

A two-level on-chip memory hierarchy as shown in Figure 1 is proposed to support the parallel hardware acceleration.

L1 $ is a write-back cache that supports *load*, *store*, and *flush* requests coming from the slave hardware threads. In Figure 1, a dedicated L1 cache is instantiated per slave thread that allows each thread to access memory independently for the maximum performance. Note that this model is complaint to the OpenMP shared memory model.

L2 $ is a write-back cache that receives *line read* and *line write* requests from L1 $ components and responds to the requests accordingly. All initial and final data of the parallel application are assumed to be kept in the L2 cache. Furthermore, according to Figure 1, the L2 $ state data is held in an on-chip memory, whereas the application data are kept in an off-chip memory accessed through a memory controller.

C. Interconnection Network

Interconnection Network (INw) is a packet-based network-on-chip network (NoC) that interconnects various components of the architecture [9].

III. CASE STUDIES

A. Matrix-Vector Multiplication

The first case study considers the matrix-vector multiplication of y = A×x, where A is an n×n matrix, and both x and y denote n×1 vectors. The parallel implementation of the matrix-vector multiplication is supported by Figure 1 as follows:

- Each hardware thread P_i, 1≤*i*≤N, starts its computation upon receiving a start request from P_0.
- Each P_i, 1≤*i*≤N, computes n/N vector elements y[k], where y[k]=A[k,:]×x requires a complete row A[k,:] of the matrix A and the whole vector x.
- The L1 cache directly attached to every P_i ($L1_i$) is loaded with n/N rows of the matrix and the vector x from the L2 cache during the computation.
- Each P_i computes its part of y[k] and stores it into its L1 cache. At the end of its computation, each P_i sends a flush request to $L1_i$ so that all dirty lines of y[k] in $L1_i$ are written back to the L2 cache.
- Each P_i waits for a flush acknowledgement from $L1_i$, and then sends a finish response to P_0. Once P_0 receives N finish responses, the matrix-vector multiplication is completed.

Note that the following components in Figure 1 will not be needed for case A: hardware threads P_i, N+1≤ *i* ≤ N+M, the corresponding interconnection networks and L1 caches. As a result, the matrix-vector multiplication is implemented as a single fork-join paradigm.

B. Vector Inner-Product

The second case study considers the vector inner-product of r = b×x, where b is a 1×n row vector, x denotes an n×1 column vector, and r is a resulting scalar value. The parallelization of the vector inner-product can be accomplished within the framework of Figure 1 as follows:

- Upon receiving a start request from P_0, each P_i, 1≤*i*≤N, computes a partial sum scalar value y[i] by means of multiplying its exclusive part of n/N elements of vectors b and x, and then performing n/N sums.
- Since each thread needs n/N elements of both vectors, $L1_i$ is loaded with n/N columns of b and n/N rows of x from the L2 cache.
- After the computation of y[i] is over, each P_i, 1≤*i*≤N, writes y[i] into $L1_{N+1}$, and then sends a finish response to P_0.
- After P_0 receives N finish responses, P_0 sends another start request to the thread P_{N+1} so that P_{N+1} can perform the final reduction sum over y[i], 1≤*i*≤N, in cache $L1_{N+1}$ and write the result r into $L1_{N+1}$.
- Finally, P_{N+1} sends a flush request to $L1_{N+1}$, waits for a flush acknowledgement from $L1_{N+1}$, and sends a finish response to P_0. Once P_0 receives this final finish response message, the vector inner-product is finished.

The hardware threads P_i, N+2≤ *i* ≤ N+M, the related networks and L1 caches in Figure 1 will not be needed for case B. Thus, the implementation of a vector-inner product requires a fork-join type of parallel execution followed by a reduction operation.

C. Matrix-Matrix Multiplication

Finally, the matrix-matrix multiplication of C = A×B, where each matrix is an n×n dense matrix, is considered as the third case study. Such a matrix multiplication, for example, can be performed as a block-matrix multiplication using (n/Q)x(n/Q) submatrices for Q=2 as shown below:

$$\begin{bmatrix} C_{11} & C_{12} \\ C_{21} & C_{22} \end{bmatrix} = \begin{bmatrix} A_{11} & A_{12} \\ A_{21} & A_{22} \end{bmatrix} \times \begin{bmatrix} B_{11} & B_{12} \\ B_{21} & B_{22} \end{bmatrix}$$

$$C_{11} = A_{11} \times B_{11} + A_{12} \times B_{21},$$

$$C_{12} = A_{11} \times B_{12} + A_{12} \times B_{22},$$

$$C_{21} = A_{21} \times B_{11} + A_{22} \times B_{21},$$

$$C_{22} = A_{21} \times B_{12} + A_{22} \times B_{22}$$

The parallel implementation of the block matrix multiplication is supported by Figure 1 as follows:

- Each P_i, $1 \leq i \leq N$, starts its computation upon receiving a start request from P_0.
- Each P_i, $1 \leq i \leq N$, deals with a single submatrix multiplication $Y_{jkl} = A_{jk} \times B_{kl}$ (for example, $Y_{111}=A_{11} \times B_{11}$, $Y_{121}=A_{12} \times B_{21}$, and so on). As a result, each P_i requires the corresponding A_{jk} and B_{kl} submatrices with dimensions of (n/Q)×(n/Q). There will be $N=Q^3$ submatrix multiplications.
- $L1_i$ is loaded with two submatrices A_{jk} and B_{kl} from the L2 cache during the submatrix multiplication.
- Each P_i completes the submatrix multiplication, stores the result submatrix Y_{jkl} into the cache $L_{N+j+l-1}$, and then sends a finish response to P_0.
- After P_0 receives N finish response messages, P_0 sends a start request to each hardware thread P_{N+i}, $1 \leq i \leq Q^2$, so that P_{N+i} can perform the final sum over Q different submatrices Y_{jkl} kept in cache $L_{N+j+l-1}$ to compute C_{jl}.
- At the end of its computation, each P_{N+i}, $1 \leq i \leq Q^2$, sends a flush request to L_{N+i} so that all dirty lines of C_{jl} in this L1 cache are written back to the L2 cache.
- P_{N+i}, $1 \leq i \leq Q^2$, waits for a flush acknowledgement from its cache, and then sends a finish response to P_0. Once P_0 receives Q^2 finish messages more, the matrix-matrix multiplication is done.

Different from case A and case B, the matrix-matrix multiplication implementation requires the use of all hardware components shown in Figure 1. Furthermore, it features two level of fork-join parallelism where the different number of threads are working on different tasks at each level.

IV. CONCLUSIONS

A parallel hardware architecture for a class of parallel applications that can be modeled by a fork-join programming model, such as OpenMP, is introduced. Its features are further highlighted on three different case studies.

Future work involves devising a compiler to generate such parallel hardware from regular OpenMP applications; measuring and reporting the performance that can be attainable by the generated parallel hardware using a set of benchmark OpenMP applications, and making this compiler to support the most of OpenMP constructs.

REFERENCES

[1] B. Chapman, G. Jost, R. van der Pas, Using OpenMP Portable Shared Memory Parallel Programming. London, UK: The MIT Press, 2008.

[2] J. Choi, St. Brown, and J. Anderson, "From software threads to parallel hardware in high-level synthesis for FPGAs," International Conference on Field-Programmable Technology (FPT'13), IEEE Press, Dec. 2013, pp. 270-277, doi: 10.1109/FPT.2013.6718365.

[3] Y. Y. Leow, C. Y. Ng, and W.F. Wong, "Generating hardware from OpenMP programs," IEEE International Conference on Field Programmable Technology, (FPT 2006), IEEE Press, Dec. 2006, pp. 73-80, doi: 10.1109/FPT.2006.270297.

[4] A. Cilardo, L. Gallo, and N. Mazzocca, "Design space exploration for high-level synthesis of multi-threaded applications," Journal of Systems Architecture, vol. 59, pp. 1171-1183, Nov. 2013, doi: 10.1016/j.sysarc.2013.08.005.

[5] A. Podobas and M. Brorsson, "Empowering OpenMP with automatically generated hardware," International Conference on Embedded Computer Systems: Architectures, Modeling and Simulation (SAMOS), IEEE Press, Jul. 2016, pp. 201-205, doi: 10.1109/SAMOS.2016.7818354.

[6] L. Sommer, J. Korinth, and A. Koch, "OpenMP device offloading to FPGA accelerators," 2017 IEEE 28th International Conference on Application-specific Systems, Architectures and Processors (ASAP 2017), IEEE Press, Jul. 2017, pp. 201-205, doi: 10.1109/ASAP.2017.7995280.

[7] L. Sommer, J. Oppermann and A. Koch, "Synthesis of interleaved multithreaded accelerators from OpenMP loops" International Conference on ReConFigurable Computing and FPGAs (ReConFig), IEEE Press, Dec. 2017, 10.1109/RECONFIG.2017.8279823.

[8] Xilinx SDAccel. [Online]. Available from https://www.xilinx.com/products/design-tools/softwarezone/sdaccel.html/ 2018/06/08.

[9] K. Ebcioglu, E. Kultursay, and M. T. Kandemir, "Method and system for converting a single-threaded software program into an application-specific supercomputer," US8,966,457B2, 2015.

[10] T. Bjerregaard and S. Mahadevan, "A survey of research and practices of network-on-chip," ACM Computing Surveys, vol. 38, pp. Jun. 2006, doi: 10.1145/1132952.1132953.

Privacy-Preserving Multicast to Explicit Agnostic Destinations

Cuong Ngoc Tran*, Vitalian Danciu*

* Ludwig-Maximilians-Universität München
Oettingenstr. 67, 80538 München, Germany
Email: {cuongtran, danciu}@mnm-team.org

Abstract—**Multicast protocols require either the participation of hosts in group management or partial address lists of the group members to be sent to end-points (hosts), thus creating a privacy issue. In our new protocol for 1:n multicast over the Internet, senders perform all group management while receivers do not require explicit support for the protocol. The protocol copes with varying degrees of support by routers in the network and avoids the disclosure of others' addresses to end-points. Performance evaluation shows a decrease of the total volume of traffic in the network of up to 1:5 as compared to unicast, suggesting suitability for applications, such as Internet Protocol Television (IP-TV), video conferences, online auctions and others.**

Keywords–Privacy-Preserving Multicast; Agnostic Destination.

I. INTRODUCTION

Applications replacing traditional broadcast services (IP-TV, IP-Radio), phone and video conferencing, and also technical services for software update or large-scale configuration may profit from an *n:m*, multicast, distribution scheme. Today, these applications still rely mostly on unicast transmission despite multicast having been available for a long time.

Typical multicast schemes are based on managed groups (e.g., [1], [2], [3]) where end-points may join the multicast group and the network forwards messages addressed to the group to all group members. Once set up, a multicast group is often symmetric in allowing any participant to address a message to all others. Unfortunately, it requires the network manager to effect configuration reflecting that a given application uses a different kind of network function, while the user is responsible for configuring the application to use multicast. The setup for services being provided across networks and thus across administrative domains always requires the co-operation of each participant domain's network managers.

A. Problem

As illustrated in Figure 1, by requiring an end-point to join and leave the multicast group that supports the desired application, the use of multicast

1) requires network management to authorize a service session and possibly setup (multicast routers),
2) requires the user to execute a network management action,
3) requires transfer of knowledge on group membership on the application level to a multicast group and
4) introduces state to the otherwise state-less (from the view of the end-point) IP communication.

A number of additional properties exacerbate the perceived drawbacks to multicast use:

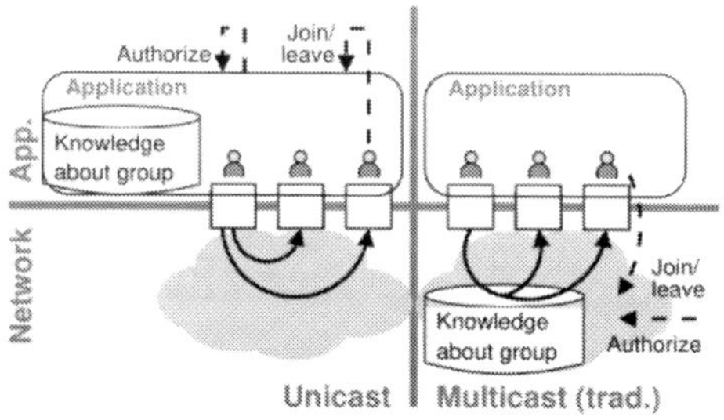

Figure 1. Knowledge and management actions in unicast and multicast.

5) If the network-level setup of multicast fails, there is no automatic fall-back to unicast: instead, the application simply fails as well.
6) All participants in a service must have multicast support.
7) Re-configuration of the application group requires re-configuration of the network.
8) Knowledge about the identities of the participants in a service session is present in the network, possibly in several administrative domains.

Therefore, applications seem to prefer unicast even with the expense of the higher transmission volume, or Application-Layer Multicast (ALM) (e.g., [4], [5]) in spite of it being application specific and requiring a network function within the application's code.

In essence, ALM reduces the *n:m* multicast pattern to the asymmetric case of *1:n* communication, where a single sender addresses a group of receivers. In this case, it is sufficient for the sender to hold knowledge about the group. Since the sender necessarily implements the application layer of the service being provided, group management may be transacted at the application level. Such communication is easily implemented over unicast transmissions. However, it requires the receiver-side configuration and does not profit from network support.

B. Contribution

We propose to combine the benefits of multicast to agnostic receivers with those of optional network support.

We introduce a protocol named Multicast to Explicit Agnostic Destinations (MEADcast) to allow sender-based multicast of IPv6 over the Internet. The novelty of MEADcast is that it protects receivers' anonymity and allows a gradual, pro-active and selective transition between multiple unicast and network-supported multicast. As the protocol favours conservative decisions, we present studies of the transmission cost in the network performed by simulating randomized as well as designed situations.

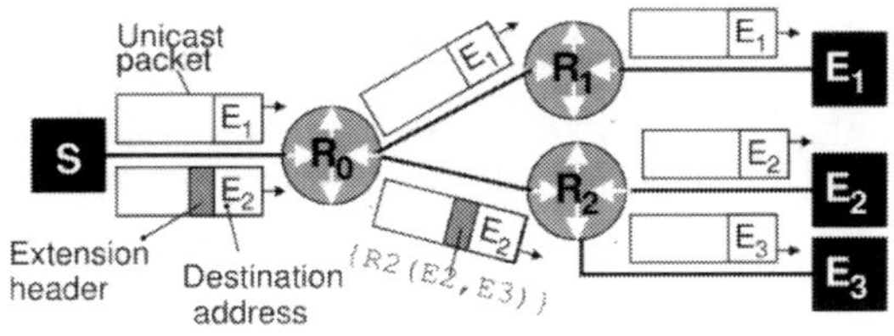

Figure 2. Multicast to agnostic receivers.

C. Technical overview

MEADcast implements a sender-centric multicast in that all knowledge about the receiver group, the network topology and the availability of MEADcast-capable routers (or the so-called MEADcast router in this paper) is gathered at and decided upon by the sender. Given an initial list of receivers, the sender commences to send data in unicast to each sender while simultaneously probing the network for the presence of MEADcast-capable routers and hence for the option to consolidate some of the unicast streams into multicast. Multicast packet headers reflect the MEADcast router responsible for translating the multicast packets into (multiple) unicast packets. Receiving end-points always receive true unicast packets either directly from the sender or generated by a MEADcast router, based on a multicast packet. Only unicast addresses are used in the protocol.

Multicast packets begin with a standard IPv6 header addressed to one of the multicast receivers on a path, followed by a Hop-by-Hop Routing Header with Router Alert. The addresses of all multicast receivers on a path as well as the MEADcast router responsible for translation are encoded into a multicast header. It is typically followed by a UDP header. The addressing pattern is similar to the one in Internet email, where one recipient is addressed directly (To:) while all recipients are included in the carbon copy (CC:) list. The protocol is designed to minimize packet duplication, and recipient list re-writing in transit routers is eliminated.

Figure 2 shows an example where a sender S transmits to three receiving end-points E_i with the aid of three MEADcast-capable routers R_j. Note that the sender transmits unicast directly to E_1, as it is the only end-point on its subtree. It transmits one multicast packet to E_2 and E_3, to be transformed into unicast by router R_2.

None of the end-points can discern the identity of the others, thus preserving privacy, or if the data has been multicasted.

D. Synopsis

Our work is inspired by Xcast [6], which is discussed along with other related work in Section II before expounding the technical properties of MEADcast in Section III. The study of the protocol's behaviour and performance, presented in Section IV, indicates that the reduction in total volume may well be worth the introduction of the mechanism. We provide a discussion of the protocol's overhead, security and application scenarios in Section V. Section VI summarizes our ideas and findings and points out further directions of research.

II. Related work

The idea of multicast was introduced decades ago and has drawn research efforts broadly. A variety of solutions have been proposed and a selection is presented here.

"Standard" multicast [1], [2], [3], [7] specifies the transmission of an IP datagram to a "host group", a set of zero or more hosts identified by a single IP destination address. It requires the network support (multicast capable router) and the receiving end-points to proactively join the "host group". The routers and end-points use the Internet Group Management Protocol (for IPv4) or Multicast Listener Discovery (for IPv6) to maintain the multicast group. The deployment of IP multicast in the Internet is yet far behind expectations due to a number of issues [8]. Amongst those are the management complexity put on end-point and the requirement of overall router upgrade, which constitute the motivation for our works.

ALM implements multicasting functionality at the application layer instead of at the network layer by using the unicasting capability of the network. In contrast to the slow deployment of IP multicast, ALM gains practical success thanks to the ease of deployment. A survey of ALM over the period 1995-2005 was given in [9]. The common approach of ALM is that the multicast participants establish an overlay topology of unicast links to serve as an overlay network on top of which multicast trees can be constructed. The drawback of ALM is the privacy of receiving end-point is not ensured, which means the identity of one end-point might be known by the other; furthermore, the data delivery of ALM depends on the end-point capability, which could not guarantee the stability and reliability. These problems are learnt in designing MEADcast.

Xcast [6] is a multicast scheme with explicit encoding of the list of destinations in the data packets, instead of using a multicast group address. Xcast supports a very large number of small multicast sessions, which makes up complementary scaling property to IP multicast, since the latter has a scalability issue for a very large number of distinct multicast groups. Xcast sends data via optimal route without traffic redundancy when Xcast-aware routers exist; otherwise, receiving end-point has to do ALM and data is sent in a daisy-chain form. The privacy of receiving end-points in the latter case is violated. Xcast limits the number of participants in a multicast session to 64, making it unsuitable for many applications. The idea of Xcast is inherited in MEADcast development while its shortcomings are remedied.

III. Protocol design

MEADcast is implemented by senders and routers. We describe the functions relevant for sender and router elements and message types and procedures necessary for the realization of these functions. A simple multicast scenario described in full illustrates the behaviour of the protocol.

The information needed to describe the protocol is the sender S, the set of end-points E_i that it transmits to, the set of MEADcast routers R_j in the network and their distance d to the sender in hops between MEADcast routers. Association is indicated by superscript, i.e., a router responsible for a subset E_k of the end-points is R^k and an end-point served by a router R_j is E^j.

A. Functions

In MEADcast, we need to distinguish two groups of functions for the sender and the router.

Sender functions include transmission of *unicast* and *multicast* messages, *initiation of discovery* of the path to an end-point and *discovery response evaluation*.

Router functions include normal *forwarding*, *decomposition* of multicast packets to unicast packets and multicast packets and *reaction to discovery* requests from a sender.

1) Discovery-related functions: Both the sender and the MEADcast router are involved in the discovery process. The goal of discovery is for the sender to determine the sequence of routers $(R_1^i, R_2^i, \cdots)$ on the path to each end-point E_i. Discovery requests and responses can be written as `req(E, d)` and `resp(E, d, R)`, respectively.

To initiate discovery, the sender addresses a MEADcast discovery request `req(E, 0)` to an end-point E. When receiving the request, every router R on the path to E increments d and forwards the discovery request `req(E, d+1)` to the next hop; at the same time, R sends a discovery response `resp(E, d+1, R)` to S. Thus, the first router R_1 on the path to E will send $(E, 1, R_1)$, the second $(E, 2, R_2)$ and so on.

S can compile the sequence $\{(E_i, d_1, R_1^i, d_2, R_2^i, \cdots), \cdots\}$ and can compute the groups of end-points to be handled by a given router with a specific distance $(R_j, d_j, E_1^j, E_2^j, \cdots)$.

2) Decomposition: Decomposition, which is specific to MEADcast router, means the transformation of a multicast packet addressed to a set of target end-points into multiple unicast and multicast packets with the same payload.

The target addresses $R_j, E_1^j, E_2^j, \cdots, R_k, E_1^k, E_2^k, \cdots$ within a multicast message are structured to denote that a router R_i is responsible for end-points E^i. During decomposition a router will send unicast packets to each of the end-points it is responsible for and send multicast packets to the routers responsible for the remaining target end-points.

When a multicast packet is created, the targets already served either by unicast or by other multicast messages are removed from the list of targets of the packet being created. The removal process can be implemented efficiently by marking removal in a bitmap and thus eliminating the need to compose a new list of targets.

B. Sender behaviour

The sender behaviour involves two phases: *MEADcast discovery* and *MEADcast data sending*.
The sender sends *MEADcast discovery request* $\texttt{req}(E_i, 0)$ to all receiving end-points and updates the network topology in the form of $(R_j, d_j, E_1^j, E_2^j, \cdots)$ whenever it receives a *MEADcast discovery response*. In the mean time, the sender also transmits data to these end-points "unicastly".
MEADcast data sending phase starts when the discovery phase is complete (e.g., after a pre-defined timeout). Based on its network topology view, the sender constructs and transmits *MEADcast data messages* containing the target addresses $(R_j, E_1^j, E_2^j, \cdots, R_k, E_1^k, E_2^k, \cdots)$ for those end-points that can be served by MEADcast routers and stops unicast data to them. In the current MEADcast design, the sender does not put the MEADcast router and its end-point in the address list if it is responsible for only one end-point since it may be a waste of the header space. That end-point is served by unicast. This is the case for E_1 in Figure 2.

It is obvious that if there is no MEADcast router responsible for any receiving end-points, the data sending phase of MEADcast operates exactly as unicast.

The discovery phase is carried out periodically so that the sender can maintain an updated view of the topology.

C. Protocol mechanics by example

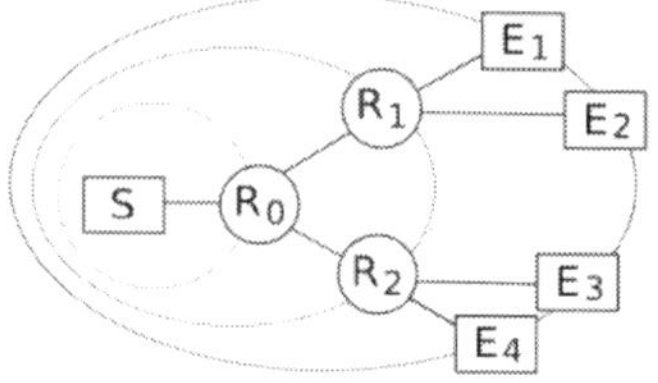

(a) Scenario 1

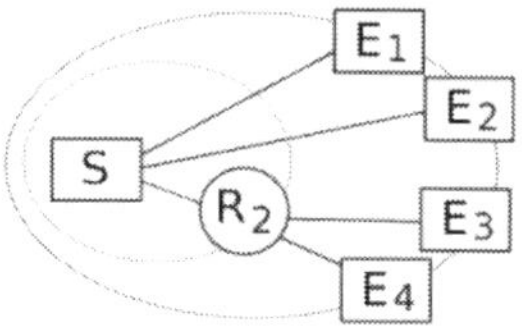

(b) Scenario 2

Figure 3. Network topology from sender viewpoint.

Figure 3 describes the network where the proposed scheme is effective, consisting of five endpoints S, E_1, E_2, E_3, E_4 and three routers R_0, R_1, R_2. Their connections are shown in Figure 3(a) (without the rings). Two different scenarios are described, the first one with all routers being MEADcast capable, the second one with only R_2 being a MEADcast router. The communications between the sender S and the recipients E_1, E_2, E_3 and E_4 via the network in the first scenario are as follows:

1) S transmits data to E_1, E_2, E_3, E_4 "unicastly".
2) S sends four different *MEADcast discovery requests* $\texttt{req}(E_i, 0)$, $i \in \{1, 2, 3, 4\}$.
3) for unicast message, R_0, R_1, R_2 simply forward it to the intended receiver.
4) R_0 receives $\texttt{req}(E_1, 0)$, it reacts to the presence of the Hop-by-Hop header and analyses the content of the MEADcast header. R_0 sends a *MEADcast discovery response* $\texttt{resp}(E_1, 1, R_0)$ to S. It also sends $\texttt{req}(E_1, 1)$ to E_1. The same procedure is carried out for $\texttt{req}(E_2, 0)$, $\texttt{req}(E_3, 0)$, $\texttt{req}(E_4, 0)$.
5) R_1 receives $\texttt{req}(E_1, 1)$, it sends $\texttt{resp}(E_1, 2, R_1)$ to S. It also sends $\texttt{req}(E_1, 2)$ to E_1. The same procedure is carried out when R_1 receives $\texttt{req}(E_2, 1)$.
6) R_2 receives $\texttt{req}(E_3, 1)$ and $\texttt{req}(E_4, 1)$, it sends $\texttt{resp}(E_3, 2, R_2)$ and $\texttt{resp}(E_4, 2, R_2)$ to S. It also sends $\texttt{req}(E_3, 2)$ to E_3 and $\texttt{req}(E_4, 2)$ to E_4.
7) E_1, E_2, E_3, E_4 receive the unicast messages normally. For the *MEADcast discovery request*, they do not understand and simply drop it.
8) S receives *MEADcast discovery responses* and updates its network topology view as $(R_0, 1, E_1, E_2, E_3, E_4), (R_1, 2, E_1, E_2), (R_2, 2, E_3, E_4)$. The topology view of sender can be illustrated by the rings in Figure 3(a), where the sender is at the center, R_0 has distance one and lies on the first ring, R_1 and R_2 are on second ring with a distance of two and all receiving end-points are always at the outermost ring.
9) S stops transmitting data via unicast and starts MEADcast data sending phase. S transmits a *MEADcast data message* with E_1 as the destination IP address and $\{R_1, E_1, E_2, R_2, E_3, E_4\}$ in the MEADcast header address list. A position field showing the position of MEADcast router in the address list and another status field

marking whether a MEADcast router has received the *MEADcast data message* are also included in the message.

10) R_0 receives the *MEADcast data message*, sees that:
    - it does not have to deliver message to any receivers since its address is not in the MEADcast address list.
    - based on the position field and status field, there are two other MEADcast routers that need to receive *MEADcast data message*. R_0 duplicates the original *MEADcast data message*, the status field of the first one is modified, indicating that R_2 has received a *MEADcast data message*. R_0 sends this message to R_1. R_0 changes the destination IP address of the second message to E_3, modifies the status field to indicate that R_1 has received a *MEADcast data message* and sends it to R_2.
11) R_1 receives a *MEADcast data message*, sees that it is responsible for E_1 and E_2. R_1 constructs two unicast messages with the data from the *MEADcast data message* and transmits each to E_1 and E_2. There is no MEADcast router that needs to receives this *MEADcast data message*.
12) R_2 receives a *MEADcast data message*, sees that it is responsible for E_3 and E_4. R_2 constructs two unicast messages with the data from the *MEADcast data message* and transmits each to E_3 and E_4. There is no MEADcast router that needs to receives this *MEADcast data message*.

The communications between the sender S and the recipients E_1, E_2, E_3 and E_4 via the network in the second scenario (only R_2 is a MEADcast router) have the same first three steps as in the first scenario. The further steps are as follows:

1) R_0 receives req(E_1,0), it reacts to the presence of the Hop-by-Hop header and analyses the content of the MEADcast header, which it does not understand. It forwards the message further to the E_1 direction. R_0 does not drop the message since the option type identifier of MEADcast header is 00 [10]. The same procedure is performed for req(E_2,0), req(E_3,0), req(E_4,0).
2) Similarly, R_1 receives req(E_1,0) and req(E_2,0), it sends these messages to E_1 and E_2.
3) R_2 receives req(E_3,0), req(E_4,0). It sends resp(E_3, 1, R_2) and resp(E_4, 1, R_2) to S. It also sends req(E_3,1) to E_3 and req(E_4,1) to E_4.
4) E_1, E_2, E_3, E_4 receive the unicast messages normally. For the *MEADcast discovery request*, they do not understand and simply drop it.
5) S receives *MEADcast discovery responses*, updates its network topology view as $(R_2, 1, E_3, E_4)$. Its network topology view is illustrated in Figure 3(b). There is no MEADcast router on the paths to E_1, E_2, only R_2 is on the paths to E_3, E_4 and it lies on the first ring of distance one. All receiving end-points are on the outermost ring.
6) S starts MEADcast data sending phase. Based on its topology view, S sees that:
    - there is no MEADcast router on the paths to E_1, E_2. S transmits data to these receivers "unicastly".
    - R_2 is on the paths to E_3, E_4. S transmits a *MEADcast data message* with E_3 as the destination IP address and $\{R_2, E_3, E_4\}$ in the MEADcast header IP address list. A position field and a status field as described in the first scenario are also included in the message.

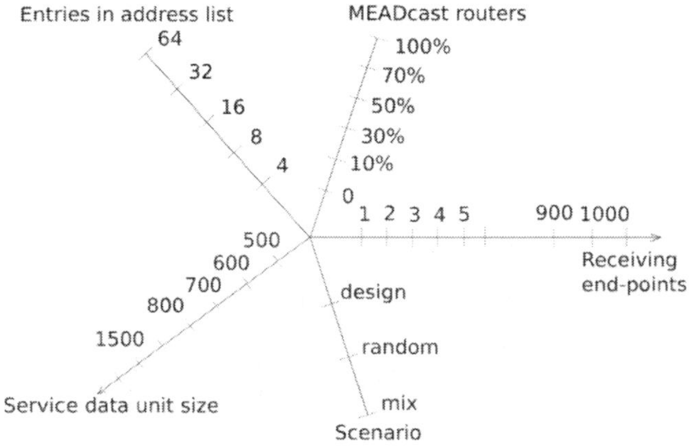

Figure 4. Parameters for experiments.

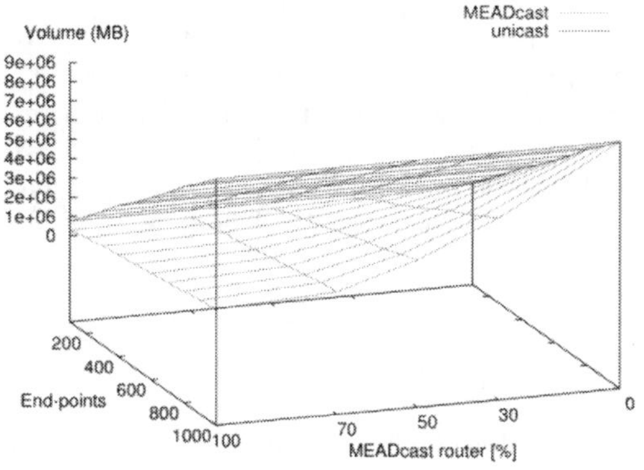

Figure 5. Total data volume of unicast and MEADcast.

7) for unicast message, R_0, R_1 simply forward it to the intended receiver.
8) R_0 receives the *MEADcast data message*, which it does not understand. It forwards the message further to the E_3 direction. R_0 does not drop the message since the option type identifier of MEADcast header is 00 [10].
9) R_2 receives a *MEADcast data message*, sees that it is responsible for E_3 and E_4. R_2 constructs two unicast messages with the data from the *MEADcast data message* and transmits each to E_3 and E_4.

IV. EVALUATION

We have performed experiments within the parameter space illustrated in Figure 4. We simulate MEADcast for 100 routers both on random network topologies with a diameter of 16 (generated by GT-ITM [11]) and on "designed", realistic topologies, using ns-2 [12]. Table I shows the total volume transmitted on all links in the network when the sender transmits a stream of 800 MB of data into the network with 500 and 1000 receiving end-points.

The number of receiving end-points and the number of MEADcast routers in the different scenarios are varied in the experiments. The impact of the service data unit size and the number of entries in the address list are discussed in Section V.

The volume gap of two approaches is plotted in Figure 5. The number of receiving end-points ranges in 100, 200...

TABLE I. TOTAL TRAFFIC VOLUME IN THE WHOLE NETWORK [MB].
* INDICATES DESIGNED TOPOLOGY.

Topology		*Unicast*	*MEADcast without discovery*	*Discovery (one time)*	*Traffic reduction [%]*
End-points	*MEADcast routers [%]*				
500	0	4,136,544	4,136,544	0.409	$(-0.x)$
	10(*)	4,136,544	1,279,936	0.813	69.1
	30	4,136,544	2,513,296	0.897	39.2
	50	4,136,544	1,698,336	1.216	58.9
	70	4,136,544	1,069,276	1.389	74.2
	100	4,136,544	902,056	2.835	78.2
1000	0	8,341,776	8,341,776	0.826	$(-0.x)$
	10(*)	8,341,776	2,525,904	1.640	69.7
	30	8,341,776	4,978,384	1.802	40.3
	50	8,341,776	3,137,972	2.462	62.4
	70	8,341,776	1,866,456	2.819	77.6
	100	8,341,776	1,552,304	5.727	81.4

to 1000.

If there is no MEADcast router, sender sends mainly unicast messages and periodically sends discovery messages which occupy only a little traffic volume over the whole network. This discovery overhead is indicated by the value "$-0.x$" in Table I and depends on how many times the discovery is performed. Hence, the traffic volume of MEADcast protocol when there is no MEADcast router is approximately that of unicast, provided that sender has large traffic to send. The gap increases when the number of receiving end-points and the percentage of MEADcast routers grow. The extreme case of 1000 end-points and 100% MEADcast routers shows the difference of 81.4% in total traffic volume.

The total traffic volume reduction is considerable in the presence of sufficient MEADcast routers, as shown by the designed cases. The link stress (the number of identical packets sent by a protocol over each underlying link in the network) [13] at the sender is reduced to an even higher degree.

V. DISCUSSION

The concepts of MEADcast require a higher degree of interaction between the network layer and its upper layers (transport and application), that merits discussion. While our simulation results indicate significant performance gains for a wide range of parameters, MEADcast scenarios may be limited by properties of the protocol or the applications using it, and routers may experience a higher control plane load. After discussing these points, we conclude with remarks on fault and security issues.

A. Relation to upper layers

Decomposition of MEADcast data packets may yield packets with different destination addresses and thus invalidate checksums in upper layer headers that include network addresses in the checksum (e.g., UDP for IPv6). For the new packet to be valid at the destination, MEADcast routers must re-compute these checksums for every new unicast packet and every new MEADcast packet with a different destination address. This issue is due to the re-use of network addresses in transport layer protocols, and problematic not only because of the increased load on routers' control plane but also because of the requirement to handle protocols other than IP.

Transport layer port numbers will differ at end-point sockets and have to be included in the MEADcast header along with the IP address of each end-point, thus creating an additional binding to the transport layer.

Network service primitives do not support addressing multiple recipients. Therefore, applications and higher protocols on the sender side must be modified to make use of MEADcast. A solution idea would be to use "regular" IGMP/IGMP6-based multicast on the first hop, thus allowing applications and higher protocols to employ multicast addressing as usual, then use a proxy function to translate between regular multicast and MEADcast before transmitting. While Path MTU discovery [14] is a standard function of the Internet, the application requirements on payload size are not readily available to allow the computation of optimum header size. We envision an interface to the network layer allowing the application to issue *hints* with respect to its intended use of the network.

We emphasize that these modifications are required for the sender only. The providers of asymmetric applications (IP-TV, Internet radio etc.) can be assumed to correctly gauge the cost and benefit of introducing modifications to consolidate the multitude of unicast flows they create presently.

B. Limitations

Inherent limitations of the approach include the maximum number of entries in the address table, the overhead introduced by the address table, the time required to establish multicast structures and load introduced in the control plane of routers.

MEADcast routers do not keep group information, thus rendering MEADcast processing stateless, while nevertheless complex in contrast to multiple flows, that may be handled by accelerators such as FPGAs.

MEADcast performs a gradual transition from a number of unicast packet flows to a (smaller) number of multicast flows as the availability of MEADcast-capable routers is discovered. Sessions that are shorter than the time for discovery not only forego the benefit of multicast but also carry the additional load for discovery; they are an application for unicast.

Given a path MTU value, the number of entries in the address table determines the remaining space for payload. If the service data units received from the upper layer is small, the sender may enlarge the number of entries, however, for large number of end-points even small payloads will require the sender to issue multiple multicast packets. Figure 6 shows the critical points where data volume is increased when the address table space of 32 entries is exhausted by one router multicasting to an increasing number of end-points. Conversely, a large address table leaves less space for payload and may lead to fragmentation, as illustrated in Figure 7.

C. Fault and security considerations

Packet loss naturally incurs a larger penalty for MEADcast than unicast, as more receivers are affected. In particular, the failure of a MEADcast path by changes in routing (by administrative action or by faults) will lead to continuous loss of packets until the periodic discovery mechanism informs the sender of the change in the network topology. A higher discovery frequency might lessen the consequences at the expense of increased control plane load in routers and an increase in the number of (albeit small) packets transmitted over a path.

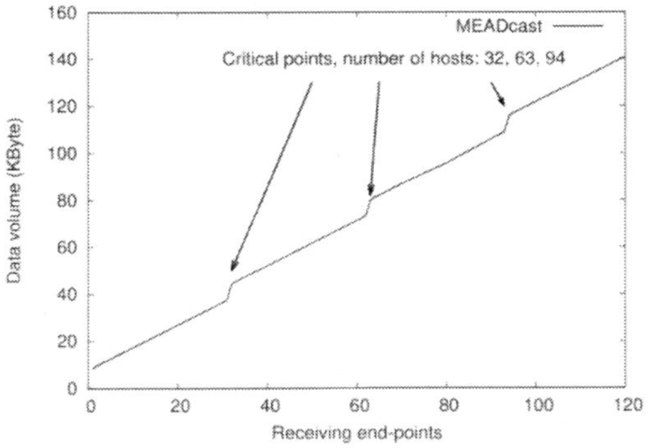

Figure 6. Total volume increased by exhausted address table.

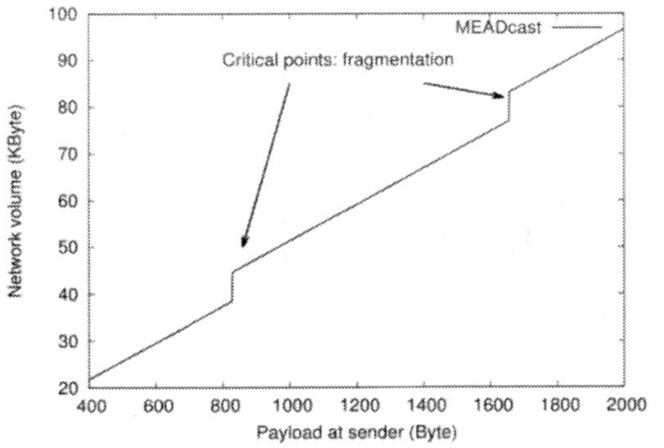

Figure 7. Fragmentation impact on total volume (1 router, 31 end-points).

Beyond the security issues noted for Xcast (see [6]), that also employs sender-based multicast, we note that the deprecation [15] of the Type 0 Routing Header in IPv6 to prevent amplification attacks suggests careful scrutiny of any mechanism, that causes Internet routers to transmit more packets than they receive. We presume our mechanism to be reasonably safe due to the following properties: *i)* the total volume of transmitted multicast data does not exceed the corresponding unicast volume for the same data, with the exception of the signalling required for fallback to unicast, *ii)* addresses are not modified by routers, i.e., data is transmitted via the same path in both unicast and multicast modes.

VI. CONCLUSION

The MEADcast protocol introduced in this paper creates a separation of concerns between the stateful sender, stateless routers and agnostic end-points. While avoiding the need of network-side group management and the transmission of address tables to end-points, multicast is automatically employed when possible, falling back on unicast, when not. MEADcast yields in our simulations a significant factor of reduction of the traffic volume of an application session compared to the same session in pure unicast, in network topologies with a sufficient number of supporting routers.

Our discussion indicates several open questions and avenues for development, including the study of the load increase in router control planes and the real-world evaluation of streaming applications based on a module implementation for the Linux kernel and the development of an interface for the management of multicast groups and parameters on the sender side. A different point of interest is the realisation of MEADcast with virtual network functions, to be used in and between Software Defined Networks (SDN).

ACKNOWLEDGMENT

The authors wish to thank the members of the Munich Network Management (www.mnm-team.org), directed by Prof. Dr. Dieter Kranzlmüller and the anonymous reviewers for valuable comments on previous versions of this paper.

REFERENCES

[1] S. Deering, "Host extensions for IP multicasting," RFC 1112 (INTERNET STANDARD), Internet Engineering Task Force, Aug. 1989, updated by RFC 2236, [retrieved: June, 2018]. [Online]. Available: http://www.ietf.org/rfc/rfc1112.txt

[2] B. Cain, S. Deering, I. Kouvelas, B. Fenner, and A. Thyagarajan, "Internet Group Management Protocol, Version 3," RFC 3376 (Proposed Standard), Internet Engineering Task Force, Oct. 2002, updated by RFC 4604, [retrieved: June, 2018]. [Online]. Available: http://www.ietf.org/rfc/rfc3376.txt

[3] H. Holbrook, B. Cain, and B. Haberman, "Using Internet Group Management Protocol Version 3 (IGMPv3) and Multicast Listener Discovery Protocol Version 2 (MLDv2) for Source-Specific Multicast," RFC 4604 (Proposed Standard), Internet Engineering Task Force, Aug. 2006, [retrieved: June, 2018]. [Online]. Available: http://www.ietf.org/rfc/rfc4604.txt

[4] S. Banerjee, B. Bhattacharjee, and C. Kommareddy, Scalable application layer multicast. ACM, 2002, vol. 32, no. 4.

[5] D. A. Tran, K. A. Hua, and T. T. Do, "A peer-to-peer architecture for media streaming," IEEE journal on Selected Areas in Communications, vol. 22, no. 1, 2004, pp. 121–133.

[6] R. Boivie, N. Feldman, Y. Imai, W. Livens, and D. Ooms, "Explicit Multicast (Xcast) Concepts and Options," RFC 5058 (Experimental), Internet Engineering Task Force, Nov. 2007, [retrieved: June, 2018]. [Online]. Available: http://www.ietf.org/rfc/rfc5058.txt

[7] W. Fenner, "Internet Group Management Protocol, Version 2," RFC 2236 (Proposed Standard), Internet Engineering Task Force, Nov. 1997, updated by RFC 3376, [retrieved: June, 2018]. [Online]. Available: http://www.ietf.org/rfc/rfc2236.txt

[8] C. Diot, B. N. Levine, B. Lyles, H. Kassem, and D. Balensiefen, "Deployment issues for the ip multicast service and architecture," IEEE network, vol. 14, no. 1, 2000, pp. 78–88.

[9] M. Hosseini, D. T. Ahmed, S. Shirmohammadi, and N. D. Georganas, "A survey of application-layer multicast protocols," IEEE Communications Surveys & Tutorials, vol. 9, no. 3, 2007, pp. 58–74.

[10] R. Hinden, "Internet protocol, version 6 (ipv6) specification," no. 8200, Jul. 2017, [retrieved: June, 2018]. [Online]. Available: http://www.ietf.org/rfc/rfc8200.txt

[11] E. W. Zegura, K. L. Calvert, and S. Bhattacharjee, "How to model an internetwork," in INFOCOM'96. Fifteenth Annual Joint Conference of the IEEE Computer Societies. Networking the Next Generation. Proceedings IEEE, vol. 2. IEEE, 1996, pp. 594–602.

[12] "The network simulator - ns-2," [retrieved: June, 2018]. [Online]. Available: https://www.isi.edu/nsnam/ns/

[13] Y.-h. Chu, S. G. Rao, S. Seshan, and H. Zhang, "A case for end system multicast," IEEE Journal on selected areas in communications, vol. 20, no. 8, 2002, pp. 1456–1471.

[14] J. McCann, S. Deering, J. Mogul, and R. Hinden, "Path mtu discovery for ip version 6," no. 8201, Jul. 2017, [retrieved: June, 2018]. [Online]. Available: http://www.ietf.org/rfc/rfc8201.txt

[15] J. Abley, P. Savola, and G. Neville-Neil, "Deprecation of Type 0 Routing Headers in IPv6," RFC 5095 (Proposed Standard), Internet Engineering Task Force, Dec. 2007, [retrieved: June, 2018]. [Online]. Available: http://www.ietf.org/rfc/rfc5095.txt

Understanding Power Measurement Capabilities on Zaius Power9

Bo Li
Virginia Tech
Blacksburg, Virginia, USA
Email: bxl4074@vt.edu

Edgar A. León
Lawrence Livermore National Laboratory
Livermore, California, USA
Email: leon@llnl.gov

Kirk W. Cameron
Virginia Tech
Blacksburg, Virginia, USA
Email: cameron@cs.vt.edu

***Abstract*—Power and energy are first-class operating concerns for data centers, emerging supercomputers, and future exascale machines. The power and energy measurement capabilities in emerging systems is critical to understand and optimize power usage according to application characteristics. In this work, we describe our evaluation of the power monitoring capabilities of the Zaius Power9 server. We highlight existing limitations of this system and report on the available power domains, measurement granularity, and sampling rate. We provide empirical power profiles that stress the memory system and the compute capabilities. Furthermore, we demonstrate high-level insights of a scientific proxy-application through its power consumption. Our goal is to provide an empirical study for the benefit of developers and researchers planning on utilizing the power capabilities of this state-of-the-art architecture.**

***Index Terms*—Power measurement; HPC; Zaius; Power9.**

I. Introduction

Power and energy are becoming first-class operating concerns for emerging supercomputers and future exascale machines. The implications of power and energy concerns for supercomputers have a broad impact ranging from managing power by utility companies to pursuing optimizations for power and energy consumption, in addition to performance, by system and application developers. One set of optimizations may include shifting power from hardware components not in the critical path to those components in the critical path of an application. Therefore, the power and energy measurement capabilities in emerging systems is critical to understand and optimize power usage according to application characteristics.

On the path to exascale computing, the U.S. Department of Energy will field two new supercomputers in 2018 featuring IBM Power9 processors, NVIDIA Volta GPUs, and the InfiniBand interconnect. For example, *Sierra*, hosted at Lawrence Livermore National Laboratory (LLNL), is expected to provide 125 petaflops within a 12 megawatt power budget. While it is possible to rely on third party solutions to monitor and profile power consumption [1]–[3], the Power9 processors enable fine-grained power measurements through an on-chip controller. In this paper, we describe our experience with power monitoring on the Zaius Power9 server. While the Zaius server targets data centers, we expect the lessons learned from this study to be useful in future power studies on supercomputers like Sierra.

The paper is organized as follows. First, Section II introduces the power measurement capabilities of interest available on the Power9 processor. Section III describes the experimental setup including the testbed platform. Then, Section IV establishes a performance baseline using several micro-benchmarks. This is followed by Section V, where we present a set of experiments to understand power consumption and its limitations focusing on two use cases: the cache hierarchy and the behavior of an application. Finally, Section VI summarizes our findings and describes future work.

II. Power Monitoring Overview

The IBM Power9 processor embeds an On-Chip Controller (OCC) to monitor system information such as the power consumption of CPU, memory, and GPUs as well as thermal data [4]. The OCC works with other components including the Autonomic Management of Energy Component (AMEC), the Analog Power Subsystem Sweep (APSS), and the Baseboard Management Controller (BMC) to read system data and to control system settings. For example, the power of system can be capped in which case the OCC monitors the power sensors and throttles the CPU and memory subsystem accordingly.

There are two ways to monitor power consumption: in-band and out-of-band [5], [6]. The out-of-band method collects the power data without the intervention of the main processor. The BMC can communicate with the OCC to get the power and sensors data, which is collected periodically by the OCC. This method allows the profiling of power consumption of a host from another system connected on the same network. Some example sensors collected by the OCC include the power consumption of each processor, the temperature of each core, the temperature of each memory DIMM, and the power consumption of GPUs.

While the out-of-band method requires the support of several hardware components including the BMC, the in-band method only relies on sampling the OCC. The OCC driver periodically copies the sensor data to main memory and makes it accessible as *hwmon* sensors. Most modern systems have sensor chips on the motherboard to support the monitor of system status (e.g., temperature, fan speed, and voltage) and use the hwmon kernel module to interact with those sensors. The OCC takes 8 ms to update a block of sensors to main memory and up to 80 ms to update all of the available sensors. For example, the OCC takes 8 ms to read processor core data and 64 ms to read DIMM memory data. One can use *lm_sensors* [7] to access these sensors. In this work, we use lm_sensors because it works with the hwmon kernel module to read hardware sensor data from user space.

III. Experimental Setup

In this work, we investigate the power measurement capabilities of the Zaius Power9 server. We conducted experiments to investigate the power measurement interfaces; characterize performance (i.e., computation, memory bandwidth, and memory latency) and power consumption using benchmarks; and demonstrate how one may apply these monitoring capabilities to a proxy application from the U.S. Department of Energy.

A. Testbed platform

Our testbed includes a Zaius Power9 server designed by Rackspace. The server has two Power9 LaGrange processors with 12 SMT-4 cores each and a total of 96 hardware threads. There are 73 different CPU clock frequencies ranging from 2.0 to 3.2 GHz. Each core has 32 KB L1 cache (data and instruction), 512 KB shared L2 cache, and 10 MB shared L3 cache. The server has 128 GB of DDR4 memory.

We use the in-band method to measure power because the Zaius board lacks an APSS. Some important features that rely on the APSS include out-of-band power profiling, setting a power cap, and measuring DRAM power.

In this work, all the power measurements were collected in-band. To avoid application interference by the power monitoring thread, we bind this thread to one of the processors and the application tasks to the other processor (there are two processors). While we could simply dedicate a core for the monitoring thread, we want to avoid any interference that could result by using the shared memory bus. In future work, we will assess this other configuration and quantify the associated overheads. The monitoring thread, thus, measures the power consumption of the second processor where the application runs.

We also measured the overhead of polling the in-band power sensors. It takes about 17 ms for each query, which means the highest sampling rate of in-band power measurement is 17 ms.

B. Benchmarks and Mini-Applications

LMBench [8] is a benchmark suite used for analyzing memory speed. We employ STREAM and LAT_MEM_RD in LMBench to measure memory bandwidth and latency, respectively. We use the OpenMP version of STREAM and the single-thread version of LAT_MEM_RD.

LULESH [9], the Livermore Unstructured Lagrange Explicit Shock Hydrodynamics mini-application, provides a simplified source code that contains the data access patterns and computational characteristics of larger hydrodynamics codes at LLNL. It uses an unstructured hexahedral mesh with two centerings and solves the Sedov problem. Because of its smaller size, LULESH allows for easier and faster performance tuning experiments on various architectures.

DGEMM from the APEX benchmark suite [10] is a simple double-precision dense-matrix multiplication code. We use it to capture floating-point computational rate.

IV. Performance Characterization

STREAM measures memory throughput and represents the practical peak bandwidth of the memory system. The performance of STREAM is dependent on a number of parameters including CPU clock frequency and the number of threads. Figure 1 shows the impact of thread concurrency and CPU frequency. In Figure 1a, we measured the throughput of STREAM-ADD (performs add operations on memory arrays) as a function of thread concurrency for two CPU frequencies. The results show that, for both CPU frequencies, STREAM obtains the highest throughput, i.e., 126 GB/s, by running with 12 threads. As we further increase the thread count, the throughput gets worse due to memory resource contention. Figure 1b shows that CPU clock frequency has a small impact on memory throughput regardless of the concurrency level.

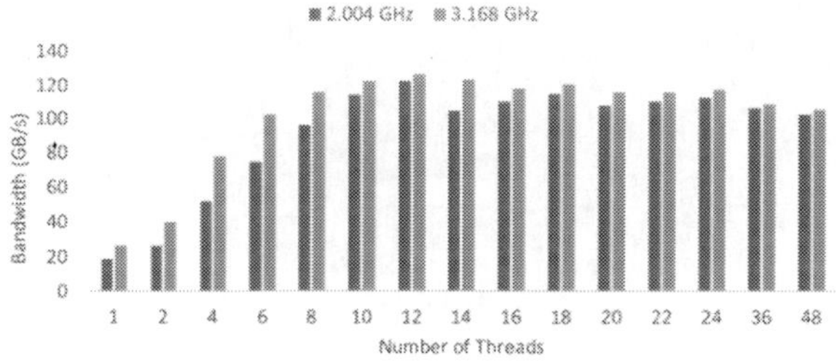

(a) STREAM-ADD under various thread concurrencies.

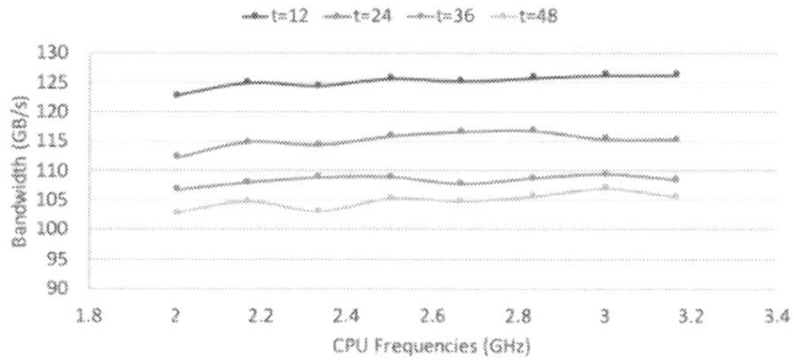

(b) STREAM-ADD under various CPU frequencies.

Figure 1. Memory bandwidth under different configurations.

LAT_MEM_RD captures memory latency by measuring the time it takes to access data residing in different levels of memory. It controls the memory level to access by varying the size of the input array and stride. Input arrays of small size fit into cache resulting in faster access latency. Main memory accesses occur when the array size is too large to fit in cache. By measuring the time to access different array sizes, LAT_MEM_RD shows the empirical latency of L1, L2, L3, and main memory.

Figure 2 illustrates the latency (in nanoseconds) of accessing the different caches and main memory. Figure 2a shows memory latency for multiple CPU frequencies. As CPU frequency affects how much time one CPU cycle takes, higher CPU frequency leads to lower latency. Focusing on a single CPU frequency, we observe that there are four groups of latency (*steps*) corresponding to the L1, L2, L3, and main memory. We used an array size of 8 GB, to ensure main memory accesses, and a stride size of 128 bytes, to match the cache line size of the Power9 processor.

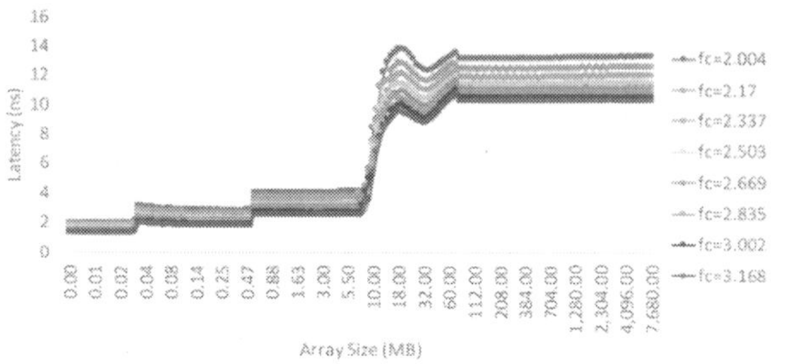

(a) Memory latency under different CPU frequencies (f_c). Array size is 8 GB and stride size is 128 bytes.

(b) Memory latency under different stride sizes. CPU frequency is 2.004 GHz and array size is 500 MB.

Figure 2. Impact on hierarchical memory latency.

Figure 2b illustrates the impact of stride size on latency. When the stride size is small, one cache line can potentially satisfy multiple data requests, thus the overall latency of multiple data accesses is lower. When the stride size is large enough, data load requests may cause more cache misses, thus the overall data access latency is higher.

V. UNDERSTANDING POWER CONSUMPTION

We rely on the OCC to measure power consumption at runtime. The granularity of power measurement is at the processor (socket) level. Since the Zaius system does not have an APSS, we can only measure core power (Vdd) and nest power (Vdn). Nest power mainly includes the on-chip interconnect and the memory controller. To account for the remaining processor power (cache, I/O, etc.), a fixed value is added to Vdd and Vdn to estimate total processor power (C):

$$Processor\_power = Vdn + Vdd + 35Watts \quad (1)$$

The fixed 35 Watts value is defined in the Machine Readable Workbook (MRW), an XML description of the machine specified by the system administrator. In addition, without an APSS power draw of main memory or GPUs are not easily accessible.

We use lm_sensors to query instant power consumption in user space. We make direct system calls to read the power sensors and get the power data back as standard output. By issuing the lm_sensors call multiple times and averaging its elapsed time, we obtained the overhead of querying sensor data: about 17 milliseconds. We wrapped the system call with a sleep timer, which can be used to change the power sampling rate. For example, if we set the sleep timer to be 100 ms, the sample rate of power profiling will be 117 ms/sample. If we set the timer to be 0 ms, we can get the highest sample rate: 17 ms/sample. If not explicitly stated, we set the sleep timer to 100 ms.

First, we profile the power consumption of DGEMM, a compute intensive benchmark, and STREAM, a memory intensive benchmark. Their power profiles are shown in Figure 3. There are two processors on our test system. As mentioned before, we bind the power monitoring process to the first processor and run the codes on the second processor to avoid application interference by the monitoring process. As shown in Figure 3, when the benchmarks start to execute the core power, Vdd, increases significantly. Interestingly, even though STREAM is memory intense, the peak core power consumption is the same as DGEMM. STREAM, however, stresses other components. For example, the nest power, Vdn, is higher and shows more dynamic variation than DGEMM. This is because the memory controller is part of Vdn. If we could measure the power consumption of main memory, we would expect to see pronounced differences between DGEMM and STREAM.

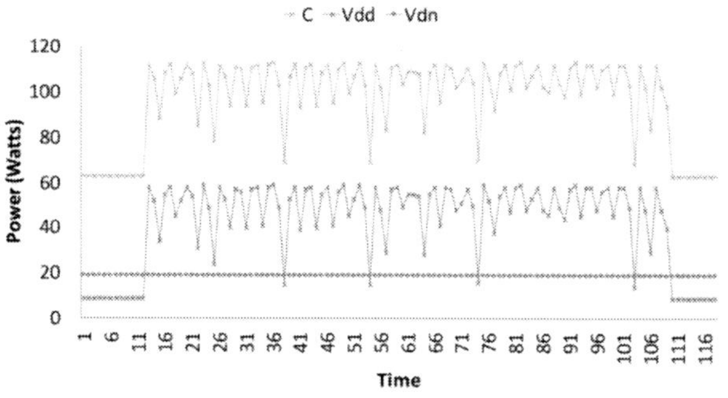

(a) DGEMM.

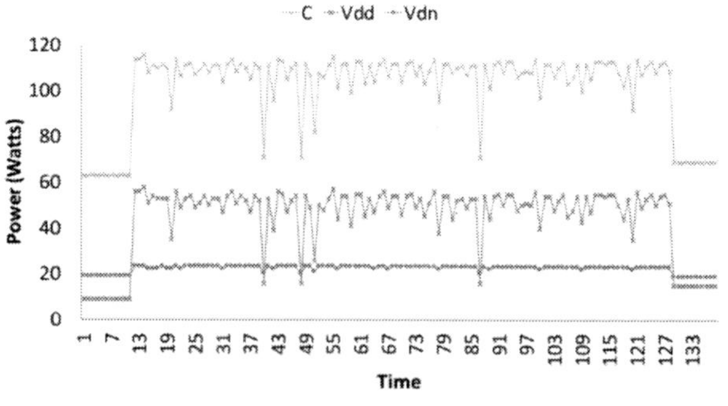

(b) STREAM.

Figure 3. Power profile of compute-intense and memory-intense benchmarks.

We also observed low points in Vdd power. This could be the result of several factors. For example, the processor has to wait for data from main memory. An idle processor consumes significantly less power than a busy processor. Other factors reducing the computational intensity of the code would affect the power consumption of the processor. Finally, we note that the total power consumption of the processor, C, follows the same pattern as Vdd because of the constant factor shown in (1) and the small or null variations in Vdn power.

A. Cache Hierarchy Power Draw

The relationship between power and memory access patterns is important for power and energy efficiency. Figure 4 shows the power profile of LAT_MEM_RD, which accesses the different levels of the memory hierarchy as a function of time. In order to stress the power consumption when the code accesses the levels of memory, we ran ten instances of LAT_MEM_RD concurrently. As the figure shows, as the benchmark accesses progress from L1 to L3, the core power consumption, Vdd, decreases. This is because load operations become slower (see Figure 2) and the code becomes less compute bound. When the application starts to access main memory, the core power continues to decrease while the nest power increases, as we would expect.

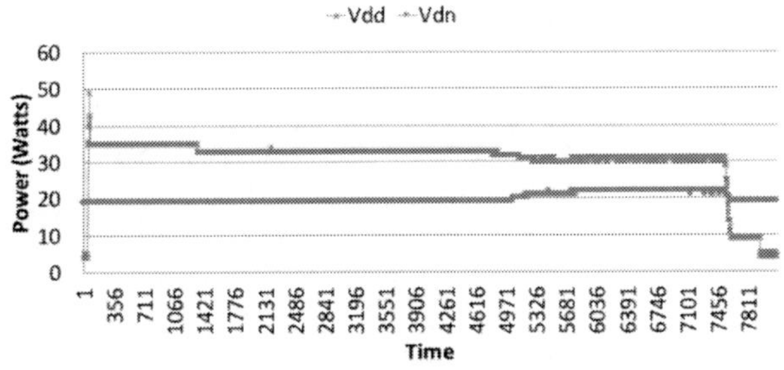

Figure 4. Power profile of the memory hierarchy.

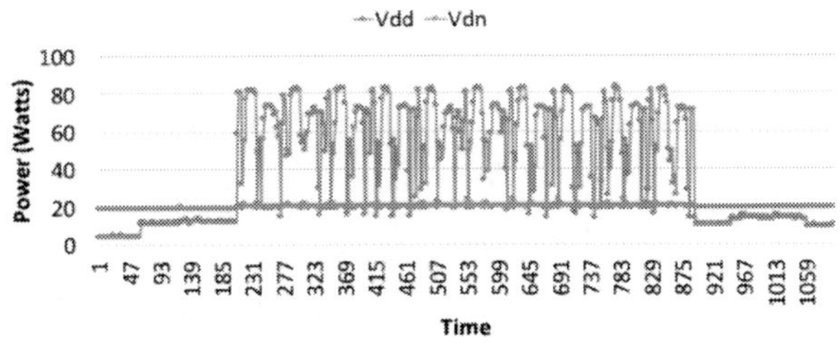

Figure 5. Power profile of LULESH.

B. Application Behavior and Power Draw

The capability of profiling power consumption for scientific applications is important for gaining insights into their behavior and identifying optimization areas [5], [9]. Figure 5 shows the power profile of LULESH with the following parameters: 48 OpenMP threads, 10 iterations, and 240 input elements. In order to capture finer power characteristics, we set the power sampling rate to the highest, i.e., 17 ms. From the power profile, we can identify 10 curves with similar patterns. They map to the 10 iterations of LULESH that do the similar computations. Within each iteration, we observe dynamic variations in core power consumption due to the different code phases of LULESH within an iteration, some of which are compute bound and others memory bound [9].

The core power profile, Vdd, also shows that the initialization and completion stages have significant lower power consumption due to the less intensive compute and memory workload. In future work, we may instrument the application to perform function-level power profiling.

VI. Summary and Future Work

In this work, we evaluated the power monitoring capabilities of a state-of-the-art Zaius Power9 server. The Power9 processor is an important architecture in both data centers and high-performance computing markets. Although there are many sensors to monitor power and energy in the Power9 processor, we were limited to only three power domains because of the lack of certain components on the Zaius board such as the APSS. Additionally, in-band power monitoring was our only option and with this a 17ms sampling rate, which may be too coarse to analyze small code fragments within an application. Despite these limitations, we were able to characterize the performance and power of this system under different configurations using a number of benchmarks to stress the compute and memory capabilities. We observed that the core power dominates the behavior of the total processor power because of a constant factor used in its calculation. Also, changes in nest power are subtle even when exercising the cache hierarchy. The power profile of LULESH represented the iterative nature of the code, as well as changes in phases based on their memory and compute utilization.

In future work, we plan to evaluate policies to shift power between the processor, memory, and the GPUs. To this end, we will investigate other ways to communicate with the OCC on the Zaius board to get access to the power of the memory system and other sensors of interest.

Acknowledgment

We thank Adi Gangidi from Rackspace and Martha Broyles, Chris Cain, and Todd Rosedahl from IBM for their support and assistance. Prepared by LLNL under Contract DE-AC52-07NA27344. LLNL-CONF-748981.

References

[1] J. H. Laros, P. Pokorny, and D. DeBonis, "PowerInsight – a commodity power measurement capability," in *International Green Computing Conference*, June 2013.

[2] B. Li, H. C. Chang, S. Song, C. Y. Su, T. Meyer, J. Mooring, and K. W. Cameron, "The power-performance tradeoffs of the Intel Xeon Phi on HPC applications," in *IEEE International Parallel Distributed Processing Symposium Workshops*, May 2014.

[3] R. Ge, X. Feng, S. Song, H. C. Chang, D. Li, and K. W. Cameron, "PowerPack: Energy profiling and analysis of high-performance systems and applications," *IEEE Transactions on Parallel and Distributed Systems*, vol. 21, no. 5, pp. 658–671, May 2010.

[4] T. Rosedahl, M. Broyles, C. Lefurgy, B. Christensen, and W. Feng, "Power/performance controlling techniques in OpenPOWER," in *High Performance Computing*. Springer International Publishing, 2017, pp. 275–289.

[5] R. E. Grant, J. H. Laros, M. J. Levenhagen, S. L. Olivier, K. Pedretti, H. L. Ward, and A. J. Younge, "Evaluating energy and power profiling techniques for HPC workloads," in *International Green and Sustainable Computing Conference*, Oct. 2017.

[6] R. E. Grant, M. Levenhagen, S. L. Olivier, D. DeBonis, K. T. Pedretti, and J. H. L. III, "Standardizing power monitoring and control at exascale," *IEEE Computer*, vol. 49, no. 10, pp. 38–46, Oct. 2016.

[7] (2018, May) The lm-sensors package. [Online]. Available: https://github.com/groeck/lm-sensors

[8] L. W. McVoy and C. Staelin, "lmbench: Portable tools for performance analysis," in *USENIX annual technical conference*, 1996, pp. 279–294.

[9] E. A. León, I. Karlin, and R. E. Grant, "Optimizing explicit hydrodynamics for power, energy, and performance," in *International Conference on Cluster Computing*, ser. Cluster'15. Chicago, IL: IEEE, Sep. 2015.

[10] (2018, Jan.) APEX benchmarks. [Online]. Available: http://www.nersc.gov/research-and-development/apex/apex-benchmarks

Data-monitoring Visualizer for Software Defined Networks

Luz Angela Aristizábal
Dept. Informatics and Computation
National University of Colombia
Manizales, Colombia
e-mail: laaristizabalq@unal.edu.co

Nicolás Toro.
Dept. Electrical, Electronics and Computation
National University of Colombia
Manizales, Colombia
e-mail: ntorog@unal.edu.co

Abstract— **Monitoring the behavior of a data network is a starting point for its analysis, and must be a constant activity that allows operators and administrators to quickly notice changes in the network. A view of the topology associated with the network traffic could speed the response to possible network failures. The study's principal contribution involves using graph signal processing theory as method to structure a signal composed of statistical data provided by the software defined network switches and establishing correspondence between the statistical traffic patterns with color.**

Keywords- Monitoring; Graph Signal Processing, Software Defined Network.

I. INTRODUCTION

The network monitors usually use lines, bars, pie charts, and area charts to show network traffic [1]. The analysis of this information takes time. It is necessary to reduce the time invested in the information monitoring analysis, by creating methods that allow for visualization of the traffic information correlation with network topology.

The goal of this investigation is to implement a mechanism that facilitates the visual detection of congestion for network managers. The proposed strategy makes use of two current technologies: Graph Signal Processing (GSP) and Software Defined Networks (SDN).

GSP is a new area of study in Digital Signal Processing that provides us with conceptual and practical tools to model complex networks and graphically show their evolution. The advantage of applying GSP in data network analysis is the possibility to relate network topology with its behavior throughout time. [2]. This form of network behavior visualization allows for timely detection of congestion levels and abrupt changes that can be consequences of failures.

With the emergence of SDN in 2008, a new prospect for the implementation of network monitors was visualized. In its operation model, each switch connected to a controller includes the generation of statistics associated with data flows circulating through its ports. This makes it possible to obtain the switches activity statistics, taken at regular intervals, which allows us to generate signals that feed the network graph model [3][4].

The principal contribution of this investigation is to show how SDN activity can be modeled with GSP theory and how one may implement an application that takes advantage of the statistical information that an SDN's nodes calculate in run-time, in order to construct a signal that characterizes network traffic.

This paper is divided in three sections: Section 1 describes the conceptual aspects of GSP and SDN involved in the development of this study. Section 2 presents the method utilized in order to graphically show the network topology associated with traffic information taken from the statistics sent by SND switches to the controller. Section 3 specifies the results analysis, and finally, the conclusions.

II. SOFTWARE DEFINED NETWORK AND GRAPH SIGNAL PROCESSING

This section will present the relevant concepts involve in the application development.

A. *Software defined networking*

SDN consists of three element types: switches, controllers, and a secure communication channel that communicates the controller with the switches. Communication between devices uses Openflow messages [5][6], as is shown in Figure 1.

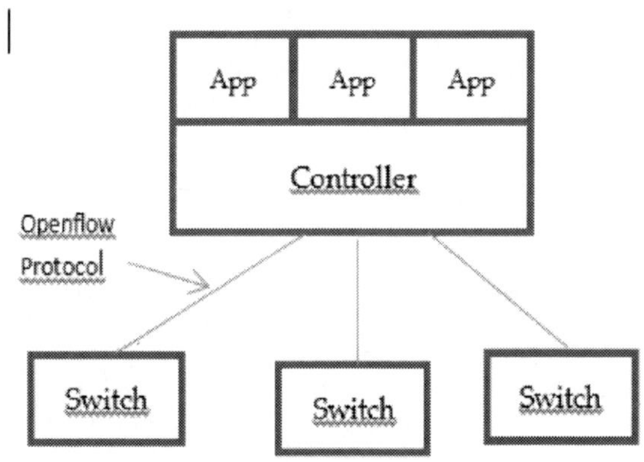

Figure 1. Structure of a Software Defined Network.

The controller periodically sends the *Statistic request* message to the switch, which answers with the message *Statistics reply* that includes: transmitted and received bytes, transmitted and received packets, and transmitted and received errors and collisions.

With this information, it is possible to form the data sequences that will constitute the network traffic signal in a specific time interval.

B. Graph Signal Processing (GSP)

A data network can be represented by a graph: G=(V,A), where V is the set of nodes, $V=\{v_0,v_1,.....v_{N-1}\}$ and A is the adjacency matrix, N number of nodes . Each v_i is a node that is connected with a v_j node. A(i,j) determines the existence of a directed edge from v_i to v_j.

For an SDN, V is the set formed by network devices, such as: switch, server, and host. A(i,j) represents a connection between the nodes or devices *i* and *j* . See Figure 2.

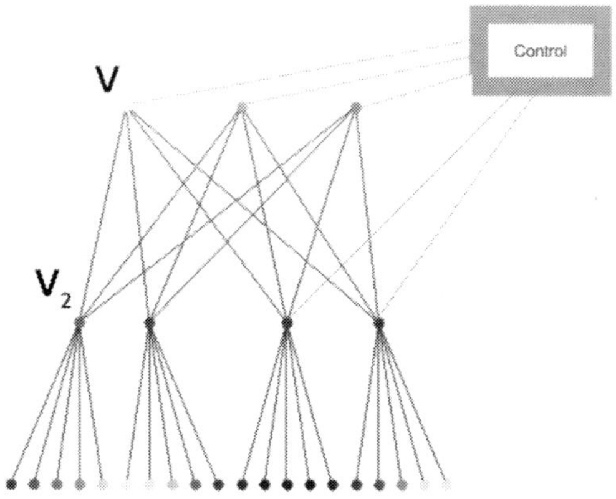

Figure 2. Data network graph.

In this case, A(1,2) has a value of one, indicating that there is a connection that relates node v_1 with node v_2.

III. DATA-MONITORING VISUALIZER

In this section, the actions taken to achieve the following two objectives will be explained:

- Associate the results of a monitoring process with network topology.
- Generate a graph structure that allows for visualization of the changes in network traffic during a time interval.

Initially, the statistics sent by the SDN switches to the controller were taken as response to the "*Statistic request*" message. With this information, a structure was formed, which contained those bytes transmitted and received by each of the devices connected to the network switches. The aim was to form an *S* signal with *T* length, which contained the information received by the controller regarding various time instances (1).

$$S_j = \{s_1, s_2, ...s_T\}$$
$$1 <= t <= T \qquad (1)$$
$$1 <= j <= N$$

Each s_t represents the transmitted bytes in a *t* time for device v_j (N is the number of network devices). The entire network visualization process is generated with value s_t for each S_j. This is:

$$MV_t = \{G(V, NS_t, A)\} \qquad (2)$$
$$0 <= t <= T$$

Where MV_t is the visualization of the entire network at time t (2), V is the set of network devices, NS_t is the signal formed by the bytes transmitted from all network devices in instant t, and A is the adjacent matrix. The algorithm implemented is shown in Figure 3.

1. From the topology of the network, generate graph
   G(V,A)
2. Read the statistics from the software defined network during time T.
3. Associate each device or network node with the signal Sj
4. For t=0:Δt:T
   for j=1:N
   NS(t,j)=V(j).s(t)
   End
   MV(t)=G(V,NS(t),A)
   end

Figure 3. Algorithm for graph generation with traffic signal.

And finally, how does color correspond to network traffic states? What color represents a congested node? What color represents a node with low traffic? Color relationships are shown in Figure 4.

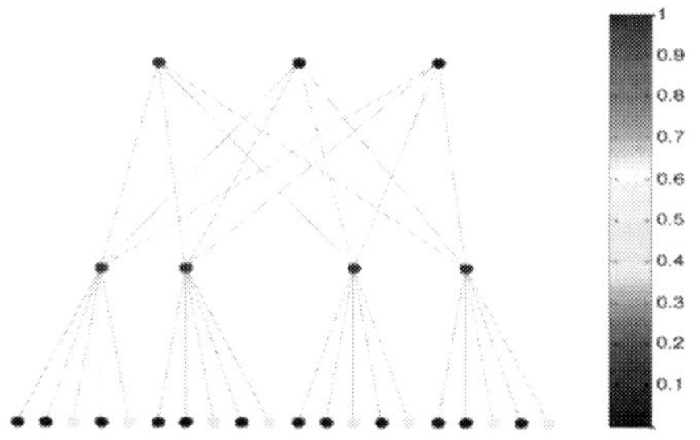

Figure 4. Correspondence between network traffic and color.

Red indicates that the node is congested, blue indicates that the node has low traffic. Thus, the lower nodes, that in the figure are green, have a moderate level of traffic.

IV. RESULTS

How was the monitoring result associated with network topology? How was it made graphically tangible? It was necessary to implement three processes:

- SDN was implemented in mininet, using a Ryu controller. The topology implemented is shown in Figure 4, in which the two first levels are openflow switches and the third level contained hosts. In order to illustrate the advantages of the proposal described in this document, some hosts don't have information flow, and others use *Iperf.* Figure 4 shows the effects of these traffic differences. The inactive hosts are blue, and the *Iperf* hosts are green.

- The statistical data was taken each 30 ms. and saved in a file. With this information the traffic signal associated with the topology was created This signal determines the color for each node in the visualization.
- The network topology was created using the matlab GSP toolbox. The statistics file was taken, and the Figure 3 algorithm was implemented. Its execution allowed viewing of color changes associated with network traffic. Figure 5 shows some of the graphs generated by the application at different moments in time.

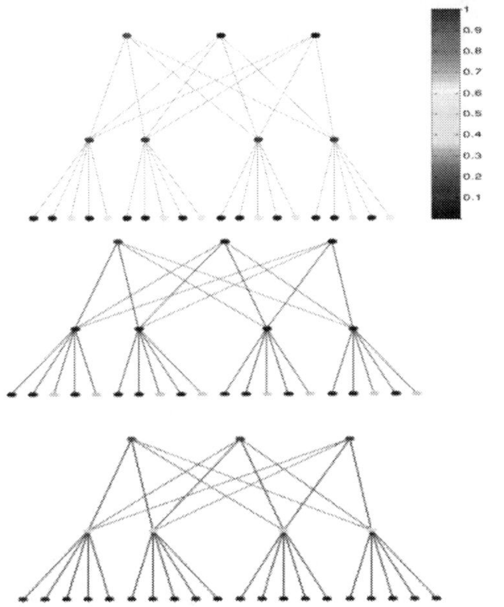

Figure 5. Three SDN colored topology frames.

In the superior graph in Figure 5,observe that the hosts are green. This indicates greater activity than those hosts which are blue, and the distribution switches have greater activity than the core switches. In the graph below, the activity is shifted from the lower nodes, the computers, to the distribution switches, and from these to the core switches.

V. CONCLUSIONS

The network must be analyzed as a dynamic system, with monitoring applications that consider time to be an essential element associate of the entire network.

The software implemented allows for visualization of the network dynamics, in animation form, which shows the way in which it changes through time. This permitted agile detection of areas or nodes with atypical behavior. The most common ways to present monitoring information, using static graphics (line, bar, pie charts, area charts, etc.), requires considerable time investment on the part of the network operator to analyze these graphics, especially when it is necessary to find the cause of a failure. With such an application, a congestion failure can be detected by simply observing the animation.

This implementation motivates to continue the investigation, creating mechanisms that automatically analyze the network graphic signal and the implementation of algorithms for traffic distribution from SDN congested areas to nearby areas less congested.

REFERENCES

[1] SevOne "Software Defined Network Monitoring" [Online] Available from https://www.sevone.com/solutions/sdn_old. [accessed: 2018-02-20]

[2] D Shumman, S. Narang, P.Frossard, A. Ortega, and P. Vanderghesynst, "The Emerging Field of Signal Processing On Graphs: Extending High- Dimensional Data Analysis to Networks and Other Irregular Domains". IEEE Signal processing Magazine, May 2013, pp 83 – 98, doi: 10.1109/MSP.2012.2235192, ISSN: 1053-5888

[3] D. Luong, A. Outtagars, and A. Hebbar, "Traffic Monotoring in Software Defined Netwoks Using Opendaylight Controller" Lecture Notes in Computer Science. LNCS, Vol. 10026. Springer. Dec 2016, pp 38-48, doi: doi.org/10.1007/978-3-319-50463. ISBN: 978-3-319-50463-6

[4] L. Niels, M. van Adrichem, C. Doer, and F. Kuiper."OpenNetMon: Network Monitoring in Openflow Software-Defined Networks". Network Archictures and Services. Delft University of Technology. IEEE Xplore. July. 2014.doi: 10.1109/NOMS.2014.6838228, ISBN: 978-1-4799-0913-1

[5] M, Jammal, T. Singh, A. Shami, R.l Asal, and Y. Li, "Software defined networking: State of the art and research challenges," Computer Networks, vol. 72, Oct 2014, pp 74-98, doi:10.1016/j.comnet.2014.07.004

[6] OpenFundation. S. Bailey, Deepak Bansal, Linda Dunbar, Dave Hood, and Zoltán Lajos Kis, "SDN Architecture Overview", [Online] Available from: https://www.opennetworking.org/images/stories/downloads/sdn-resources/technical-reports/SDN-architecture-overview-1.0.pdf. [accessed: 2018-03-05]

[7] A. Sandryhaila and F. Moura, "Discret Signal Processing: on Graph". IEEE Transacion signal processing. Vol 61. No 7. April. 2013, pp 1644 -1656, doi: 10.1109/TSP.2013.2238935.

[8] N. Le Magoarou, J. Paratte, D. Shuman, V. Kalofolias, P. Vanderghesynst, and D. Hammond, "GSPBOX: A toolbox for Signal Processing on Graphs", ArXiv e-prints. Mar 2016, [Online] Available from: https://arxiv.org/abs/1408.5781v2

[9] A. Sandryhaila and F. Moura, "Discret Signal Processing: on Graph" Proceedings of the Sixth International Conference on Advances in Computer-Human Interactions (ACHI 2013) IARIA, Feb. 2013. Nice France, pp. 7-12, ISSN: 2308-4138, ISBN: 978-1-61208-250-9

Forecasting Transportation Project Frequency using Multivariate Regression with Elastic Net Regularization

Alireza Shojaei, Hashem Izadi Moud and Ian Flood
M. E. Rinker, Sr. School of Construction Management, University of Florida
Gainesville, Florida, USA.
Email: a.shojaei@ufl.edu, izadimoud@ufl.edu, flood@ufl.edu

***Abstract*—Knowledge of the number of upcoming projects and their impact on the company plays a significant role in strategic planning for project-based companies. The current horizon of planning for companies working on public projects are the latest advertised projects for bidding, which in many cases is reported less than a year in advance. This provides a very short-term horizon for strategic project portfolio planning. In this research, a multivariate regression model with elastic net regularization, using economic indices and other environmental factors, is built for Florida Department of Transportation (FDOT) projects to forecast the number of projects they will advertise in the future. The results show that, of the predictors considered, unemployment rate in the construction sector and the Brent oil price are the most significant variables in forecasting FDOT's future project frequency.**

Keywords-Multivariate Regression; Elastic Net Rugularization; Strategic Planning; Project Portfolio Management, Forecasting.

I. INTRODUCTION

Construction companies, as with many other companies working in project-based industries, such as IT, are usually managing multiple projects concurrently while looking for new projects to maintain their business. The task of managing current (ongoing) projects while obtaining projects for continuous business is called Project Portfolio Management (PPM). A crucial part of the management of a portfolio is to make sure that the company resources and on-going projects are optimally balanced to ensure that not only each project meets its objectives but also the whole organization meet its overall goals. Management needs to make sure that they maximize the utilization of their resources by minimizing idle time while not accepting more work than they can complete effectively.

The majority of the literature focuses on internal uncertainties that pertain to PPM. In other words, the most explored aspect of the uncertainties in PPM is the relationships between the projects within the portfolio and the interaction between the current ongoing projects and possible future projects to measure their compatibility in terms of resource demand, and other criteria. However, environmental factors, such as economic conditions and specific industry conditions (for instance, the number of workers in construction) can have a significant impact on the portfolio and company's overall performance. This study aims to integrate the environmental uncertainties and uncertainties regarding the unknown future projects, so that companies can apply this approach in their mid-term to long-term strategic planning. Martinsuo's [1] review of PPM frameworks showed that the uncertainty and continual changes in a company's portfolio has a significant negative correlation with its success. As a result, if users can reduce the extent of the uncertainties in their planning and have a more robust portfolio, it could greatly help their success. In summary, this paper proposes a regression model for forecasting frequency of FDOT's future projects, which helps the user to estimate the number and timing of tendered projects in the future. The novelty of this approach is the consideration of environmental uncertainties in the model and the provision of quantitative insights into the unknown future.

The rest of this paper is organized as follows. Section II describes the impact of uncertainty on PPM and how unknown future projects can impact strategic planning. Section III describes the modeling approach followed in this paper. Section IV addresses the regression model for forecasting the number of projects in the future. Section V presents the conclusions and identifies future directions for the research.

II. UNKNOWN FUTURE PROJECTS AND PORTFOLIO STRATEGIC PLANNING

Planning is vital to the success of any construction entity. In the public sector, governmental agencies try to forecast the needed equity in advance in order to successfully plan the number of their future projects. Historically, governmental agencies have had a short-sighted view towards predicting the future; mainly due to uncertainty in the size of the next year's budget. The process of planning the future is costly, slow and traditionally based on historic-data on past projects. This process is usually projected one year in advance as budgetary issues restrict the ability of governmental agencies to define the scope, number, and types of projects that are needed in later years. In the private sector, the process of defining future projects (in terms of scope, number and types) is better planned compared to the public sector. However, this planning process is still far from ideal.

In project management, the process of targeting goals for multiple projects in a portfolio of a company is referred to as PPM. PPM is defined as *"dealing with the coordination and control of multiple projects pursuing the same strategic goals and competing for the same resources, whereby managers prioritize among projects to achieve strategic benefit"* [2]. PPM deals with two significant tasks, which are complementary: (1) reinforcing investment decisions by helping companies to select projects that optimize their return on investment and risks associated with them as a whole [3]; and (2) optimizing the allocation of resources across different projects within portfolios in order to meet project goals and minimize risks [4]. The key to effective implementation of PPM within any construction entity is information. The unknown nature of the future is a primary factor that can undermine the success of the PPM process [5].

Uncertainty may influence the success of any organization in any discipline [6][7]. In project management, uncertainty is referred to as the degree of accuracy in determining future work processes, resource variation and work output [8]. The Project Management Institute (PMI) introduces risk management to the broader context of portfolio management. However, PMI does not provide many direct and specific guidelines, recommendations, plans or procedures on how to effectively manage future uncertainties at the portfolio level. Risk management at the portfolio level is restricted to naming only a few risk management techniques. PMI only suggests some vague guidelines on how to detect, monitor and handle uncertainties [5].

At the scientific level, managing uncertainties in projects has usually been handled by analyzing historical project data. Many methods and approaches have been used to collect and analyze historical data to find trends that might help understand how uncertainty impacts the success of projects and/or portfolios. Trippi et al. [9] suggest using Artificial Intelligence (AI) in portfolio management. Henriksen and Traynor [10] developed algorithms to allocate risks and other criteria in project selection and portfolio management. More advanced analysis methods, such as multi-agent modeling [11], multi-objective binary programming [12] and use of Bayesian Networks [13] have also been introduced by researchers to analyze the uncertainty and/or allocated different risks associated with projects at the project and/or portfolio levels. However, incorporating future project forecasts in portfolio planning with consideration of unknown environmental uncertainties remains largely unexplored.

III. MODELING APPROACH

The literature [5][7][14] has looked at forecasting unknown future projects with a univariate modeling approach where the number of future projects are forecasted solely based on the past values of the number of projects. This study builds upon this work by forecasting unknown future projects using multivariate regression in order to incorporate environmental uncertainties in a forecast. The data used in this case study is obtained by text mining FDOT's historical project letting database. The database covers 12 years (from 2003 to 2015) containing 2816 projects. The features extracted from the database are each project letting date, cost, and duration. Table 1 provides a pool of candidate independent variables including macroeconomics and construction indices compiled from the literature [5][7][14], which were available at the monthly level and did not have any missing values for the explored time frame. Table 1 also provides the abbreviation for each variable and the sources from which they have been obtained. These factors are considered in the regression modeling as the dependent (explanatory) variables.

The integrity and continuity of the data are important as it is a time series. As a result, random cross validation was not appropriate, and a rolling forecast origin approach was adopted for cross-validation, as illustrated in Figure 1. The data were divided into two sections, training and testing. The training period starts with three years and increases by one year in each iteration while the testing period remains steady as the three consecutive years after the training set. In other words, seven models are trained, and the average error is considered as the result of cross-validation.

TABLE I. CANDIDATE INDEPENDENT VARIABLES.

Variable name	Abbreviation of variable	Source
Dow Jones industrial average Vol	DJI	Yahoo Finance
Dow Jones industrial average Closing	DJIC	Yahoo Finance
Money Stock M1	MS1	Federal Reserve System
Money Stock M2	MS2	Federal Reserve System
Federal Fund Rate	FFR	Federal Reserve Systems
Average Prime Rate	APR	Federal Reserve System
Producer Price Index for All Commodities	PPIACO	U.S. Bureau of Labor Statistics
Building Permit	BP	U.S. Bureau of Census
Brent Oil Price	BOP	U.S. Energy Information Administration
Consumer Price Index	CPI	U.S. Bureau of Labor Statistics
Crude Oil Price	COP	U.S. Energy Information Administration
Unemployment Rate	UR	U.S. Bureau of Labor Statistics
Florida Employment	FE	U.S. Bureau of Labor Statistics
Florida Unemployment	FU	U.S. Bureau of Labor Statistics
Florida Unemployment Rate	FUR	U.S. Bureau of Labor Statistics
Florida Number of Employees in Construction	NFEC	U.S. Bureau of Labor Statistics
Number Housing Started	HS	U.S. Bureau of Census
Unemployment Rate Construction	URC	U.S. Bureau of Labor Statistics
Number of Employees in Construction	NEC	U.S. Bureau of Labor Statistics
Number of Job Opening in Construction	JOC	U.S. Bureau of Labor Statistics
Construction Spending	CS	U.S. Census Bureau
Total Highway and Street Spending	THSS	Federal Reserve System

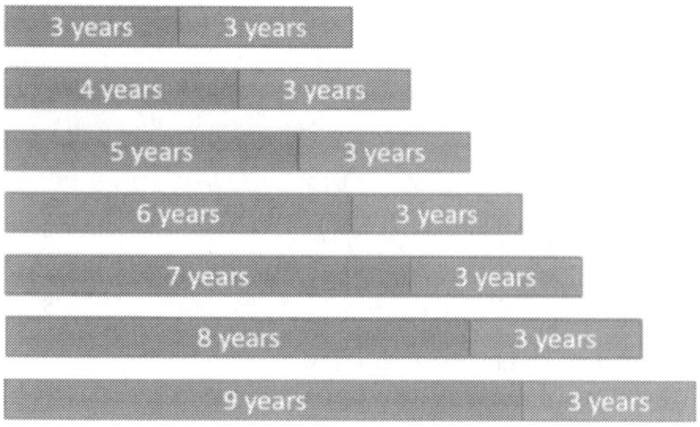

Figure 1. Forecast on a rolling origin cross-validation.

A. *Exploratory data analysis*

To develop the multivariate models, a better understanding of the data characteristics was first necessary, and that information was gained through an exploratory data analysis and the identification of potentially relevant predictors.

The first exploratory analysis consisted of a correlation analysis. Figure 2 provides the correlation plot of the variables. The color indicates the magnitude of the correlation, and the direction of the ellipse illustrates the direction of the relationship. Furthermore, the concentration of the ellipse tells us about the degree of the linear relationship between the variables. Project frequency is represented by "freq" in the last row and column. It appears that none of the exploratory variables had a strong linear relationship with the project frequency.

B. *Feature selection and feature importance*

Feature selection is the process of selecting the most relevant predictors and removing irrelevant variables from the pool of potentially useful predictors. Depending on the model's structure, feature selection can improve a model's accuracy. This process can be carried out by measuring the contribution of each variable to the model's accuracy, and then removing irrelevant and redundant variables while keeping the most useful ones. In some cases, irrelevant features can even reduce a model's accuracy. In general, there are three approaches to feature selection: the filter method, wrapper method, and embedded method.

Embedded methods implement feature selection and model tuning at the same time. In other words, these machine learning algorithms have built-in feature selection elements. Examples of embedded method implementations include LASSO and elastic net. Regularization is a process in which the user intentionally introduces bias into the training, preventing the coefficients from taking large values. This method is especially useful when the number of variables is high. In such a situation, the linear regression is not stable and in which a small change in a few variables results in a large shift in the coefficients. The LASSO approach uses L1 regularization (adding a penalty equal to the magnitude of the coefficient), while ridge regression uses L2 regularization (adding a penalty equal to the square of the magnitude of the coefficient). Elastic net uses a combination of L1 and L2. Ridge regression is effective in reducing a model's variance by minimizing the summation of the square of the residuals. The LASSO method minimizes the summation of the absolute residuals. The LASSO approach produces a sparse model that minimizes the number of coefficients with non-zero values. As a result, this approach has implicit feature selection. The generalized linear method implemented in the next section uses elastic net. This approach incorporates both L1 and L2 regularization and thus has implicit feature selection.

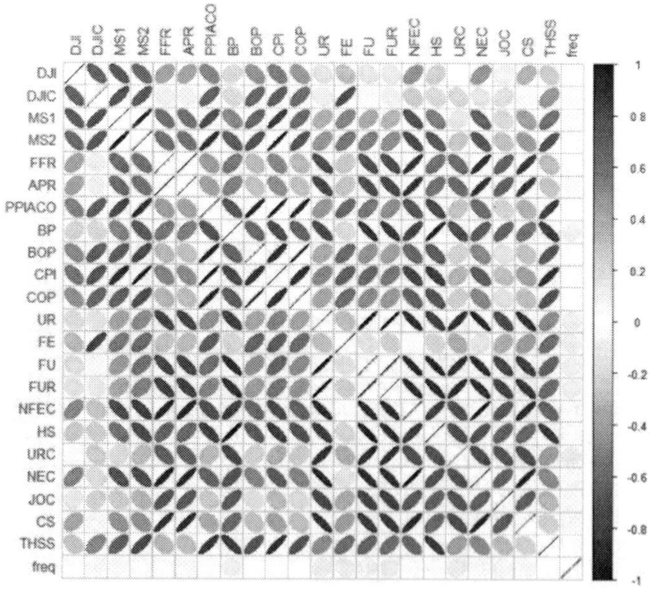

Figure 2. Correlation plot.

Feature reduction methods, such as principal component analysis (PCA), are widely used in studies to reduce the number of independent variables. The output of such methods is a reduced set of new variables extracted from the initial variables while attempting to maintain the same information content. However, using these methods can drastically decrease the ability to interpret the significance of each input, which in itself can be very beneficial. For example, in this study knowing that oil price has a significant impact on the frequency of the projects compared to construction spending can provide valuable insight both for policy makers and contractors. As a result, the authors have chosen not to implement feature reduction methods, such as PCA.

Looking at the correlation between independent variables and the dependent variable, it became evident that a filter method using a correlation analysis was not useful, as all the variables had a nonsignificant relationship with the project frequency. As a result, an elastic net approach is used in the next section.

IV. Regression Model

The general process of model optimization and feature selection consisted of first defining a set of model parameter values to be evaluated. Then, the data was preprocessed in accordance with a 0-1 scale to make sure the high value in some variables are not skewing the model's coefficient and other variables importance. For each parameter set, the cross-validation method discussed earlier served to train and test the model. Finally, the average performance was calculated for each parameter set to identify the optimal values for the parameters.

Ordinary linear regression is based on the underlying assumption that the model for the dependent variable has a normal error distribution. Generalized linear models are a flexible generalization of the ordinary linear regression that allows for other error distributions. In general, they can be applied to a wider variety of problems than can the ordinary linear regression approach. Generalized linear models are defined by three components: a random component, a systematic component, and a link function. The random component recognizes the dependent variable and its corresponding probability distribution. The systematic component recognizes the independent variables and their linear combination, which is called the linear predictor. The link function identifies the connection between the random and systematic components. In other words, it pinpoints how the dependent variable is related to the linear predictor of the independent variables.

Ridge regression uses an L2 penalty to limit the size of the coefficient, while LASSO regression uses an L1 penalty to increase the interpretability of the model. The elastic net uses a mix of L1 and L2 regularization, which makes it superior to the other two methods in most cases. Using a combination of L1 and L2, the elastic net can produce a sparse model with few variables selected from the independent variables. This approach is especially useful when multiple features with high correlations with each other exist.

A generalized linear model was fit to the data using the cross-validation method discussed earlier. Alpha (mixing percentage) and lambda (regularization parameter) were the tuning parameters. Alpha controls the elastic net penalty, where $\alpha=1$ represents lasso regression, and $\alpha=0$ represents ridge regression. Lambda controls the power of the penalty. The L2 penalty shrinks the coefficients of correlated variables, whereas the L1 penalty picks one of the correlated variables and removes the rest. Figure 3 illustrates the results of the generalized linear model (for each set of parameters 7 models according to cross-validation method is trained and the average error is assigned to the set of parameters under study), optimized by minimizing the RMSE with controlling alpha and lambda. The optimized parameters were $\alpha=1$ and $\lambda= 0.56$. The authors also tested λ higher than 0.56 up to 1, however, the coefficients were not well-behaved beyond lambda=0.56.

Figure 4 depicts the LASSO coefficient curves. Each curve represents a variable. The path for each variable demonstrates its coefficient in relation to the L1 value. The coefficient paths more effectively highlight why only two variables were significant in the generalized linear model. When two variables were excluded, all other coefficients became zero at the L1 normalization, and this arrangement yielded the best performance. Figure 5 offers the variable importance for the generalized linear model with all the variables. Only the unemployment rate in construction industry, the Brent oil price, and the unemployment rate (total) had non-zero coefficients. However, the unemployment rate (total) seemed to be relatively insignificant.

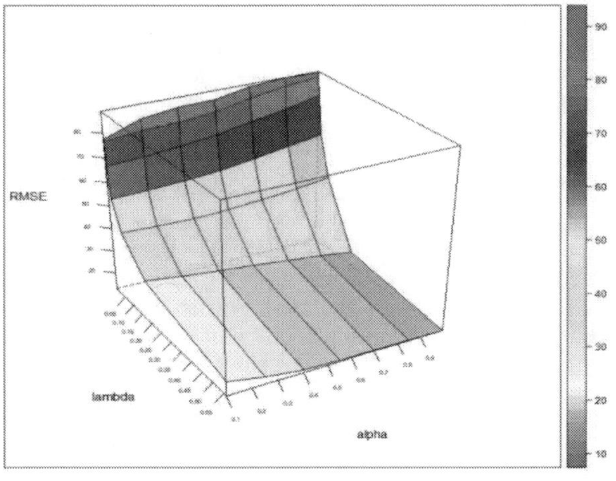

Figure 3. Generalized linear method optimization.

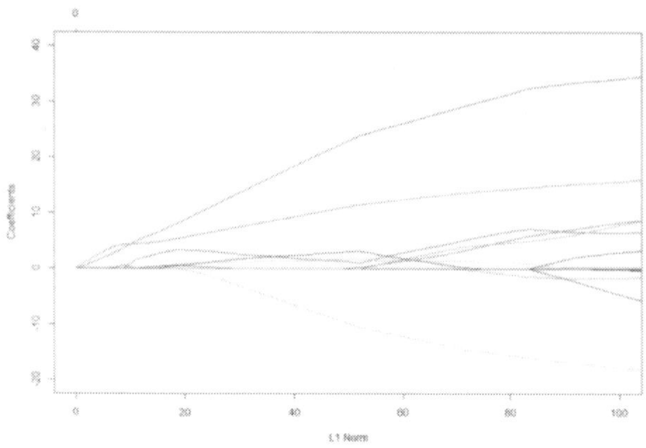

Figure 4. Lasso coefficient curve.

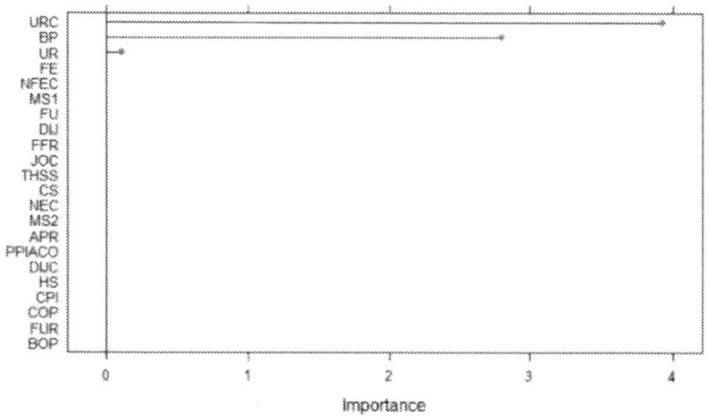

Figure 5. Variable importance of the generalized linear model.

To further prune the generalized linear model, another model with only the unemployment rate in the construction sector and the Brent oil price was trained and tested. Table 2 contains the optimized parameters (coefficients and intercept) for the generalized linear models. The general unemployment rate had a low coefficient and, upon pruning it, the authors saw an improvement in the performance of the model. The most important variable was unemployment rate in construction having the highest coefficient of 4.03.

Table 3 illustrates the performance of the optimized general linear model using a different dataset on the cross-validation sections. It was evident that excluding the unemployment rate improved the model's performance over most of the cross-validation data sections. It is notable that the pruned model performed much better in data section 1 which had the highest error and produced a more evenly distributed error among the different data sections tested. The only variables contributing to the final linear model were the unemployment rate in the construction sector and the Brent oil price.

Table 4 provides a comparison between the regression models proposed in this study and some other univariate models studied previously by the authors [5]. Comparing the error terms shows that the regression model is not outperforming some of the univariate models, such as Autoregressive Moving Average (ARMA). However, it comes close to the best performing example and it provides insight regarding the impact of environmental uncertainties on future project streams and thus could be valuable in long term strategic planning.

It is important to note that the result of this model is the frequency of FDOT's unknown future projects, about which the user would otherwise have no information. Having reliable estimates with known error margins regarding unknown future projects can arguably provide more insight in strategic planning for a company's future compared to the current conjecture-based decision making. It should be noted that the accuracy of the model as long as the model is stable (the error is not systematic but random) is acceptable. The model is forecasting an unknown-unknown variable in the future for which there is no information available regarding their existence. However, users can use the output of this model including the error margin as inputs to their strategic planning.

TABLE II. PARAMETERS OF THE GENERALIZED LINEAR MODELS.

Variables	Coefficients	Coefficients (Pruned by one variable)
URC	3.94	4.03
BP	2.80	2.77
UR	0.11	-----
Intercept	17.14	17.16

TABLE III. PERFORMANCE OF THE GENERALIZED LINEAR MODEL.

Error term	RMSE		MAE	
Feature set	All	Pruned	All	Pruned
1	16.13	9.78	13.24	10.8
2	11.58	11.94	9.64	8.56
3	13.86	13.69	11.6	8.01
4	13.16	13.14	10.82	8.25
5	12.07	10.94	9.55	10
6	11.03	10.27	8.53	8.6
7	10.89	10.87	8.6	11.28
Average	12.67	11.52	10.28	9.36

TABLE IV. PERFORMANCE COMPARISON OF DIFFERENT MODELS.

Model	RMSE	MAE
Regression	11.52	9.36
ARMA(8,8)	10.715	8.45
ARMA(12,12)	11.556	9.23
AR(8)	10.925	8.48
Exponential MA (8)	11.404	9.02

The output of this research can provide quantitative insight as a foundation for future planning. It should be noted that this model is not a standalone portfolio management framework, rather it is a supplement to existing models. For example, knowing that there is likely to be a decrease or increase in the number of projects in the future can help a company prepare in terms of consolidating or expanding its resources and assets.

V. Conclusion and Future Work

The importance and impact of upcoming projects on a project portfolio has been established in previous published work. However, little work has been done considering the uncertainties regarding incorporating unknown future projects in long term strategic planning. In this paper, an approach for incorporating environmental uncertainties for forecasting the number of unknown future projects is presented. A multivariate regression model with elastic net regularization was used to forecast FDOT's unknown future projects using economic and construction indices. The results indicate that the approach can reduce the impact of uncertainties on their portfolio and thus enable development of a more robust plan with a better strategic plan. The generalized linear model indicated that the best explanatory variables were the unemployment rate in the construction sector and the Brent oil price. The regression model's performance is no better than other methods tried earlier by the authors, such as a univariate autoregressive moving average model [5] regressing on project frequency's past value. However, this regression model provides insight regarding the impact of environmental uncertainties on future project streams and thus could be valuable in long term strategic planning. The regression model presented in this literature only considers the linear relationship between the variables. Exploring non-linear modeling techniques, such as neural networks for capturing more complicated relationships between the variables would be the next logical step in this research. The model developed in this study is limited to FDOT projects. However, new regression models specific for other databases can be built by following the same steps and adopting appropriate alternative sets of independent variables.

References

[1] M. Martinsuo, "Project portfolio management in practice and in context," Int. J. Proj. Manag., vol. 31, no. 6, pp. 794–803, Aug. 2013.

[2] R. G. Cooper, S. J. Edgett, and E. J. Kleinschmidt, "Portfolio management in new product development: Lessons from the leaders—I," Res. Manag., vol. 40, no. 5, pp. 16–28, 1997.

[3] H. Markowitz, "Portfolio Selection," J. Finance, vol. 7, no. 1, pp. 77–91, Mar. 1952.

[4] J. S. Pennypacker and L. D. Dye, "Project Portfolio Management and Managing Multiple Projects : Two Sides of the Same Coin ?," in Managing Multiple Projects: Planning, Scheduling, and Allocating Resources for Competitive Advantage, CRC Press, 2002, pp. 1–10.

[5] A. Shojaei and I. Flood, "Stochastic forecasting of project streams for construction project portfolio management," Vis. Eng., vol. 5, no. 1, p. 11, 2017.

[6] Y. Petit and B. Hobbs, "Project portfolios in dynamic environments: Sources of uncertainty and sensing mechanisms," Proj. Manag. J., vol. 41, no. 4, pp. 46–58, Sep. 2010.

[7] A. Shojaei and I. Flood, "Stochastic Forecasting of Unknown Future Project Streams for Strategic Portfolio Planning," in Computing in Civil Engineering 2017, 2017, pp. 280–288.

[8] J. Dahlgren and J. Soderlund, "Modes and mechanisms of control in Multi-Project Organisations: the R&D case," Int. J. Technol. Manag., vol. 50, no. 1, p. 1-22, 2010.

[9] R. R. Trippi, P. By-Lee, and K. Jae, Artificial intelligence in finance and investing: state-of-the-art technologies for securities selection and portfolio management. McGraw-Hill, Inc., 1995.

[10] A. D. Henriksen and A. J. Traynor, "A practical r&d project-selection scoring tool," IEEE Trans. Eng. Manag., vol. 46, no. 2, pp. 158–170, May 1999.

[11] J. A. Araúzo, J. Pajares, and A. Lopez-Paredes, "Simulating the dynamic scheduling of project portfolios," Simul. Model. Pract. Theory, vol. 18, no. 10, pp. 1428–1441, Nov. 2010.

[12] A. F. Carazo, et al. "Solving a comprehensive model for multiobjective project portfolio selection," Comput. Oper. Res., vol. 37, no. 4, pp. 630–639, Apr. 2010.

[13] R. Demirer, R. R. Mau, and C. Shenoy, "Bayesian networks: a decision tool to improve portfolio risk analysis," J. Appl. Financ., vol. 16, no. 2, p. 106, 2006.

[14] A. Shojaei and I. Flood, "Extending the Portfolio and Strategic Planning Horizon by Stochastic Forecasting of Unknown Future Projects," in The Seventh International Conference on Advanced Communications and Computation, INFOCOMP 2017, 2017, no. c, pp. 64–69.

Qualitative and Quantitative Risk Analysis of Unmanned Aerial Vehicle Flights over Construction Job Sites

Hashem Izadi Moud, Alireza Shojaei, Ian Flood, Xun Zhang and Mohsen Hatami
M. E. Rinker, Sr. School of Construction Management
University of Florida
Gainesville, Florida, United States of America
Email: izadimoud@ufl.edu, a.shojaei@ufl.edu, flood@ufl.edu, xzz0032@ufl.edu, mohsen.hatami@ufl.edu

***Abstract*—Unmanned Aerial Vehicles (UAVs) have been used on construction job sites for a variety of purposes for more than a decade. But the risks and hazards of flying UAVs on construction job sites has never been quantitatively or qualitatively evaluated. While the general aviation industry has been using sophisticated analysis techniques to quantitatively assess the risks of general aviation industry flights over the general population for decades, the risks of UAV flights over this group has never been quantitatively assessed. UAVs are being used in construction activities on a regularly without proper risk assessment. There is no action plan in place, by either construction managers or safety officers, to design UAV flights based on safety measures. This paper presents the first known quantitative and qualitative analyses of UAV flight risks for construction job sites. A quantitative model for UAV flight risk assessment is presented and tested, using the Monte Carlo simulation technique, for an actual construction job site. A qualitative risk assessment of UAV flights is also presented by combining the Federal Aviation Administration (FAA) rules, regulations and guidelines concerning UAV flights, with the safety needs and specifications of UAV flights on a construction job site. The techniques introduced in this paper can be used by construction managers and safety officers to take safety into account when planning UAV flights over construction job sites. This paper further argues that using techniques and methods introduced in this research paper could potentially make UAV flights in any environment safer and more reliable.**

Keywords-Unmanned Aerial Vehicle, UAV, Monte Carlo Simulation, Risk Assessment, UAV flight risk

I. Introduction

Unmanned Aerial Vehicles (UAVs), commonly referred to as drones, have been used in the construction industry for over ten years [1]–[3]. The versatility of UAVs enables users to capture different types of data (typically visual) easily from angles which might not be possible without such a device. The relatively low cost of new generations of UAVs along with the possibility of having different sensors attached to them, such as high resolution and thermal cameras, RFID readers, and laser scanners, have played a crucial role in their proliferation in construction research and practice. The applications explored for using UAVs in construction includes construction progress monitoring [4], [5], overall site monitoring [6], structural health inspection [7]–[11], surveying job sites and building 3D models [12], infrastructure asset management [13]–[16], urban monitoring [17], material tracking [18], sustainable energy production management [19], and construction safety [20]. The applications and use of UAVs have increased exponentially while the safety risks associated with UAV flights have not been studied thoroughly.

As a general approach, the risks associated with flying UAVs over a job site can be divided into two categories:

1. *direct hazards*, such as the falling of the UAV and falling debris from a collision of a UAV with other objects [21][22]; and
2. *indirect hazards*, such as the invasion of personal space [23][24], diverting the attention of workers due to the UAVs' sound and motion (thereby increasing their cognitive load while performing their tasks [25]–[27]), and invasion of a workers' personal space [28].

The construction industry is often critiqued for its high rate of fatalities and poor safety record. The total number of work-related fatalities in the United States in 2015 was 4,836, 20% of which occurred within construction (more than any other industry). From construction, falls, slips and trips are the highest cause of fatal incidents, with 364 cases. Transportation incidents were the second highest cause (with 226 cases) and contact with objects came third (with 159 cases) [29]. These statistics show the importance of the role of equipment in construction safety and establish the need for better monitoring and regulation of their use. Safe use of construction equipment, such as excavators, loaders, and cranes has been thoroughly regulated due to prolong use in construction. In contrast, new equipment introduced to the job sites, such as UAVs, do not have specific regulations in place for managing their safety in use. Flying UAVs can be challenging in any environment. Construction job sites are dynamic systems that are constantly changing. These constant changes could make flying UAVs even more challenging, potentially introducing more hazards to construction activity. The lack of a comprehensive qualitative and quantitative methodology for risk assessment of UAVs on construction sites coupled with a rapid increase in their use poses a new safety threat that requires attention. This paper proposes and evaluates quantitative and qualitative approaches for modeling the safety risks related to UAV flights over construction job sites. The method is applied to a case study from a building project at the University of Florida to demonstrate the methods application and significance.

This paper is organized as follow. In Section 2, rules and regulations regarding UAV flights in the United States are presented. Section 3 discusses the risks of UAV flights. Section 4 introduces the use of Monte-Carlo simulation for modeling uncertainty in the flight path environment. Section 5 presents a quantitative application of risk assessment of UAV flights in a case study. The last section concludes the study with a discussion of the results and of a simple qualitative approach to UAV flights risks within construction.

II. RULES AND REGULATIONS GOVERNING UAV FLIGHTS IN THE UNITED STATES

In the US, the Federal Aviation Industry (FAA) is the main agency for managing civil aviation. The FAA regulates the Unmanned Aerial Systems (UASs) (a broader category for UAVs) flights by dividing the UAV uses into the following two main categories: (1) fly for hobby purposes and (2) fly for commercial use. UAS Flight rules issued by FAA are as follow [30][31]:

A. *Fly under the Special Rule for Model Aircraft (Section 336)*

- Only used for entertainment or hobby purposes.
- The model aircraft need to be registered.
- Follow community-based safety guidelines and fly within the programming of a national community-based organization.
- The weight limit of the aircraft is 55 lbs., unless certified by a community-based organization.
- Flying range cannot exceed visual line-of-sight.
- Never fly near other aircraft.
- The airport and air traffic control tower must be notified in advance if a model aircraft is flying within 5 miles of an airport.
- Never fly near emergency response efforts.

B. *Fly under the FAA's small UAS Rule (Part 107)*

- Fly for recreational or business use.
- The drone must be registered.
- Require a remote pilot certificate issued by the FAA.
- Weight of drone under 55 lbs.
- Flight speed at or under 100 mph.
- Flying range cannot exceed visual line-of-sight.
- Never fly near other aircraft or over people.
- Do not fly in controlled airspace near airports until you get the permission from FAA.
- Fly only during daylight or civil twilight.
- Flying height limit is 400 feet.
- Never fly from a moving vehicle, unless in a sparsely populated area.

Generally, to simplify the most critical aspects of these rules, this paper makes the following assumptions: (1) the construction site used as the case study is not close to the 5-mile radius of any airport; (2) all UAV flying regulations are being followed; (3) UAV flights are taking place within the line-of-sight of the pilot; (4) UAV specifications comply with FAA regulations, and more importantly (5) UAVs are not flying through the space over people's heads for safety consideration. These assumptions are specifically highlighted in the qualitative risk analysis that is provided in the discussion and conclusion sections.

III. RISKS OF UAV FLIGHTS

A. *Quantifying Risks of UAV Flights*

Quantifying risks associated with UAV flights over construction job sites is a crucial factor in determining the safety of UAVs flights over construction project zones. By having a quantifiable analysis of UAV flight risks, construction managers and superintendents and in general decision makers in this industry, based on reliable metrics, are able to assess the extent of risks related to UAV flights. Also, a quantifiable risks analysis of UAV flights will give insurance companies a better insight into the value, extent and severity of risks associated with UAV flights on construction job sites. In this paper, based on the Clothier and Walker [22] approach, the authors define a model to measure and describe ground fatality expectation. The model only measures and enumerates the risk of expected ground fatalities based on falling UAVs or falling debris.

While this model quantifies the direct risks of falling UAVs, or debris, it does not consider the indirect risks associated with UAV flights. Some of the indirect risks that are not considered in this model but could have a significant impact on the general risks of UAV flights are: (1) threatening workers' personal space, (2) threatening privacy of workers and (3) potential distraction of workers due to noise and motion.

Clothier and Walker [22] formalized the ground fatality expectation model as below:

$$SO = MR * \varphi * AL \tag{1}$$

where: SO is the safety objective in terms of the number of fatalities per flight hours; φ is the population density of the area under the flight path of the UAV; AL is the lethal area, which is determined by the circular area of the maximum length of UAV diameter plus a (safety) buffer; and MR is the mishap rate, calculated according to (2).

$$MR = SFR + MC\mathit{Debris} + \mathit{Other} \tag{2}$$

where: SFR is the system failure rate per flight hour; MC*Debris* is the quantity of debris from a possible midair collision per flight hour, and *Other* is the other hazards that might result in fatality risks.

Based on [1], the fatality rate, which is expected in the industry of common air travels, is generally bounded to $1*10^{-06}$ or in other words one casualty for every million flight hours. However, due to a lack of data about the causalities, fatalities and injuries caused by UAVs around the world, it is not possible for the authors to establish a fatality rate for UAV flights. For this reason, the same safe rate of fatality as the general aviation industry (one in a million flight hours) was adopted.

B. *Qualitative Risks of UAV Flights*

As discussed in Section 2, FAA established a series of general rules and regulations for UAV flights within the national air space. Two of these rules and regulations are specifically important for the construction industry: (1) never fly a UAV out of the pilot's line of sight and (2) never fly a UAV over a populated area, which means that it is illegal to fly a UAV over people's heads. Based on these specific regulations, the authors developed a qualitative safety map for UAV flights over the job site that has been used as a case study in this research and is presented in the analysis section.

IV. USING MONTE CARLO SIMULATION AS A RISK ASSESSMENT METHOD

Risk and uncertainty are prevalent throughout every construction project [32]. It is necessary to conduct quantitative risk analysis to evaluate failure and safety risks to provide a platform as a means of decision making. A dichotomy of risk assessment techniques is into deterministic and probabilistic methods [33]. Deterministic methods ignore uncertainty, while probabilistic methods are able to take into account unexplained variances in factors as diverse as time, weather, spatial demands, and labor performance [34]. Due to the fact that in this study, several uncertainty elements including behavior of the UAVs and the work area conditions are part of the assumptions, a probabilistic method was adopted. The Monte-Carlo method is a commonly adopted probabilistic technique in the construction industry due to the high levels of uncertainty and the large financial investments in this type of work [35]. Mooney [36] defines Monte-Carlo simulation as a computerized mathematical approach that enables researchers to perform quantitative risk analysis through a decision making process. The approach replaces point estimates with random variables drawn from representative probability density functions [37], refining the results through a large sampling of possible outcomes [38]. Occupational safety and health risks and associated hazards can be modeled using Monte-Carlo by considering the stochastic nature of the problems[39]. Baudry [40] suggested using a range-based Multi-Actor Multi-Criteria Analysis as a scenario that addresses the group decision making under high uncertainty, to consider different viewpoints of the stakeholders. Later, the binocular optical axis parallel detection method was used by Ying [41] to analyze the error factors and establish a model based on Monte-Carlo simulation. Applying this method, and given different values for corresponding coordinates, the analysis is conducted [41]. Podgorny [42], using a Monte-Carlo based model, examined three-dimensional radiative transfer over inhomogeneous surface albedo including open water, sea ice, and melt ponds by flying UAVs over these areas The goal of this study was to investigate the influence of surface feature erraticism on the energy budget of the lower troposphere ice–ocean system. Also, Monte-Carlo simulation has been used to determine and examine the active relationship between the factors leading to an accident and the recompense paid for it [42]-[44]. In a real-time location-based Monte Carlo simulation, Li et al. [45] used historical data to forecast the safety hazard level on a separate level based on time and position. On construction job sites, small UAVs require safety consideration due to uncertain operational conditions, such as their weak structural shape that may cause instability and failure in windy weather, their potential for operational errors, as well as their high maneuverability and potential for mechanical failures. Recently, Plioutsias et al. [46] concluded in a research paper that current commercial UAVs are far from being able to meet safety requirements. To simulate collision and other hazards between one or multiple UAVs operating on construction sites and their bordering area, the Monte-Carlo simulation method offers both flexibility and potential accuracy in modeling. This method is playing an important role in modeling uncertainties, such as the movement of different kinds of object on a construction site and environmental factors, such as wind [47]-[50].

V. ANALYSIS OF THE CASE STUDY

A. *Analysis of Quantifying Risks of UAV Flights*

In this section, a Monte Carlo Simulation is used to assess the risk of flying UAVs over construction job sites, which is referred to as the Safety Objective (SO) as described by (1) above. Mishap Rate (MR), the Lethal Area (A_L) and the density of population (φ) are needed to find the SO in each area. MR is the variable with the least empirical data as there is not much information recorded on the MR of UAVs. In this analysis, it is assumed that the UAV lifetime, or the duration over which the possibility of a crash exists, is normally distributed, with a range between 100 hours and 10,000 hours, a mean of 5,050 hours, and standard deviation of 1,650 hours. MR is referred to as the rate of failed UAV flights in a given flight hour lifetime for a UAV. In this case, the normal productive life of a UAV is estimated to be in this range. As a result, MR is calculated as one crash in a UAV's lifetime: 1 / (lifetime of UAV in flight hours).

A_L is the area that has the potential for lethal impact from the UAV or debris if the UAV crashes. Typically, it is calculated by using the longest dimension of a UAV. In this case, considering the fact that most of the UAVs flying over construction job sites are commercially available, it is presumed that A_L can assume a value between 0.3 m and 1.8 m. Thus, an even distribution across a diameter with a minimum of 0.3 m and maximum of 1.8 m is used in the simulation. The density (φ) represents the number of personnel on the site divided by the area of the location that a UAV flies over. In this study, it is assumed that only construction workers are present at the job site. Due to a lack of empirical data it is estimated that the number of construction personnel on the job site varies between 2 and 14 with a normal distribution (a mean of 8, a standard deviation of 2). The density is calculated for Area 1 to Area 4 by dividing the sampled number of construction workers for each zone by its area. The area of each location that a UAV can fly over is calculated and shown in Figures 1 and 2. The area surrounding the job site is divided into Area 1 through Area 4 using the logic of FAA regulations regarding safe UAV flights, which prohibits UAV flights over head of people, in this case construction personnel.

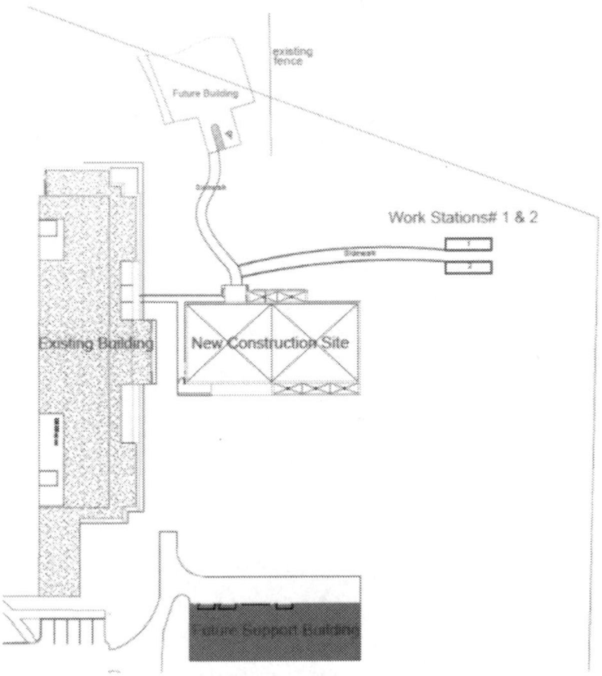

Figure 1. General layout of the construction site

Thus, considering the pathways that construction personnel routinely commute between work stations and the job site, four separate areas are drawn as separate areas that UAVs can fly over. Due to these regulations, UAVs cannot fly from one of these areas to another because they need to fly over a construction personnel pathway, which is prohibited by FAA regulations. A Monte Carlo simulation was run using the Palisade @Risk 7.5. The number of simulation iterations was controlled for convergence of the mean and standard deviation of the SO (safety objective) results for each area. The simulation was run until it reached convergence with 95% confidence and 5% tolerance. The convergence was checked every 600 iterations. The simulation reached convergence at 174,000 iterations. The results of the Monte Carlo simulation are summarized as follows:

- Area 1 (Figures 3 and 4):
  - Mean: 2.746E-006
  - Mode: 2.634E-007
  - Median: 1.900E-006
  - Standard deviation: 2.716E-005

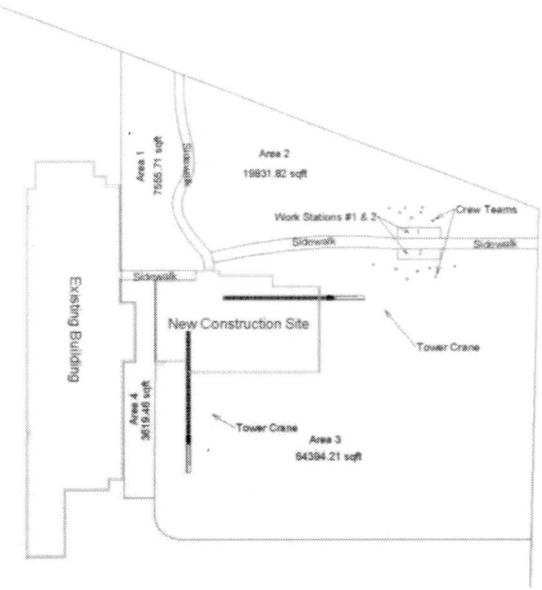

Figure 2. Simplified layout for analysis

  -
- Area 2 (Figures 5 and 6):
  - Mean: 1.042E-006
  - Mode: 8.349E-008
  - Median: 7.248E-007
  - Standard deviation: 1.029E-005
- Area 3 (Figures 7 and 8):
  - Mean: 3.217E-007
  - Mode: 3.078E-008
  - Median: 2.232E-007
  - Standard deviation: 3.414E-006
- Area 4 (Figures 9 and 10):
  - Mean: 5.670E-006
  - Mode: 5.512E-007
  - Median: 3.972E-006
  - Standard deviation: 5.328E-005

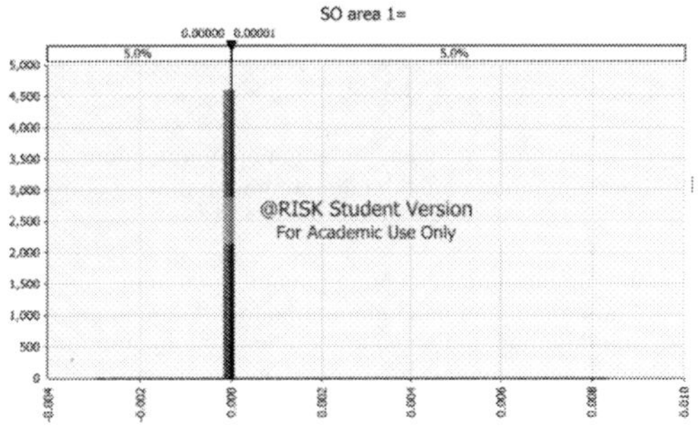

Figure 3. SO result of area 1 from simulation

Figure 4. Zoomed in SO result of area 1 from simulation

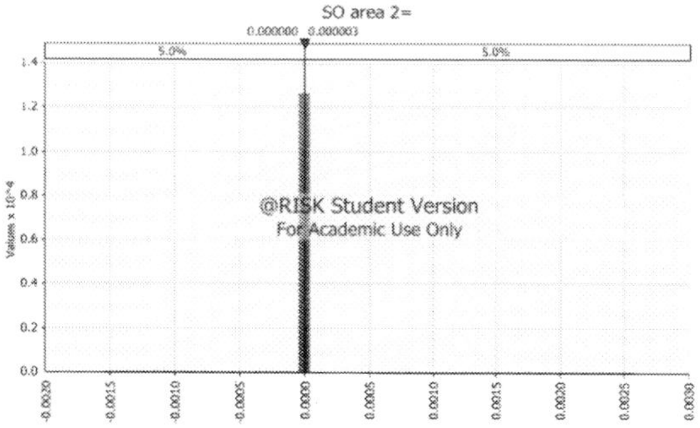

Figure 5. SO result of area 2 from simulation

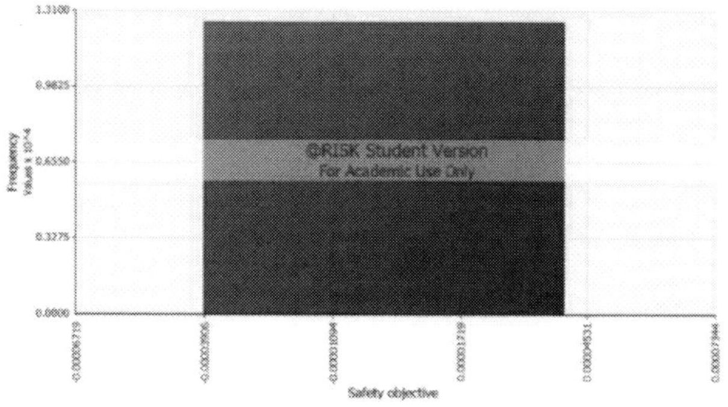

Figure 6. Zoomed in SO result of area 2 from simulation

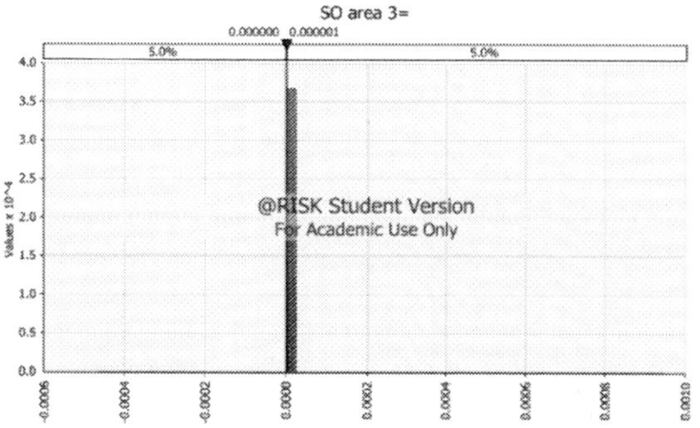

Figure 7. SO result of area 3 from simulation

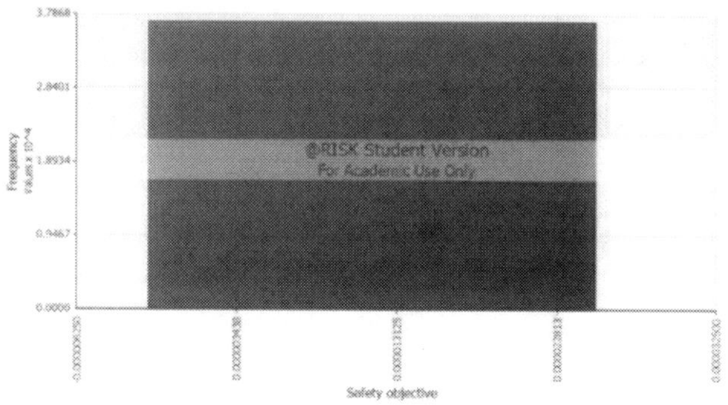

Figure 8. Zoomed in SO result of area 3 from simulation

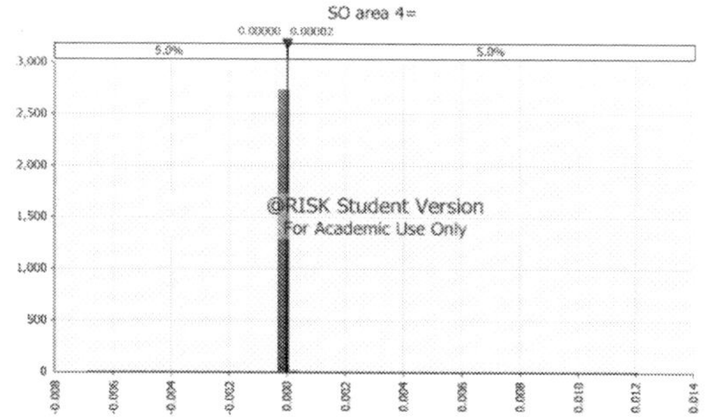

Figure 9. SO result of area 4 from simulation

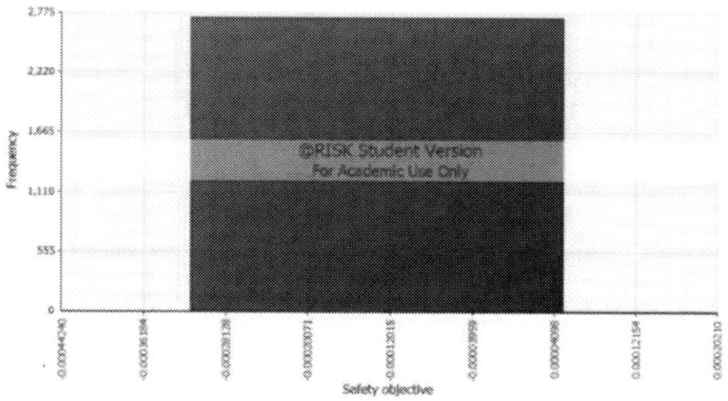

Figure 10. Zoomed in SO result of area 4 from simulation

B. *Analysis of Qualititative Risks of UAV Flights*

The FAA regulations prohibit flying over head of peoples' heads. Thus, in Figure 1, we need to restrict the areas that are safe for UAV flights. This logic leads to Figure 2, where each area is restricted by the workers' pathways that act as borders between each area. Taking FAA regulations into account, the following issues need to be considered in developing a qualitative risk assessment color-coded map for UAV flights:

- UAV no-fly zone areas are shown in red. These are the areas that are absolutely forbidden for UAVs to fly over/on due to federal rules.
- The area immediately adjacent to the red areas are shown in orange as it is risky to fly close to a no-fly zone.

- Any existing construction equipment is shown with orange as it is risky to fly over, on or adjacent to moving objects.
- In this example, there are two tower cranes which, by nature, are constantly moving in three dimensions.

Considering these facts, a color-coded safety map using green for safe to fly areas, orange for risky to fly areas, and red for no-fly zones, is constructed and shown in Figure 11. Authors believe that this is the first UAV safety heat map for construction that qualitatively categorizes the relative risks of UAV flights over job sites.

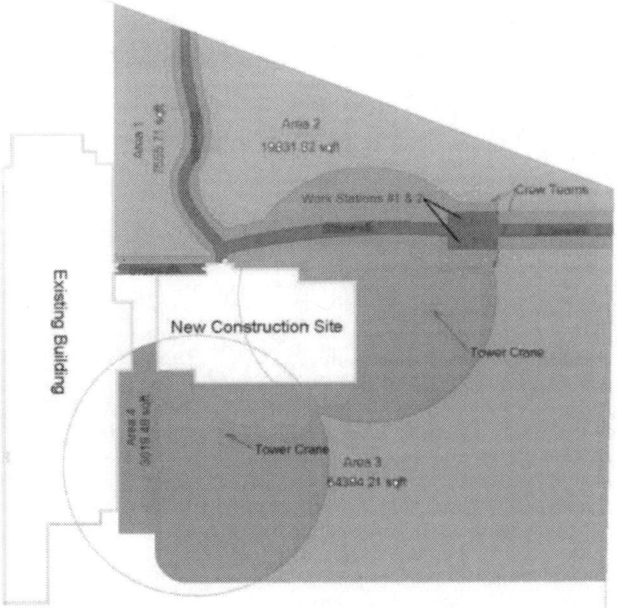

Figure 11. A color-coded map showing the qualitative risks of flying UAVs in a construction job site, where green represents the minimum risk, orange represents the medium risk and red represents high risk or no-fly zones.

VI. DISCUSSION AND CONCLUSION

This paper presents qualitative and quantitative risk analyses of UAVs flights over construction job site environments. It is the first known study discussing risks of UAVs flights over construction job sites using a Monte-Carlo simulation as a well-known qualitative analysis and also a quantitative analysis based on FAA rules and regulations.

By using Monte-Carlo simulation, it is shown that the risks of flying a UAV (with a given probability of UAV size, over an active construction job site, with a given probability of construction crew presence) the mean risk of a fatality incident varies from 5.670E-006. In other words, this predicts more than five fatalities in a million flight hours, to 1.042E-006 (almost one fatality in a million flight hours). Based on Clothier and Walker [22], the general aviation industry fatality rate is restricted to *one fatal incident in one million flight hours*. While it is not truly accurate to propagate the fatality rate of the general aviation industry to the UAV industry, authors use the general aviation industry as a reference to compare the risks due to the lack of data on qualitative risks of UAV flights. By comparing the simulation results to the general aviation industry restricted fatality rate, which is one fatality in a million flight hours, it is seen in the case study that most areas have higher than normal fatality risks of flights. Thus, it is up to construction managers or safety officer to decide on the appropriateness of UAV flights on this construction site.

So far, a quantitative method has been presented that provides a specific number for expected fatalities per million UAV flight hours. Using this quantitative method, it is straightforward for anyone (whether or not they have knowledge of risk assessment and/or expertise in UAV flights) to determine whether it is safe to fly a UAV within specific zone. This provides safety managers, project managers, owners and insurance companies with valuable insight on the safety of proposed UAV flights.

The FAA rules and regulations prohibit UAVs to fly over peoples' heads, over or close to airports and set a series of specific guidelines regarding UAVs operations. Combing these FAA guidelines with safety specification of UAVs flights in construction job site environments, such as higher risk of UAV collision in proximity of tower cranes, a qualitative color-coded safety map is generated that shows the relatively safer areas for UAV flights, using green, compare to medium UAV flight risks areas, with orange color, and no-fly zones, or the highest risks of UAV flights zones with red. Figure 11 presents this qualitative safety map. Areas above sidewalks, pathways and construction personnel work stations are shaded as red, as it is not safe to fly a UAV over these areas. The work radius of tower cranes is marked with two distinct circles. Areas in proximity of tower cranes are shaded in orange, as it is risky to fly UAVs in close proximity to tower cranes. The areas that are shaded green are the ones without any known safety hazards. This simple map can be used when no data is available regarding the number of workers present on site and/or when general assessment of safe-fly-zones and no-fly-zones are being performed.

These two analyses, qualitative and quantitative, enable construction managers, safety officers and insurance companies to detect, explore and address the risks of UAV flights in construction job site environments, which will help the construction industry to better manage the safety concerns of UAV flights.

REFERENCES

[1] Y. Ham, K. K. Han, J. J. Lin, and M. Golparvar-Fard, "Visual monitoring of civil infrastructure systems via camera-equipped Unmanned Aerial Vehicles (UAVs): a review of related works," Vis. Eng., vol. 4, no. 1, p. 1, 2016.

[2] P. Liu et al., "A review of rotorcraft unmanned aerial vehicle (UAV) developments and applications in civil engineering," Smart Struct. Syst., vol. 13, no. 6, pp. 1065–1094, 2014.

[3] M. Zucchi, "Drones: A Gateway Technology to Full Site Automation | 2015-06-10 | ENR." [Online]. Available: https://www.enr.com/articles/9040-drones-a-gateway-technology-to-full-site-automation?v=preview. [Accessed: May 30th 2018].

[4] K. Han, J. Lin, and M. Golparvar-Fard, "A formalism for utilization of autonomous vision-based systems and integrated project models for construction progress monitoring," in Proceedings of 2015 Conference on autonomous and robotic construction of infrastructure, 2015, pp. 118–131.

[5] J. J. Lin, K. K. Han, and M. Golparvar-Fard, "A framework for model-driven acquisition and analytics of visual data using UAVs for automated construction progress monitoring," in Computing in Civil Engineering 2015, 2015, pp. 156–164.

[6] M.-C. Wen and S.-C. Kang, "Augmented reality and unmanned aerial vehicle assist in construction management," in Computing in Civil and Building Engineering (2014), 2014, pp. 1570–1577.

[7] C. Eschmann, C.-M. Kuo, and C. Boller, "Unmanned Aircraft Systems for Remote Building Inspection and Monitoring," Proc. 6th Eur. Work. Struct. Heal. Monit. July 3-6, 2012, Dresden, Ger., vol. 2, pp. 1–8, 2012.

[8] N. Kerle, J. Fernandez Galarreta, and M. Gerke, "Urban structural damage assessment with oblique UAV imagery, object-based image analysis and semantic reasoning," in Proc., 35th Asian conference on remote sensing, 2014.

[9] N. Michael et al., "Collaborative mapping of an earthquake-damaged building via ground and aerial robots," J. F. Robot., vol. 29, no. 5, pp. 832–841, 2012.

[10] G. Morgenthal and N. Hallermann, "Quality Assessment of Unmanned Aerial Vehicle (UAV) Based Visual Inspection of Structures," Adv. Struct. Eng., vol. 17, no. 3, pp. 289–302, 2014.

[11] K. S. Pratt et al. "Use of tethered small unmanned aerial system at Berkman Plaza II collapse," in Safety, Security and Rescue Robotics, 2008. SSRR 2008. IEEE International Workshop on, 2008, pp. 134–139.

[12] S. Siebert and J. Teizer, "Mobile 3D mapping for surveying earthwork projects using an Unmanned Aerial Vehicle (UAV) system," Autom. Constr., vol. 41, pp. 1–14, 2014.

[13] A. Ellenberg, A. Kontsos, F. Moon, and I. Bartoli, "Bridge related damage quantification using unmanned aerial vehicle imagery," Struct. Control Heal. Monit., vol. 23, no. 9, pp. 1168–1179, Sep. 2016.

[14] C. Eschmann, C.-M. Kuo, C.-H. Kuo, and C. Boller, "High-resolution multisensor infrastructure inspection with unmanned aircraft systems," ISPRS-International Arch. Photogramm. Remote Sens. Spat. Inf. Sci., no. 2, pp. 125–129, 2013.

[15] N. Metni and T. Hamel, "A UAV for bridge inspection: Visual servoing control law with orientation limits," Autom. Constr., vol. 17, no. 1, pp. 3–10, 2007.

[16] S. Rathinam, Z. W. Kim, and R. Sengupta, "Vision-based monitoring of locally linear structures using an unmanned aerial vehicle," J. Infrastruct. Syst., vol. 14, no. 1, pp. 52–63, 2008.

[17] R. Qin, "An object-based hierarchical method for change detection using unmanned aerial vehicle images," Remote Sens., vol. 6, no. 9, pp. 7911–7932, 2014.

[18] B. Hubbard et al., "Feasibility study of UAV use for RFID material tracking on construction sites," in Proc. 51st ASC Annu. Int. Conf, 2015.

[19] R. R. Murphy et al., "Use of remotely operated marine vehicles at Minamisanriku and Rikuzentakata Japan for disaster recovery," 9th IEEE Int. Symp. Safety, Secur. Rescue Robot. SSRR 2011, pp. 19–25, 2011.

[20] J. Irizarry, M. Gheisari, and B. N. Walker, "Usability assessment of drone technology as safety inspection tools," J. Inf. Technol. Constr., vol. 17, no. 12, pp. 194–212, 2012.

[21] N. D. Opfer and D. R. S. PE, "Unmanned aerial vehicle applications and issues for construction," in 121st ASEE Annual Conference and Exposition, pp. 1-16, 2014.

[22] R. A. Clothier and R. A. Walker, "Determination and evaluation of UAV safety objectives,". Bristol, United Kingdom: 21st International Unmanned Air Vehicle Systems Conference, 2006.

[23] R. Clarke, "Understanding the drone epidemic," Comput. Law Secur. Rev., vol. 30, no. 3, pp. 230–246, 2014.

[24] R. L. Finn and D. Wright, "Unmanned aircraft systems: Surveillance, ethics and privacy in civil applications," Comput. Law Secur. Rev., vol. 28, no. 2, pp. 184–194, 2012.

[25] F. Christiansen, L. Rojano-Doñate, P. T. Madsen, and L. Bejder, "Noise levels of multi-rotor unmanned aerial vehicles with implications for potential underwater impacts on marine mammals," Front. Mar. Sci., vol. 3, p. 277, 2016.

[26] C. F. Liew and T. Yairi, "Quadrotor or blimp? Noise and appearance considerations in designing social aerial robot," in Human-Robot Interaction (HRI), 2013 8th ACM/IEEE International Conference on, 2013, pp. 183–184.

[27] G. Sinibaldi and L. Marino, "Experimental analysis on the noise of propellers for small UAV," Appl. Acoust., vol. 74, no. 1, pp. 79–88, 2013.

[28] B. A. Duncan and R. R. Murphy, "Comfortable approach distance with small unmanned aerial vehicles," in RO-MAN, 2013 IEEE, 2013, pp. 786–792.

[29] "Census of Fatal Occupational Injuries (CFOI) - Current and Revised Data." [Online]. Available: https://www.bls.gov/iif/oshcfoi1.htm. [Accessed: 20-Apr-2018].

[30] Federal Aviation Administration. Getting Started: 2 Options for Flying Your Drone. [Online]. Available from:https://www.faa.gov/uas/getting_started/ 2018.04.21

[31] Federal Aviation Administration. Fly under the small UAS Rule. [Online]. Available from:https://www.faa.gov/uas/getting_started/part_107/ 2018.04.21.

[32] P. A. Thompson and J. G. Perry, Engineering Construction Risks: A Guide to Project Risk Analysis and Assessment

Implications for Project Clients and Project Managers. Thomas Telford, 1992.

[33] T. Öberg and B. Bergbäck, "A Review of Probabilistic Risk Assessment of Contaminated Land (12 pp)," J Soils Sediments, vol. 5, no. 4, pp. 213–224, Oct. 2005.

[34] A. S. Akintoye and M. J. MacLeod, "Risk analysis and management in construction," International Journal of Project Management, vol. 15, no. 1, pp. 31–38, Feb. 1997.

[35] A. S. Akintoye and M. J. MacLeod, "Risk analysis and management in construction," International journal of project management, vol. 15, no. 1, pp. 31–38, Feb. 1997.

[36] C. Z. Mooney, Monte Carlo Simulation. SAGE Publications, 1997.

[37] E. Gómez-Lázaro et al., "Probability Density Function Characterization for Aggregated Large-Scale Wind Power Based on Weibull Mixtures," Energies, vol. 9, no. 2, p. 91, Feb. 2016.

[38] J. H. Smid, D. Verloo, G. C. Barker, and A. H. Havelaar, "Strengths and weaknesses of Monte Carlo simulation models and Bayesian belief networks in microbial risk assessment," International Journal of Food Microbiology, vol. 139, pp. S57–S63, May 2010.

[39] V. Sousa, N. M. Almeida, and L. A. Dias, "Risk-based management of occupational safety and health in the construction industry – Part 2: Quantitative model," Safety Science, vol. 74, pp. 184–194, Apr. 2015.

[40] G. Baudry, C. Macharis, and T. Vallée, "Range-based Multi-Actor Multi-Criteria Analysis: A combined method of Multi-Actor Multi-Criteria Analysis and Monte Carlo simulation to support participatory decision making under uncertainty," European Journal of Operational Research, vol. 264, no. 1, pp. 257–269, Jan. 2018.

[41] J. Ying and B. Liu, "Binocular optical axis parallelism detection precision analysis based on Monte Carlo method," in Fourth Seminar on Novel Optoelectronic Detection Technology and Application, 2018, vol. 10697, p. 1069719.

[42] I. Podgorny, D. Lubin, and D. K. Perovich, "Monte Carlo Study of UAV-Measurable Albedo over Arctic Sea Ice," Journal of Atmospheric and Oceanic Technology, vol. 35, no. 1, pp. 57–66, Jan. 2018.

[43] R. Y. M. Li, K. W. Chau, and D. C. W. Ho, "Dynamic Panel Analysis of Construction Accidents in Hong Kong," Asian Journal of Law and Economics, vol. 8, no. 3, pp. 1–9, Dec. 2017.

[44] I. M. Shohet, M. Luzi, and M. Tarshish, "Optimal allocation of resources in construction safety: Analytical-empirical model," Safety Science, vol. 104, pp. 231–238, Apr. 2018.

[45] H. Li, X. Yang, F. Wang, T. Rose, G. Chan, and S. Dong, "Stochastic state sequence model to predict construction site safety states through Real-Time Location Systems," Safety science, vol. 84, pp. 78–87, 2016.

[46] A. Plioutsias, N. Karanikas, and M. M. Chatzimihailidou, "Hazard Analysis and Safety Requirements for Small Drone Operations: To What Extent Do Popular Drones Embed Safety?," Risk Analysis, vol. 38, no. 3, pp. 562–584, Mar. 2018.

[47] D. Alejo, J. A. Cobano, G. Heredia, and A. Ollero, "An Efficient Method for Multi-UAV Conflict Detection and Resolution Under Uncertainties," in Advances in Intelligent Systems and Computing, vol. 417, L. P. Reis, A. P. Moreira, P. U. Lima, L. Montano, and V. Muñoz-Martinez, Eds. Cham: Springer International Publishing, 2016, pp. 635–647.

[48] S. P. Cook and D. Brooks, "A Quantitative Metric to Enable Unmanned Aircraft Systems to Remain Well Clear," Air Traffic Control Quarterly, vol. 23, no. 2–3, pp. 137–156, Apr. 2015.

[49] J. A. Douthwaite, A. De Freitas, and L. S. Mihaylova, "An interval approach to multiple unmanned aerial vehicle collision avoidance," in 2017 Sensor Data Fusion: Trends, Solutions, Applications (SDF), 2017, no. April, pp. 1–8.

[50] A. Mcfadyen, T. Martin, and L. Mejias, "Simulation and modelling tools for quantitative safety assessments of unmanned aircraft systems and operations," in 2016 IEEE Aerospace Conference, 2016, vol. 2016-June, pp. 1–12.

[51]

A Simplex Algorithm with the Smallest Index Rule for Concave Quadratic Programming

Mohand Bentobache, Mohamed Telli and Abdelkader Mokhtari

Laboratory of Pure and Applied Mathematics
University of Laghouat, 03000, Laghouat, Algeria
Email: m.bentobache@lagh-univ.dz

Abstract—**In this work, we propose a new algorithm called "Simplex Algorithm with the Smallest Index Rule" for finding a local minimum of a concave quadratic function subject to linear equality and nonnegativity constraints. First, we present and prove a new sufficient and necessary condition for local optimality, then we describe the developed algorithm and we give a numerical example for illustration purpose. In order to prove the efficiency of our algorithm, we developed an implementation using MATLAB, then we conducted numerical experiments on randomly generated and Rusakov's concave quadratic test problems. The obtained numerical results show that our algorithm outperforms the branch and bound algorithm suggested by Rusakov in terms of CPU time and it gives the global optimal solution for the Rusakov's test problems. Furthermore, it gives the global optimum for some generated test problems and it finds, for other problems, a local minimizer which can be used to initialize global optimization algorithms.**

Keywords–Concave quadratic programming; Local minimum; Global minimum, Simplex algorithm, Numerical experiments.

I. INTRODUCTION

The Concave Quadratic Programming (CQP) problem consists in minimizing a concave quadratic function under a convex polyhedron delimited by linear constraints. This optimization problem has important theoretic and practical aspects. Indeed, many practical problems are modeled as CQP problems, we can cite the quadratic assignment problem [1], missile flight testing [2], etc.

Unlike the convex quadratic programming problem, this problem is difficult to solve since a local optimal solution is not in general a global one. Therefore, in many research articles, the authors developed algorithms for approximate the global optimum of the problem. The first algorithm for solving the problem is suggested by Tuy [3]. The principle of the Tuy's algorithm is to compute a new linear constraint, called Tuy cut, in order to eliminate points in feasible region, which can not be global optimal solutions. Later, many algorithms are developed: branch and bound algorithms [4][5], cutting plane algorithms [6], successive underestimating method [7], metaheuristic algorithms [8], etc.

The majority of the proposed global optimization algorithms starts by a local optimal solution. It is proved in [9] that a local optimal solution of the problem is an extreme point of the convex polyhedron corresponding to the linear constraints. Hence, in this work we suggest a new algorithm called "Simplex Algorithm with the Smallest Index Rule" (SASIR) for finding an extreme point, which is a local minimum for the considered problem. The principle of our algorithm is similar to the one of the simplex algorithm of linear programming [10]: it starts by an initial extreme point obtained using some existing initialization technique of the simplex method, then it moves in each iteration from one extreme point to a new one having a better value of the quadratic objective function and finally it stops when a local optimality condition is satisfied.

In order to test the efficiency of our method, we have implemented it in MATLAB and conducted numerical experiments on Rusakov's test problems [5] inspired from practical problems arising in the area of missile flight testing and a set of randomly generated test problems with known global minimum and size varying from 100 constraints and 120 variables up to 200 constraints and 240 variables. The obtained numerical results are very encouraging. Indeed, our algorithm gives a local optimum which is also global for Rusakov's test problems and it outperforms the Rusakov's algorithm implemented in his software [11] in terms of CPU time. Furthermore, SASIR finds the global optimum for some randomly generated test problems in reasonable amount of time and it gives, for other test problems, a local minimizer which can be used as initial point for global optimization algorithms.

The paper is organized as follows: in Section II, we present the problem, we give some definitions and we recall some fondamental results of concave quadratic programming. In Section III, we present and prove the suggested local optimality criterion. In Section IV, we describe and justify the suggested algorithm. Moreover, we illustrate our approach with a numerical example. In Section V, we present some numerical results in order to compare our algorithm with the branch and bound algorithm of Rusakov [5] which uses the Tuy cut. Finally, Section VI concludes the paper and gives some future works.

II. PRESENTATION OF THE PROBLEM AND DEFINITIONS

The concave quadratic programming problem with equality and nonnegativity contraints is presented in the following form:

$$\begin{aligned} &\min f(x) = \tfrac{1}{2}x^T Dx + c^T x, \\ &\text{subject to} \quad Ax = b,\ x \geq 0, \end{aligned} \tag{1}$$

where D is an $(n \times n)$ real symmetric negative semidefinite matrix, c and x are n-vectors; A is a matrix of dimension $m \times n$, with $Rank(A) = m < n$.

- Let us define the following sets of indices:

$$I = \{1, 2, \ldots, m\},\quad J = \{1, 2, \ldots, n\},\quad J = J_B \cup J_N,$$

$$J_B \cap J_N = \emptyset, \quad |J_B| = m, \quad K = \{1, \dots, n-m\}.$$

We can partition the vectors x, c and the matrix A as follows:

$$x = \begin{pmatrix} x_B \\ x_N \end{pmatrix}, \; x_B = (x_j, j \in J_B), \; x_N = (x_j, j \in J_N),$$

$$c = \begin{pmatrix} c_B \\ c_N \end{pmatrix}, \; c_B = (c_j, j \in J_B), \; c_N = (c_j, j \in J_N),$$

$$A = (a_{ij}, i \in I, j \in J) = (a_j, j \in J), \; a_j = \begin{pmatrix} a_{1j} \\ \vdots \\ a_{mj} \end{pmatrix},$$

$$A = (A_B, A_N), \; A_B = A(I, J_B), \; A_N = A(I, J_N).$$

• We denote the feasible region of problem (1) by

$$S = \{x \in \mathbb{R}^n : \; Ax = b \; \text{ and } x \geq 0\}.$$

• A vector $x \in S$ is called a feasible solution for the problem (1).
• Let $J_B \subset J$ be a subset of indices such that $|J_B| = |I| = m$. The matrix $A_B = A(I, J_B)$ is said to be a basis matrix if $\det(A_B) \neq 0$. Then the feasible solution $x = \begin{pmatrix} x_B \\ x_N \end{pmatrix}$, with $x_B = A_B^{-1}b \geq 0$ and $x_N = 0$ is called a Basic Feasible Solution (BFS).
• A BFS x is said to be nondegenerate if $x_j > 0, \; j \in J_B$.
• Let $A_B = A(I, J_B)$ be a basis matrix, $J_N = J \setminus J_B$ and x the corresponding BFS. Let $j_0 \in J_N$, $j_1 \in J_B$ be two indices, and $\bar{J}_B = (J_B \setminus \{j_1\}) \cup \{j_0\}$, $\bar{A}_B = A(I, \bar{J}_B)$, such that $det(\bar{A}_B) \neq 0$. Let $\bar{x}$ be the BFS corresponding to the new basis matrix $\bar{A}_B$. Hence, we say that the basic feasible solutions x and $\bar{x}$ are adjacent.
• Let x^* be a feasible solution for problem (1). We say that x^* is a local minimizer if it exists a neighborhood $N(x^*)$ of x^*, such that $\forall x \in N(x^*) \cap S$, $f(x^*) \leq f(x)$. The vector x^* is said to be a global minimizer if $f(x^*) \leq f(x)$, $\forall x \in S$.
Let us recall the following fundamental result [9]:

Theorem 1. *Let f be a concave function defined on the bounded, closed convex set Ω. If f has a minimum over Ω, then it is achieved at an extreme point of Ω.*

• Since D is negative semidefinite, the quadratic function f is concave. Therefore, the global minimizer is achieved at an extreme point of the convex polyhedron S. This leads us to give the following definitions: let A_B^* a basis matrix and x^* the corresponding BFS, we denote by $\mathcal{N}(x^*)$ the set of all basic feasible solutions, which are adjacent to x^*. We say that x^* is a local minimizer for problem (1), if it satisfies $f(x^*) \leq f(x)$, $\forall x \in \mathcal{N}(x^*)$. We say that x^* is a global minimizer for problem (1), if for any BFS $x \in S$, we have $f(x^*) \leq f(x)$.
• Let J_B be a set of basic indices for problem (1) and $J_N = J \setminus J_B$. We define the following vectors and matrices:

$$\bar{b} = (\bar{b}_i, i \in I) = A_B^{-1}b, \; \bar{A} = (\bar{a}_k, \; k \in K) = -A_B^{-1}A_N, \quad (2)$$

$$Z = \begin{pmatrix} \bar{A} \\ I_{n-m} \end{pmatrix} \text{ and } Q = (q_{ij}, \; i, j \in K) = Z^T \bar{D} Z, \quad (3)$$

where I_{n-m} represents the identity matrix of order $n-m$ and $\bar{D} = P^T D P$, P is the permutation matrix obtained by permuting columns of the identity matrix I_n with respect to the partition (J_B, J_N). Note that the matrix Q is negative semidefinite. Indeed, $\forall y \in \mathbb{R}^{n-m}$, we have

$$y^T Q y = y^T Z^T \bar{D} Z y = (Zy)^T \bar{D} (Zy) \leq 0.$$

Moreover, we note that the diagonal elements of a negative semidefinite matrix are less than or equal to zero. Indeed, $\forall y \in \mathbb{R}^{n-m} : y^T Q y \leq 0$. Particularly, for $y = e_k$, where e_k is the vector with all its components equal to zero except for the kth component, it is equal to 1. Hence, we get $y^T Q y = q_{kk} \leq 0$.
• A vector $d \in \mathbb{R}^n$ is said to be a feasible direction for problem (1) if it satisfies $Ad = 0$.

III. Increment Formula of the Objective Function

Using results presented in [12][13][14] on linear and convex quadratic programming, we can deduce the increment formula of the objective function for the concave quadratic programming problem (1), when we move from a BFS to an adjacent one.

Let A_B be a basis matrix for problem (1) and $x = \begin{pmatrix} x_B \\ x_N \end{pmatrix} = \begin{pmatrix} \bar{b} \\ 0 \end{pmatrix}$ the corresponding BFS. Let $\bar{x} = \begin{pmatrix} \bar{x}_B \\ \bar{x}_N \end{pmatrix}$ be an arbitrary feasible solution (not necessarily basic) and $f(\bar{x})$ the value of the objective function at $\bar{x}$.
Since $\bar{x}$ is feasible, we can write:

$$A_B\bar{x}_B + A_N\bar{x}_N = b \Leftrightarrow \bar{x}_B = A_B^{-1}b - A_B^{-1}A_N\bar{x}_N = \bar{b} + \bar{A}\bar{x}_N. \quad (4)$$

The objective function value at $\bar{x}$ is

$$f(\bar{x}) = \begin{pmatrix} c_B \\ c_N \end{pmatrix}^T \begin{pmatrix} \bar{x}_B \\ \bar{x}_N \end{pmatrix} + \frac{1}{2} \begin{pmatrix} \bar{x}_B \\ \bar{x}_N \end{pmatrix}^T \bar{D} \begin{pmatrix} \bar{x}_B \\ \bar{x}_N \end{pmatrix} \quad (5)$$

By replacing the expression of $\bar{x}_B$ in equation (5), we get

$$\begin{aligned} f(\bar{x}) &= c_B^T\bar{b} + (c_N^T + c_B^T\bar{A})\bar{x}_N + \frac{1}{2}\begin{pmatrix} \bar{b} \\ 0 \end{pmatrix}^T \bar{D} \begin{pmatrix} \bar{b} \\ 0 \end{pmatrix} \\ &\quad + \begin{pmatrix} \bar{b} \\ 0 \end{pmatrix}^T \bar{D} \begin{pmatrix} \bar{A}\bar{x}_N \\ \bar{x}_N \end{pmatrix} \\ &\quad + \frac{1}{2}\begin{pmatrix} \bar{A}\bar{x}_N \\ \bar{x}_N \end{pmatrix}^T \bar{D} \begin{pmatrix} \bar{A}\bar{x}_N \\ \bar{x}_N \end{pmatrix} \\ &= c_B^T\bar{b} + \frac{1}{2}\begin{pmatrix} \bar{b} \\ 0 \end{pmatrix}^T \bar{D} \begin{pmatrix} \bar{b} \\ 0 \end{pmatrix} \\ &\quad + \left[c_N^T + c_B^T\bar{A} + \begin{pmatrix} \bar{b} \\ 0 \end{pmatrix}^T \bar{D} \begin{pmatrix} \bar{A} \\ I_{n-m} \end{pmatrix} \right] \bar{x}_N \\ &\quad + \frac{1}{2}\bar{x}_N^T \begin{pmatrix} \bar{A} \\ I_{n-m} \end{pmatrix}^T \bar{D} \begin{pmatrix} \bar{A} \\ I_{n-m} \end{pmatrix} \bar{x}_N. \\ &= f(x) + \left[c_N^T + c_B^T\bar{A} + \begin{pmatrix} \bar{b} \\ 0 \end{pmatrix}^T \bar{D}Z \right] \bar{x}_N \\ &\quad + \frac{1}{2}\bar{x}_N^T Z^T \bar{D} Z \bar{x}_N. \end{aligned}$$

Thus, the objective function increment takes the following final form:

$$f(\bar{x}) - f(x) = l^T\bar{x}_N + \frac{1}{2}\bar{x}_N^T Q \bar{x}_N, \quad (6)$$

where

$$l^T = c_N^T + c_B^T\bar{A} + v^T Z, \text{ with } v^T = \begin{pmatrix} \bar{b} \\ 0 \end{pmatrix}^T \bar{D}. \quad (7)$$

Remark 1.
• *If we denote by* $\bar{D} = (\bar{d}_{ij},\ i,j \in J)$ *and* $v = (v_j, j \in J)$, *then the components of the n-vector v are computed as follows:*

$$v_j = \sum_{i=1}^{m} \bar{b}_i \bar{d}_{ij},\ j = 1, 2, \ldots, n.$$

• *When* $D = 0$, *the problem (1) becomes a linear program and the increment of the objective function becomes:*

$$f(\bar{x}) - f(x) = l^T\bar{x}_N = (c_N^T + c_B^T\bar{A})\bar{x}_N = (c_N^T - c_B^T A_B^{-1} A_N)\bar{x}_N.$$

So, the vector l is equal to the reduced costs vector in the simplex method of linear programming.

Let us denote by

$$J_N = \{j_1, j_2, \ldots, j_{n-m}\} \text{ and } J_B = \{j'_1, j'_2, \ldots, j'_m\}.$$

So, if $k \in K$, then j_k represents the index of position k in J_N, and if $s \in I$, then j'_s represents the index of position s in J_B.
We introduce the following notations:

$$\bar{a}_{j_k} = (\bar{a}_{ij_k}, i \in I) = -A_B^{-1} a_{j_k}. \quad (8)$$

$$\theta_{i_k} = \min_{i \in I} \theta_i^k, \text{ with } \theta_i^k = \begin{cases} \frac{-\bar{b}_i}{\bar{a}_{ij_k}}, & \text{if } \bar{a}_{ij_k} < 0; \\ +\infty, & \text{otherwise.} \end{cases} \quad (9)$$

$$\theta_0^k = \begin{cases} \frac{-2l_k}{q_{kk}}, & \text{if } q_{kk} < 0; \\ -\infty, & \text{if } q_{kk} = 0 \text{ and } l_k > 0; \\ +\infty, & \text{otherwise.} \end{cases} \quad (10)$$

The following theorem gives us a sufficient and necessary condition for the local optimality of the BFS x.

Theorem 2. *The condition*

$$\forall k \in K : \theta_0^k \geq \theta_{i_k} \quad (11)$$

is sufficient for the local optimality of the BFS x and it is also necessary when x is nondegenerate.

Proof:
Sufficient condition. Let $\bar{x}$ be an arbitrary adjacent BFS to x and assume that the basis matrix corresponding to $\bar{x}$ is $\bar{A}_B = A(I, \bar{J}_B)$, where $\bar{J}_B = (J_B \setminus \{j'_s\}) \cup \{j_r\}$.
We assume that condition (11) holds. We have

$$f(\bar{x}) - f(x) = l^T\bar{x}_N + \frac{1}{2}\bar{x}_N^T Q \bar{x}_N.$$

However, for the BFS $\bar{x}$, we have $\bar{x}_{j_k} = 0, k \neq r$ and $\bar{x}_{j_r} = \theta_s \geq 0$. Since $\theta_0^r \geq \theta_s$, we get

$$f(\bar{x}) - f(x) = l_r\bar{x}_{j_r} + \frac{1}{2}q_{rr}\bar{x}_{j_r}^2 = l_r\theta_s + \frac{1}{2}q_{rr}\theta_s^2 \geq 0.$$

Necessary condition. Assume that x is nondegenerate and the condition (11) is not satisfied, i.e.,

$$\exists r \in K : \theta_0^r < \theta_{i_r} \quad (12)$$

Thus, we can move to a new BFS $\bar{x}$, such that $f(\bar{x}) < f(x)$. Indeed, we can improve the point $x = \begin{pmatrix} x_B \\ x_N \end{pmatrix} = \begin{pmatrix} A_B^{-1}b \\ 0 \end{pmatrix}$, by increasing the value of the component x_{j_r} by a positive number θ and letting the other nonbasic components equal to zero. Thus, we obtain a new point $\bar{x} = \begin{pmatrix} \bar{x}_B \\ \bar{x}_N \end{pmatrix}$, such that

$$\bar{x}_N = x_N + \theta e_r = \theta e_r,$$
$$\bar{x}_B = \bar{b} + \bar{A}\bar{x}_N = \bar{b} + \bar{A}(\theta e_r) = \bar{b} + \theta\bar{a}_{j_r},$$

where e_r represents the $(n-m)$-vector of zeros except for the component r, it is equal to 1. The positif number θ can be chosen in such a way that the new point $\bar{x}$ remains feasible:

$$\bar{x}_N = \theta e_r \geq 0,\ \bar{x}_B = \bar{b} + \theta\bar{a}_{j_r} \geq 0,$$

and the objective function decreases:

$$f(\bar{x}) - f(x) = l_r\theta + \frac{1}{2}q_{rr}\theta^2 < 0.$$

Indeed, using the nondegeneracy assumption ($\bar{b}_i > 0, i \in I$), we get $\theta_s = \theta_{i_r} = \min_{i \in I}\{\theta_i^r\} > 0$, then condition $\theta_0^r < \theta_s$ implies that the number θ can be chosen in the interval $]0, \theta_s]$ if $\theta_0^r \leq 0$, or in the interval $]\theta_0^r, \theta_s]$, otherwise. Hence, we get $\bar{x} \geq 0$ and $f(\bar{x}) < f(x)$. Therefore, the BFS x is not a local minimizer. ■

IV. AN ITERATION OF SASIR

Let x be an initial BFS of the problem (1). An iteration of the algorithm SASIR consists in moving from the BFS x to a new BFS $\bar{x}$, with $f(\bar{x}) \leq f(x)$ following the descent feasible direction used in the the simplex method for linear programming. The algorithm stops when the local optimality criterion (11) is satisfied.

A. Computing the feasible descent direction

We define the following set of indices:

$$K^* = \{k \in K : \theta_0^k < \theta_{i_k}\}. \quad (13)$$

Two cases can occur:
Case 1. If $K^* = \emptyset$, then the algorithm stops. The BFS x is a local minimizer.
Case 2. If $K^* \neq \emptyset$, then we choose an index $j_r \in J_N$ that satisfies the smallest index rule, i.e., we choose the index r that satisfies

$$r = \min\{k,\ k \in K^*\}$$

and we compute the feasible descent direction d as follows:

$$d_N = e_r,\ d_B = \bar{a}_{j_r}, \quad (14)$$

where j_r corresponds to the index of position r in J_N.
Note that the direction d is a feasible direction because it satisfies $Ad = 0$.
We move along the direction d with a steplength $\theta^* = \theta_{i_r}$, to achieve a new BFS $\bar{x} = x + \theta^* d$, with a better objective function value:

$$f(\bar{x}) = f(x) + l_r\theta^* + \frac{1}{2}q_{rr}(\theta^*)^2 \leq f(x).$$

Then, we proceed to the change of the basis:

$$\bar{J}_B = (J_B \setminus \{j'_s\}) \cup \{j_r\}, \ s = i_r.$$

We start a new iteration with the new BFS $\bar{x}$ and the new basis matrix $\bar{A}_B = A(I, \bar{J}_B)$.

B. Algorithm SASIR

(1) Compute $\bar{b}$, $\bar{A}$, Z, Q and the vector l with formulas (2)-(3) and (7);

(2) (Computing the entering index)
For every index k in K, compute θ_{i_k} and θ_0^k with relations (9)-(10); then compute the set K^* with relation (13);
Cas 1. If $K^* = \emptyset$, then the algorithm stops with a local minimizer x.
Cas 2. If $K^* \neq \emptyset$, then
compute the entering index j_r corresponding to the index of position r in J_N, with the smallest index rule, i.e., $r = \min\{k, \ k \in K^*\}$, and set the leaving index $s = i_r$;

(3) (Computing the direction and the steplength)
Compute the direction d with formula (14);
set the steplength $\theta^* = \theta_s = \theta_{i_r}$;

(4) (Change of the current solution)
Set

$$\bar{x} = x + \theta^* d, \ f(\bar{x}) = f(x) + l_r \theta^* + \frac{1}{2} q_{rr} (\theta^*)^2;$$

(5) (Change of the current basis)
Set

$$\bar{J}_B = (J_B \setminus \{j'_s\}) \cup \{j_r\};$$

(6) Set $x = \bar{x}$, $J_B = \bar{J}_B$ and go to step (1).

Remark 2.

• *Under the nondegeneracy assumption, our algorithm moves from one BFS x to a new one $\bar{x}$, with $f(\bar{x}) < f(x)$. Since the number of extreme points of the convex polyhedron S is finite, our algorithm finds a local optimum in a finite number of steps.*

• *We can choose the entering index j_r with the best improvement rule:*

$$\Delta f_r = \max\{\Delta f_k, k \in K^*\}, \ \textit{with} \ \Delta f_k = l_k \theta_{i_k} + \frac{1}{2} q_{kk} \theta_{i_k}^2.$$

This rule gives the maximal local improvement of the objective function. In other words, we move from the current extreme point to the adjacent one with the best objective function value. However, some preliminary numerical experiments show that this version of the algorithm consumes much time than the version SASIR presented above.

C. Numerical example

Consider the following concave quadratic program [14]:

$$\begin{array}{ll} \min & f(x) = -x_1 - 2x_2 - x_1^2 - 3x_2^2, \\ \text{subject to} & -x_1 + x_2 + x_3 = 3, \\ & x_1 - x_2 + x_4 = 6, \\ & x_1 + 2x_2 + x_5 = 12, \\ & x_j \geq 0, \ j = \overline{1,5}. \end{array}$$

We have

$$I = \{1, 2, 3\}, \ J = \{1, 2, 3, 4, 5\}, \ K = \{1, 2\}.$$

$$c = \begin{pmatrix} -1 \\ -2 \\ 0 \\ 0 \\ 0 \end{pmatrix}, \ D = \begin{pmatrix} -2 & 0 & 0 & 0 & 0 \\ 0 & -6 & 0 & 0 & 0 \\ 0 & 0 & 0 & 0 & 0 \\ 0 & 0 & 0 & 0 & 0 \\ 0 & 0 & 0 & 0 & 0 \end{pmatrix},$$

$$A = \begin{pmatrix} -1 & 1 & 1 & 0 & 0 \\ 1 & -1 & 0 & 1 & 0 \\ 1 & 2 & 0 & 0 & 1 \end{pmatrix}, \ b = \begin{pmatrix} 3 \\ 6 \\ 12 \end{pmatrix}.$$

We start SASIR with the following initial BFS:

$$J_B = \{3, 4, 5\}, \ J_N = \{1, 2\}, \ x_B^T = (3, 6, 12),$$
$$x_N^T = (0, 0), \ x^T = (0, 0, 3, 6, 12), \ f(x) = 0.$$

First iteration :
We have

$$A_B = I_3, \ A_N = \begin{pmatrix} -1 & 1 \\ 1 & -1 \\ 1 & 2 \end{pmatrix}, \ c_B^T = 0_{\mathbb{R}^3}, \ c_N^T = (-1, -2).$$

Computing the vectors $\bar{b}$, l and the matrices $\bar{A}$, Z, Q:

$$\bar{b} = A_B^{-1} b = b, \ \bar{A} = -A_B^{-1} A_N = \begin{pmatrix} 1 & -1 \\ -1 & 1 \\ -1 & -2 \end{pmatrix},$$

$$Z = \begin{pmatrix} \bar{A} \\ I_2 \end{pmatrix} = \begin{pmatrix} 1 & -1 \\ -1 & 1 \\ -1 & -2 \\ 1 & 0 \\ 0 & 1 \end{pmatrix},$$

$$\bar{D} = \begin{pmatrix} 0 & 0 & 0 & 0 & 0 \\ 0 & 0 & 0 & 0 & 0 \\ 0 & 0 & 0 & 0 & 0 \\ 0 & 0 & 0 & -2 & 0 \\ 0 & 0 & 0 & 0 & -6 \end{pmatrix}, \ Q = Z^T \bar{D} Z = \begin{pmatrix} -2 & 0 \\ 0 & -6 \end{pmatrix},$$

$$v = \begin{pmatrix} \bar{b} \\ 0 \end{pmatrix}^T \bar{D} = 0_{\mathbb{R}^5}, \ l^T = c_N^T + c_B^T \bar{A} + v^T Z = (-1, -2).$$

Computing the entering and leaving indices:
We compute θ_{i_k} and θ_0^k for $k \in \{1, 2\}$:

$$\theta_{i_1} = \min\{\theta_1^1, \theta_2^1, \theta_3^1\} = \min\{+\infty, 6, 12\} = \theta_2^1 = 6,$$
$$\theta_{i_2} = \min\{\theta_1^2, \theta_2^2, \theta_3^2\} = \min\{3, +\infty, 6\} = \theta_1^2 = 3,$$
$$\theta_0^1 = -\frac{2l_1}{q_{11}} = -1, \ \theta_0^2 = -\frac{2l_2}{q_{22}} = -2/3.$$

So,

$$K^* = \{k \in K : \theta_0^k < \theta_{i_k}\} = \{1, 2\}.$$

We choose r with the smallest index rule, we get

$$r = \min\{k, \ k \in K^*\} = \min\{1, 2\} = 1 \Rightarrow r = 1, \ s = i_1 = 2.$$

So, the entering index is the index of position $r = 1$ in J_N, i.e., $j_1 = 1$ and the leaving index is the index of position s in J_B, i.e., $j'_2 = 4$.

Computing the feasible descent direction and the steplength: We have

$$d_N = (0,1)^T, \ d_B = \bar{a}_2 = (-1,1,-2)^T,$$
$$d^T = (1,0,1,-1,-1), \ \theta^* = \theta_{i_1} = 6.$$

Computing the new solution $\bar{x}$ and the new value of the objective function $f(\bar{x})$:

$$\bar{x} = x + \theta^* d = (6,0,9,0,6)^T, \ f(\bar{x}) = -42 < f(x).$$

Change of the basis:

$$\bar{J}_B = (J_B \setminus \{4\}) \cup \{1\} = \{3,1,5\}, \ \bar{J}_N = \{4,2\}.$$

Second iteration :
We have

$$J_B = \{3,1,5\}, \ J_N = \{4,2\}, \ x^T = (6,0,9,0,6),$$
$$f(x) = -42, \ A_B = \begin{pmatrix} 1 & -1 & 0 \\ 0 & 1 & 0 \\ 0 & 1 & 1 \end{pmatrix}, \ A_N = \begin{pmatrix} 0 & 1 \\ 1 & -1 \\ 0 & 2 \end{pmatrix},$$
$$c_B = (0,-1,0)^T, \ c_N = (0,-2)^T.$$

Computing the matrices $\bar{A}$, Z, Q and the vector l:

$$Z = \begin{pmatrix} -1 & 0 \\ -1 & 1 \\ 1 & -3 \\ 1 & 0 \\ 0 & 1 \end{pmatrix}, \ Q = \begin{pmatrix} -2 & 2 \\ 2 & -8 \end{pmatrix}, \ l = \begin{pmatrix} 13 \\ -15 \end{pmatrix}.$$

We compute θ_{i_k} and θ_0^k, $k \in \{1,2\}$:

$$\theta_{i_1} = \{9,6,+\infty\} = \theta_2^1 = 6, \ \theta_0^1 = 13,$$
$$\theta_{i_2} = \{+\infty,+\infty,2\} = \theta_3^2 = 2, \ \theta_0^2 = -15/4.$$

So,

$$K^* = \{k \in K : \theta_0^k < \theta_{i_k}\} = \{2\}.$$

We choose r with the smallest index rule, we get

$$r = \min\{k, \ k \in K^*\} = 2 \Rightarrow r = 2, \ s = i_2 = 3.$$

So, the entering index $j_2 = 2$ and the leaving index is $j_3' = 5$.
Computing the feasible descent direction and the steplength:

$$d^T = (1,1,0,0,-3), \ \theta^* = \theta_{i_2} = 2.$$

Computing the new BFS $\bar{x}$ and the new value of the objective function $f(\bar{x})$:

$$\bar{x} = x + \theta^* d = (8,2,9,0,0)^T, \ f(\bar{x}) = -88 < f(x).$$

Change of the basis:

$$\bar{J}_B = (J_B \setminus \{5\}) \cup \{2\} = \{3,1,2\}, \ \bar{J}_N = \{4,5\}.$$

Third iteration :
We have

$$J_B = \{3,1,2\}, \ J_N = \{4,5\}, \ x^T = (8,2,9,0,0),$$
$$f(x) = -88, \ A_B = \begin{pmatrix} 1 & -1 & 1 \\ 0 & 1 & -1 \\ 0 & 1 & 2 \end{pmatrix}, \ A_N = \begin{pmatrix} 0 & 0 \\ 1 & 0 \\ 0 & 1 \end{pmatrix},$$
$$c_B = (0,-1,-2)^T, \ c_N = (0,0)^T.$$

Computing the matrices Z, Q and the vector l:

$$Z = \begin{pmatrix} -1 & 0 \\ -2/3 & -1/3 \\ 1/3 & -1/3 \\ 1 & 0 \\ 0 & 1 \end{pmatrix}, Q = \begin{pmatrix} -14/9 & 2/9 \\ 2/9 & -8/9 \end{pmatrix},$$
$$l = (20/3, \ 31/3)^T.$$

We compute θ_{i_k} and θ_0^k, $k \in \{1,2\}$:

$$\theta_{i_1} = \{9,12,+\infty\} = \theta_1^1 = 9, \ \theta_0^1 = 60/7,$$
$$\theta_{i_2} = \{+\infty,24,6\} = \theta_3^2 = 6, \ \theta_0^2 = 93/4.$$

So,

$$K^* = \{k \in K : \theta_0^k < \theta_{i_k}\} = \{1\}.$$

We choose r with the smallest index rule, we get

$$r = \min\{k, \ k \in K^*\} = 1 \Rightarrow r = 1, \ s = i_1 = 1.$$

So, the entering index is $j_1 = 4$ and the leaving index is $j_1' = 3$.
The feasible descent direction and the steplength are:

$$d^T = (-2/3, 1/3, -1, 1, 0), \ \theta^* = \theta_{i_1} = 9.$$

Computing the new BFS $\bar{x}$ and the new value of the objective function $f(\bar{x})$:

$$\bar{x} = x + \theta^* d = (2,5,0,9,0)^T, \ f(\bar{x}) = -91 < f(x).$$

Change of the basis:

$$\bar{J}_B = (J_B \setminus \{3\}) \cup \{4\} = \{4,1,2\}, \ \bar{J}_N = \{3,5\}.$$

Fourth iteration:
We have

$$J_B = \{4,1,2\}, \ J_N = \{3,5\}, \ x^T = (2,5,0,9,0), \ f(x) = -91.$$
$$A_B = \begin{pmatrix} 0 & -1 & 1 \\ 1 & 1 & -1 \\ 0 & 1 & 2 \end{pmatrix}, \ A_N = \begin{pmatrix} 1 & 0 \\ 0 & 0 \\ 0 & 1 \end{pmatrix},$$
$$c_B = (0,-1,-2)^T, \ c_N = (0,0)^T.$$

Computing the matrices Z, Q and the vector l:

$$Z = \begin{pmatrix} -1 & 0 \\ 2/3 & -1/3 \\ -1/3 & -1/3 \\ 1 & 0 \\ 0 & 1 \end{pmatrix}, \ Q = \begin{pmatrix} -14/9 & -2/9 \\ -2/9 & -8/9 \end{pmatrix},$$
$$l = (22/3, \ 37/3)^T.$$

We compute θ_{i_k} and θ_0^k, $k \in \{1,2\}$:

$$\theta_{i_1} = \min\{9,+\infty,15\} = \theta_1^1 = 9, \ \theta_0^1 = 66/7,$$
$$\theta_{i_2} = \min\{+\infty,6,15\} = \theta_2^2 = 6, \ \theta_0^2 = 111/4.$$

So,

$$K^* = \{k \in K : \theta_0^k < \theta_{i_k}\} = \emptyset.$$

Therefore, the local optimal BFS and the corresponding objective function value are:

$$x^* = (2,5,0,9,0)^T, \ f(x^*) = -91.$$

Let us remark that the local minimizer found by our algorithm in this example is also global.

V. NUMERICAL EXPERIMENTS

In order to compare our algorithm with the algorithm of Rusakov, we have developed an implementation with MATLAB2017a on a PC with a processor Intel Pentium Dual-Core 2.20 GHz and 4 Go of RAM. The Rusakov's algorithm is a branch and bound algorithm which uses the Tuy cut. It is implemented in his free software [5][11]. Note that the Rusakov's test problems have one constraints and n bounded variables and the available free version of the software is limited to one constraint and 20 bounded variables, that is why we have done numerical experiments on small size test problems. Numerical results on Rusakov's test problems are presented in Table I.

In order to test the performance of our algorithm on medium size test problems, we have generated concave quadratic test problems with known global optimum using the generation procedure presented in [15], see Table II.

The notations in the first row of Tables I and II : m, n, $niter_j$, opt_j, $cput_j$ represent respectively number of constraints, number of variables, number of iterations, the optimum found, the CPU time for Algorithm j, where Algorithm 1 is the SASIR algorithm and Algorithm 2 is the Rusakov's algorithm. In Table II, $gopt$ represents the global optimum of the corresponding test problem and "Mean" represents the average CPU time and the average number of iterations for each problem size.

TABLE I: NUMERICAL RESULTS ON RUSAKOV'S TEST PROBLEMS.

n	Algorithm 1 (SASIR)			Algorithm 2 (Rusakov)	
	$niter_1$	opt_1	$cput_1$ (s)	opt_2	$cput_2$ (s)
5	4	-11.0694	0.0031	-11.0694	1.1298
10	6	-40.8382	0.0041	-40.8382	2.0481
15	9	-88.9456	0.0051	-88.9456	6.1074
18	10	-127.0726	0.0075	-127.0726	9.7121
20	11	-156.1234	0.0092	-156.1234	11.5236

TABLE II: NUMERICAL RESULTS ON RANDOMLY GENERATED TEST PROBLEMS.

Prob	$m \times n$	$niter_1$	opt_1	$gopt$	$cput_1$ (s)
1	100 × 120	40	-9.5894	-6.2500	0.1439
2	100 × 120	2	-4.3225	-0.0625	0.0217
3	100 × 120	**30**	**-1.5625**	**-1.5625**	**0.2773**
4	100 × 120	**39**	**-4.0272**	**-4.0272**	**0.5287**
5	100 × 120	3	-2.2500	-0.1600	0.0247
6	100 × 120	6	-1.9492	-1	0.0330
7	100 × 120	14	-2.9417	-2.2500	0.0564
8	100 × 120	2	-23.6580	-0.3600	0.0240
9	100 × 120	**18**	**-3.0625**	**-3.0625**	**0.0552**
10	100 × 120	**20**	**-1.7778**	**-1.7778**	**0.0786**
Mean	100 × 120	37.2	-	-	0.0988
11	200 × 240	2	-12.2500	-0.1600	0.0426
12	200 × 240	2	-11.6224	-0.3600	0.0394
13	200 × 240	18	-10.5901	-4.0000	0.4594
14	200 × 240	2	-9.8212	-0.4900	0.0386
15	200 × 240	2	-15.4605	-0.3600	0.0387
16	200 × 240	2	-57.4326	-0.0400	0.0389
17	200 × 240	**27**	**-4**	**-4**	**0.5332**
18	200 × 240	2	-11.3498	-0.6400	0.0454
19	200 × 240	5	-39.3321	-0.1600	0.0824
20	200 × 240	2	-1.4400	-0.2304	0.0409
Mean	200 × 240	6.4	-	-	0.1359

We have started our algorithm by the extreme point, with objective function equal to zero. Table I shows clearly that our algorithm has succesfully found the global optimum for the Rusakov's test problems. Moreover, the simplex algorithm with the smallest index rule outperforms the branch and bound algorithm of Rusakov in terms of CPU time. Table II shows that our algorithm has found the global optimum for 5 generated test problems in a short CPU time (test problems 3,4,9,10 and 17). However, for other test problems, our algorithm gives a local minimizer which can be used for the initialization of the global optimization algorithms.

VI. CONCLUSION

In this work, we have adapted the simplex algorithm of linear programming for finding a local optimum of a concave quadratic function subject to linear and nonnegativity contraints. In order to stop the algorithm, we suggested a simple sufficient and necessary condition for local optimality of the current extreme point. Numerical experiments on Rusakov and randomly test problems show that our algorithm is very fast and can find the global optimum for some problems. In a future work, we will combine our algorithm with an existing global optimization algorithm in order to find the global optimum of medium and large-scale concave quadratic programming problems.

REFERENCES

[1] E. L. Lawler, "The Quadratic Assignment Problem," Management Sci., vol. 9, no. 4, 1963, pp. 586–599, ISSN: 1526-5501.

[2] A. I. Rusakov, "An Improved Reduction Algorithm to Check Hypotheses for the Multicollinear Regression Model," Automation and Remote Control, vol. 62, no. 5, 2001, pp. 762–771, ISSN: 1608-3032.

[3] H. Tuy, "Concave Programming under Linear Constraints," Dokl. Akad. Nauk SSSR English translation in Soviet Math. Dokl., vol. 5, 1964, pp. 1437–1440, ISSN: 1531-8362.

[4] R. Horst, "An Algorithm for Nonconvex Programming Problems," Math. Programming, vol. 10, 1976, pp. 312–321, ISSN: 1436-4646.

[5] A. I. Rusakov, "Concave programming under the simplest linear constraints," Computational Mathematics and Mathematical Physics, vol. 43, no. 7, 2003, pp. 951–960, ISSN: 0044-4669.

[6] H. Konno, "Maximization of a Convex Quadratic Function under Linear Constraints," Math. Programming, vol. 11, 1976, pp. 117–127, ISSN: 1436-4646.

[7] K. L. Hoffman, "A Successive Underestimating Method for Concave Minimization Problems," Ph.D. thesis, The George Washington University, 1975.

[8] H. Konno, C. Gao, and I. Saitoh, "Cutting plane/tabu searh algorithms for low rank concave quadratic programming problems". Journal of Global Optimization, vol. 13, no. 3, 1998, pp. 225–240, ISSN: 1573-2916.

[9] D. G. Luenberger and Y. Ye, Linear and nonlinear programming. Third edition, New York, NY, USA: Springer-Verlag, 2008, ISBN: 978-0-387-74502-2.

[10] G. B. Dantzig, Linear Programming and Extensions. Princeton University Press, Princeton, N.J., 1998, ISBN: 978-0-691-05913-6.

[11] A. I. Rusakov, "Concave software manual," URL: http://www.rusakov.donpac.ru/index1.htm [accessed: 2018-05-02].

[12] N. Ikheneche, Support Method for the Minimization of a Convex Quadratic Function. Master thesis, University of Bejaia (in french), 2004, (in french).

[13] M. Bentobache and M. O. Bibi, Numerical Methods of Linear and Quadratic Programming: Theory and Algorithms. French Academic Editions, Germany, 2016, ISBN: 978-3-8416-4112-0 (in french).

[14] A. Chikhaoui, B. Djebbar, A. Belabbaci, and A. Mokhtari, "Optimization of a quadratic function under its canonical form". Asian journal of applied sciences, vol. 2, no. 6, 2009, pp. 499–510, ISSN: 1996-3343.

[15] N. V. Thoai, "On the construction of test problems for concave minimization algorithms," Journal of Global Optimization, vol. 5, no. 4, 1994, pp. 399–402, ISSN: 1573-2916.

Mixing Power Consumption for Hulled Millet in an Agitated Drum Dryer with Discrete Element Method

Tibor Poós, Dániel Horváth
Department of Building Services and Process Engineering, Faculty of Mechanical Engineering
Budapest University of Technology and Economics
Budapest, Hungary
poos@mail.bme.hu, daniel.horvath.nk@gmail.com

Kornél Tamás
Department of Machine and Product Design, Faculty of Mechanical Engineering
Budapest University of Technology and Economics
Budapest, Hungary
tamas.kornel@gt3.bme.hu

Abstract— **There are several technologies in the agricultural, food, chemical and pharmaceutical industries for mixing granular materials. In these processes the homogenization of the particle fractions or the prevention of arch building process play very important roles. To select appropriate mixers' motors installed in certain devices, it is necessary to specify the rotational speed of the mixer and the power requirement of the propulsion engine. This selection is a difficult task nowadays for mechanical engineers without measurement or an appropriate method for the estimation of power requirement. In researches available in the literature, the determination of the mixing power requirement is solely analytical and only for devices of universal design and geometry, in the case of mixing of certain substances. The main purpose of this research is to improve a simulation model for determining the power requirement of an agitated drum dryer, which can be generally used for modeling the mixing process of granular materials with various moisture content. In this study, laboratory measurements were made by mixing hulled millet and the results were approximated by the simulations based on discrete element method (DEM). In order to give an exact estimation of the power requirement of a given mixer, accurate geometry of the drum dryer and the appropriate micromechanical and physical parameters of the discrete particle assembly are required. In laboratory tests, the mixing power requirements of the agitated drum dryer were measured at various rotational speeds (0.48 ÷ 1.58 rev/s) using hulled millet with different moisture contents on wet basis (9.6 ÷ 29.5%) with different drum loading factors (5 ÷ 25%). Based on results it can be stated that the mixing power requirement is greatly influenced by the moisture content of the granular material and the rotational speed of the agitator. The preliminary DEM simulations and parameter sensitivity studies revealed which micromechanical parameters of the contact model should be changed in order to simulate the power requirements with good approximation.**

Keywords- hulled millet; agitated drum dryer; moisture content; mixing; discrete element method

I. INTRODUCTION

In the agricultural, food, chemical and pharmaceutical industries the mixing of granular materials is often encountered, and it can be carried out in e.g., agitated drum dryers and basic material homogenizer rotary drums. In order to achieve the appropriate drying speed, and in the case of homogenization, to select the time of operation to achieve a uniform particle distribution, it is necessary to strive for the proper setting of the mixer's rotational speed. However, mixing may result in deterioration, breakage, or fragmentation of the grains, which should also be taken into account when choosing mixer design and operating parameters, including the speed of rotation. The measuring equipment required for the laboratory tests of the mixing process is costly and the measurements carried out on them are time consuming and labor intensive, so the simulation of mixing is becoming increasingly important today. To describe the mixing of the set, the mechanical properties of the materials used in the operation and the geometric parameters of the granules and the mixing apparatus are also required.

Bridgwater [1] collected the mixer geometries used to mix powders and granular materials and the phenomena occurring during operations and the researches which describe them. As a result, he found that studies of easily bulking materials without internal cohesion and hard-to-bulk materials with internal cohesion require further research. In an experiment with a horizontal shaft drum dryer, the migration of the particles was investigated between regions of the blades [1]. Between the volumes of the paddle-suspension elements, it was observed the amount of tracer-bound particles passed through the volume bounded by the other two paddle suspension elements. It was considered an event when a particle with a tracer passed through another volume. During the investigations, movements within the grain aggregation were high-lighted, but the internal displacements of the different humidity and cohesion sets have not been studied. Furthermore, the power required for mixing was not analyzed, but rather the quality of mixing was in focus.

Alchikh-Sulaiman et al. [2] analyzed the mixing of mono-disperse, bidisperse, tridisperse, and polydisperse granules in a drum dryer using discrete element method, which simulation results were compared with laboratory measurements. With the validated calculation model, the effects of drum rotation speed, grain size and initial filling rate on mixing quality were investigated. The Hertz-Mindlin contact model was used in the simulations, but the modeling of cohesive granular assemblies and the effect of the grain size were not dealt with.

Researches found in the literature have shown that a more precise description of mixing in the drum dryers requires further research and a small number of researchers have studied the effect of moisture content of agricultural granular materials on mixing power consumption. Thus, the aim of this research was to create a DEM model that is suitable for simulating the measured mixing power requirement results achieved with a laboratory agitate.

II. MATERIAL AND METHODS

Before the measurements were started, the test material has been prepared. The grains were cleansed from the dust, broken particles, and other contaminants and to achieve the desired moisture content they were pre-moistened.

A. *Material*

During the measurements, the hulled millet (Figure 1) was used. It is an appropriate agricultural material for measurements, because it has low granule size deviation, hydrophilic, properly homogeneous material structure with close to regular spherical geometry, wettable multiple times and relatively inexpensive.

Figure 1. Hulled millet

First the material was cleaned with a wind-separating device and an assembly of nearly the same particle size distribution was created. A rotating drum uniquely prepared for homogenous wet-ting of the material was used. Approximately 12 dm^3 of millet and the desired volume of water was loaded in the drum and agitated for 5 hours at predetermined intervals. To determine the resulting moisture content, a small sample was placed in a drying oven at 105 °C for 24 hours and the initial and final mass of the material was weighed. The geometric dimensions of the hulled millet were determined by sieve analysis. Based on measurements, it could be stated that the characteristic size of hulled millet (equivalent to regular sphere diameter) was ~ 1.8 mm.

B. *Laboratory equipment and measurement method*

The measurements of the mixing power consumption were performed on a horizontal axial agitated drum dryer. The electric power input by the mixing motor was measured with a special three phase Datcon PQRM5100-31 type meter at 1 s sampling intervals and recorded on a computer.

The intermittently operated agitated drum dryer consists of a 756 mm long, 250 mm wide and 275 mm U-shaped drum shown in Figure 2, which is covered by a flat plate. On the axis of the drum shaft, there are 22 mixing blades, each 20 mm high, 50 mm wide, and the horizontal angle of the plates is 10 degrees. The speed of the mixer can be adjusted in a wide range (0÷95 1/min) with a frequency inverter. The measurement started by filling the pre-moistened granular material into the drum. The volume of the drum is 47.4 dm3. After loading the material, the device was covered with a flat plate and then the engine was started at a given speed while the electrical power input was measured. At a given filling rate, with the given moisture content, the mixing speeds during the measurements were as follows: 0:48; 0.63; 0.79; 0.95; 1:11; 1:27; 1:43; 1.58 rev/s. Approximately the mixer was operated for one minute at a given speed, then it was turned to a higher speed, so all the cases were measured. The mixing power was recorded by the performance transmitter, from which the idle power was deducted.

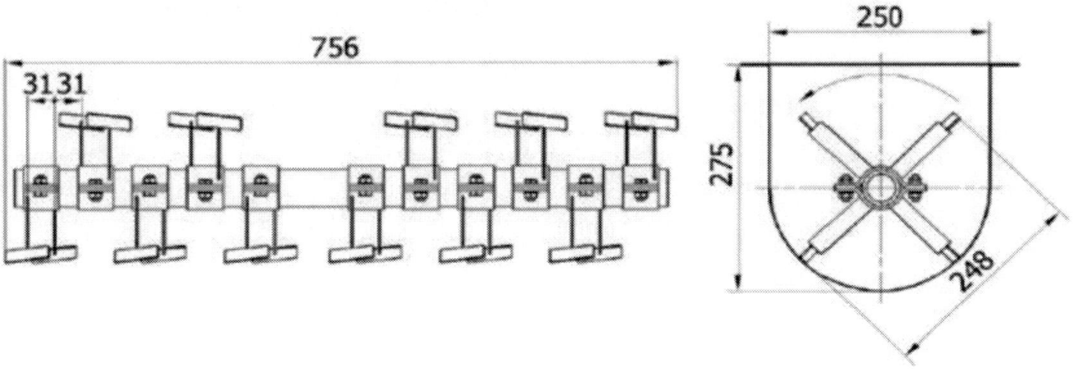

Figure 2. The design and dimensions of the mixer and the drum

TABLE I. THE PARAMETERS OF THE HULLED MILLET UTILIZED FOR THE DEM SIMULATIONS

Chosen granule diameter [mm]	Measured moisture content (wet basis) [%]	Measured granule density [kg/m^3]	Calibrated elasticity modulus [MPa]	Measured internal friction angle [°]	Calibrated strengths of the cohesion [kPa]	Calibrated dimensionless strengths of the cohesion [1]
10±1*	22.5	2092 [6]	2000	40.3 [6]	61 [7]	0.05 [7]

* The real mean diameter of the hulled millet was 1.8 mm [6].

In order to determine the nullperformance, null measurements were performed at each speed. The data per minute for a given setting was averaged and the idle power consumption was deducted from it which was considered to be the mixing power consumption for the given conditions.

C. Discrete element method

In this research, the Yade [3] open source discrete element software was used in which the modeling is done in Python. Several types of so-called motors, such as particle con-tact models, were available to describe the rheological processes

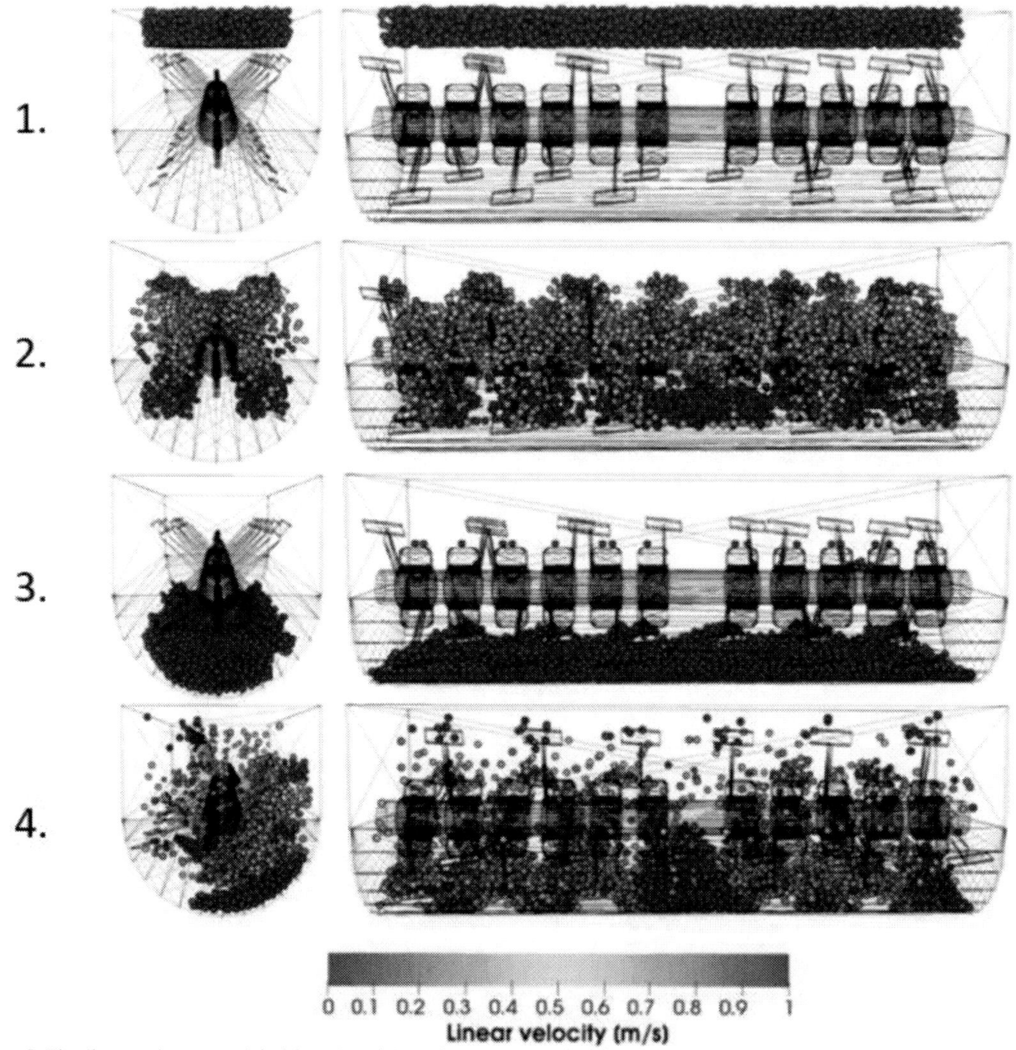

Figure 3. The discrete element model of the agitated drum dryer (1. generating the particle assembly, 2. gravity deposition of the assembly, 3. activation of the cohesive contacts, 4. start of the mixing)

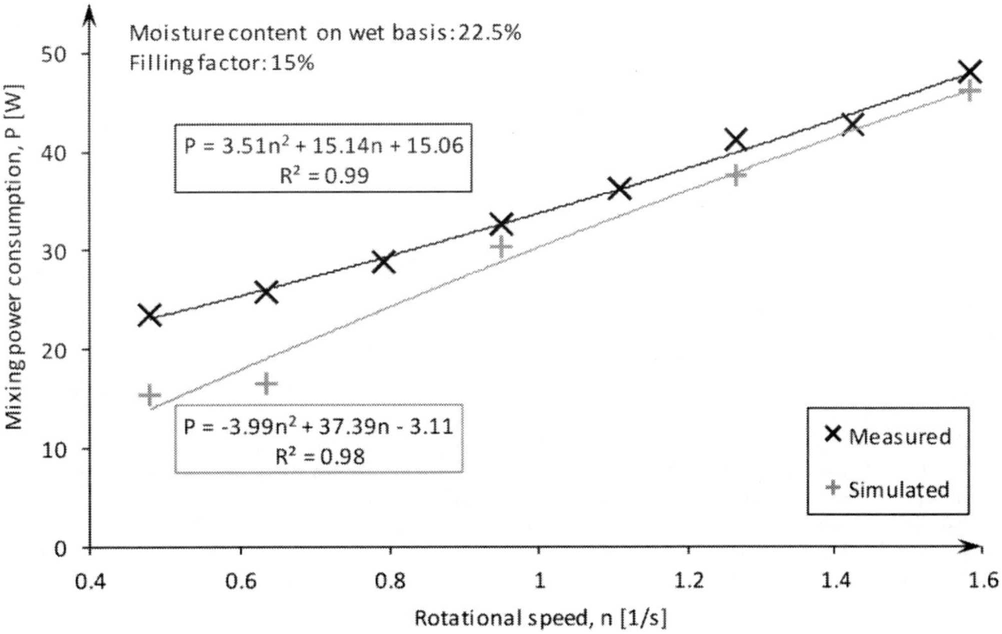

Figure 4. The measured and the simulated mixing power consumption in the case of hulled millet with a filling rate of 15% and 22.5% moisture content on wet basis depending on the rotational speed

between the particles (eg. frictional, cohesive and capillary, etc.). In the model the frictional-cohesive (CohFrictMat) contact model was utilized [4] due to the nature of the task being investigated, which is suitable for simulating the cohesion due to moisture in the granular material. Table II summarizes the parameters of the equipment's material used in the simulations, which were taken from the material properties of the steel [5].

TABLE II. THE DEM PARAMETERS OF THE EQUIPMENT'S MATERIAL [5]

Density [kg/m³]	Young's modulus [GPa]	Poisson's ratio [1]	Friction angle [°]
7750	200	0.3	40.1

The description of the connections between the drum and the particles was defined only by frictional relations. The mixing's global parameter settings for the discrete element simulations are summarized in Table III.

TABLE III. THE GLOBAL PARAMETERS OF THE DEM SIMULATIONS

Fill factor [%]	Global damping [1]	Number of particles [pcs]	Coefficient of critical time step [1]	Time step [s]
15	0	3713	0.7	$3.58 \cdot 10^{-5}$

The time step is divided by the proportional factor and it is equal to the critical time step defined by Yade software [3]. All other global parameters were left in the default setting.

III. RESULTS

The dimensions and setting parameters of the granules utilized during the simulation of the mixing process are summarized in Table I, which was determined by static measurements and simulation calibrations in previous studies [6]–[8]. In the present study the Young's modulus of the particles were modified in order to bring the simulated results closer to the real measured ones.

Because of the small size of millet grains, during the simulations, hundreds of thousands of particles would be needed, which the software could not handle with the available computing capacity at the appropriate simulation time. Thus the diameter of the particles was increased. The first stage of the simulation is to generate the particles with the filling rate (Figure 3/1). Then the gravity deposition of the assembly starts (Figure 3/2). It lasts until the magnitude of the unbalance force ratio drops below 0.001 (Figure 3/3). During the next phase, cohesion relationships between the particles will be activated, which will be re-activated each time for every new particle contact. Finally, at a given rotational speed, the mixing starts (Figure 3/4). The sampling of the torque applied to the axis was performed at every second for 30 seconds by the discrete element software.

The mixing power consumption can be calculated in terms of torque and rotational speed. Out-standing simulation performance data from the particles hitched by the mixing blades and walls of the drum were excluded during the

TABLE IV. RELATIVE ERRORS OF MEASURED AND SIMULATED MIXING POWER CONSUMPTIONS

Rotational speed, [rev/s]	Mixing power consumption, [W]		Relative Error, [%]
	Measured	*Simulated*	
0.48	23.46	15.3	34.8
0.63	25.82	16.5	36.1
0.95	32.58	30.32	6.9
1.27	41.09	37.51	8.7
1.58	48.02	46.04	4.1

evaluation. Typically, these values were 0W and above 100W. The measurement and simulation results of the mixing are shown in Figure 4, where polynomial function can be applied to the obtained values.

It can be stated that the results of the simulation model of the mixer underestimated the measured power requirements at lower rotational speeds (0.48; 0.63; 0.79 rev/s), while at higher rotational speeds (0.95; 1.11; 1.43; 1.58 rev/s) the simulated results approached them appropriately. The reason for this is probably the fact that at lower rotational speeds mass transport is typical, while at higher rotational speeds impulse transport is common. Table IV summarizes the relative errors of the mixing power consumptions obtained by the measurements and the simulations.

Further calibration of the simulation model is required, in which parameter sensitivity tests have to be performed. Density correction due to porous volume change may be a solution in increasing particle size. In this case, while it is not advisable to change the density of the material by varying the particle sizes during mixing of different granular assemblies together, it is indispensable to simulate the mixing power consumption in order to mix the same mass as during the actual measurements. In addition, slight distortion of the geometric shape of the particles can also be a solution for the simulations of mixing power consumption at low rotational speeds, as using a more intersecting form of grain particles than the ball, the movable mass can be increased.

IV. CONCLUSION

In this research, the mixing power consumption of a horizontal axis agitated drum dryer was determined by laboratory measurements of the mixed moisture-containing hulled millet. With discrete element method the mixing apparatus and its operation were modeled taking into account the operating parameters used during the measurement. Simulation of the mixing was carried out by means of previous measured material parameters and simulational calibrations, and by modifying the modulus of elasticity of the particles. The results of the measurements and the simulations were compared. The mixing power consumption increased polynomial by increasing the rotational speed. It was found that the mixer's simulation model underestimated the measurement results at lower rotational speeds (0.48; 0.63; 0.79 rev/s) while at the higher rotational speeds (0.95; 1.11; 1.43; 1.58 rev/s) they approached them reasonably due to the former being mainly mass transport, and the latter being mainly impulsive transport. Further calibrations are required in which parameter sensitivity tests are performed in the granular assembly to give a more accurate description of the mass transport phenomenon due to the mixing. In the DEM model, the greater relative errors measured at lower rotational speeds could be solved by taking into consideration the changes in the porous volume due to the increase in the particle size, and the slight distortion of the geometric shape of the particles

ACKNOWLEDGEMENTS

This work was supported by Gedeon Richter's Talentum Foundation (19-21, Gyömrői street, 1103, Budapest, Hungary), and by the Hungarian Scientific Research Fund (NKFIH/PD-116326) and the Higher Education Excellence Program of the Ministry of Human Capacities in the frame of Water science & Disaster Prevention research area of Budapest University of Technology and Economics (BME FIKP-VÍZ).

REFERENCES

[1] J. Bridgwater, "Mixing of powders and granular materials by mechanical means—A perspective," *Particuology*, vol. 10, no. 4, pp. 397–427, 2012.

[2] B. Alchikh-Sulaiman, M. Alian, F. Ein-Mozaffari, A. Lohi, and S. R. Upreti, "Using the discrete element method to assess the mixing of polydisperse solid particles in a rotary drum," *Particuology*, vol. 25, pp. 133–142, Apr. 2016.

[3] V. Šmilauer *et al.*, "Dem formulation. In Yade Documentation 2nd ed.," *Yade Proj.*, p. 37, 2015.

[4] F. Bourrier, F. Kneib, B. Chareyre, and T. Fourcaud, "Discrete modeling of granular soils reinforcement by plant roots," *Ecol. Eng.*, vol. 61, no. Part C, pp. 646–657, 2013.

[5] J. Horabik and M. Molenda, "Parameters and contact models for DEM simulations of agricultural granular materials: A review," *Biosyst. Eng.*, vol. 147, no. Supplement C, pp. 206–225, Jul. 2016.

[6] D. Horváth, "Statikus berendezésekben mozgó szemcsés anyaghalmaz modellezése," presented at the Tudományos Diákköri Konferencia, Budapesti Műszaki és Gazdaságtudományi Egyetem, 2017.

[7] T. Poós, D. Horváth, and K. Tamás, "The compare of angles of repose with discrete element method and measurement," in *8th International Scientific Conference*, Trebinje, Bosnia-Herzegovina, 2017, pp. 65–70.

[8] T. Poós, D. Horváth, and K. Tamás, "Modeling the movement of the granular material in a static equipment with discrete element method," presented at the International Scientific Conference on Advances in Mechanical Engineering (ISCAME 2017), Debrecen, Hungary, 2017.